Faith Rewarded

THE STORY OF ST ANDREW'S SCOTS MEMORIAL, JERUSALEM

– WALTER T DUNLOP –

An environmentally friendly book printed and bound in England by
www.printondemand-worldwide.com

www.fast-print.net/store.php

FAITH REWARDED:
THE STORY OF ST ANDREW'S SCOTS MEMORIAL, JERUSALEM

A catalogue record for this book is available from the British Library

ISBN 978-178456-111-6

This edition published 2014 by
Fastprint Publishing of Peterborough, England.

Dedicated
to all
Ministers and Staff
of
St Andrew's Church and Hospice, Jerusalem
and to
the many whose story this is.

Contents

Foreword

I HAVE an olive wood box brought back from Palestine by my grandfather at the end of the First World War. I have often sat proudly beneath the painting of General Allenby in the lounge of the Guest House in Jerusalem and told proudly the story of my grandfather marching into Jerusalem with Allenby on his famous entry in 1917. Unfortunately, now I have read Walter Dunlop's book I have discovered I was making it up! The 52nd Lowland Division, whatever their achievements during the Palestine Campaign, were not there on that historic day.

St Andrew's Scots Memorial Church in Jerusalem is, I think, one of only two Church of Scotland churches built as a war memorial. Its building is one of the best things ever to come out of a Presbytery meeting. On the very week the British Army took Jerusalem the Presbytery of Edinburgh met in an atmosphere of national euphoria. An elder, apparently on the spur of the moment, proposed that "to celebrate the occasion funds should build and endow a Scots Kirk of St Andrew, the Apostle, in the Holy City". And so it was to be.

In this book you will learn of Ninian Hill, the Greenock businessman who was the elder in question at Edinburgh Presbytery. His story fully deserves the attention paid to it. Without his vision, his determination and his energy the project would never have taken shape. There were plenty to oppose it; and it took years and years to raise the money. The countless reports from architects and disputes with contractors over the next thirteen years make it clear that complications with building projects in that part of the world are no new thing for the Church of Scotland! The church and guest house stand today on a splendid site and I have met no-one who is not thrilled with the beauty and appropriateness of the building.

The original plan was that a college be attached to the church, so that candidates for the ministry of the Church of Scotland could study there during their training. That plan was never realised. After my very first visit to Jerusalem I suggested something similar, but that plan was never realised either. It is good that in recent times more opportunities have been made available for ministers to enrich their education with opportunities to learn in Israel and the Occupied Territories.

Walter Dunlop has quarried a large number of primary sources of real historical interest in writing this book. There are, of course, minutes of Assembly committees; there are letters to the press – sometimes hot-blooded letters!; there are government documents and correspondence; and there are many – often very moving – personal memories. There is a gripping story of eight-year-old Tanya Gardiner Scott, whose father was twice minister at St Andrew's, at the time of the 1967 war is striking. She and her parents were living and working in circumstances of real personal danger and she recaptures vividly the shock and fear and the great noise of the fighting raging all around. Even more dramatic is the story of the church and minister in 1948. Shortly before the war reached its most violent, the Mayor of Jerusalem, Richard Graves, attended worship at St Andrews and was moved and uplifted by the sermon preached by the Moderator of the General Assembly. . Not long after, the minister, Rev Clark Kerr, found himself "in solitary confinement" in the church with no safe way for days and days as the bombs were bursting all around and bullets were hitting the church very frequently. Church of Scotland ministers in Jerusalem have had to face very grave challenges of different kinds and in different ways have displayed remarkable courage.

This book concentrates on the stories and the history from the beginnings of St Andrew's Scots Memorial Church until 1967. There are hints of another book in the closing chapters. Hints of new developments in the story of the congregation in the last fifty years and of some exceptional people who have been involved with the congregation in that time. More and more this has become a story shaped by the political circumstances of Jerusalem and by the occupation of the Palestinian Territories. The Scots Memorial Church has played a very important part in building partnerships with Palestinian churches and organisations. It has also been one of the consciences of the Church of Scotland in its continuing work and prayer for justice and peace in Israel and Palestine. That part of the story of this great church deserves a book in itself. On the evidence of this book, Walter Dunlop is the man to write the next one also.

Very Rev. Andrew R.C. McLellan, C.B.E., D.D.

Introduction

IN 2011, I received an email from the Rev. George Shand, Minister of St Andrew's Church in Jerusalem, asking if I could assist a student at the Hebrew University in Jerusalem with her research into St Andrew's Church for her M.A. in Historical Geography. Being retired and with time on my hands I readily agreed. I discovered that even after nearly twenty-five years of close involvement with St Andrew's Church and Hospice, thinking that I had a good knowledge of the buildings and their history, the result of my research into the Church records and archives proved eye opening. In conversation with George we agreed that such material and information discovered should not be left to melt back into the Minutes and files but should be compiled within a publication which, hopefully, would be of interest to a wider audience. This book is the result. It is not intended to be an academic piece of work. It is simply the story of an enterprise unique in the history of the Church of Scotland, a story of faith, commitment and persistence in the face of considerable obstacles in Scotland and in Palestine and Israel.

The book details the first fifty years of the history of the Memorial, from 1917 to approximately 1967, the year of the Six Day War. This is followed by a chapter summarising of the development of the Church of Scotland's ministry in Israel and Palestine subsequent to the War to the present day.

It is important to note that this is not the first publication providing some historical background to the Memorial. In 1999 Major Sandy Goodwin produced a wonderful booklet relating aspects of the story of St Andrew's from a personal perspective. The Church of Scotland and the Society of Friends of St Andrew's, Jerusalem, published a booklet celebrating the Jubilee of the Memorial, 1930 to 1980, written by Brigadier the Lord Ballantrae. Sheila Watson tells of the work of the Hospice in a little publication "60 Years of Hospitality 1930-1990". Each are unique, each have something different to reveal and, together with this book, they complement each other.

One of the many challenges in assisting the student in Jerusalem and writing this book has been locating the records relating to the Memorial. I am most grateful to the departmental staff of the Church of Scotland's

World Mission Council for their patience with me as I spent many days over many weeks in their office trawling through Minute books and files. The jewel was the discovery of the unbound detailed typed minutes of the Memorial Committee and its Sub-Committees from its first meeting in January 1919 until 1964 when the Committee was subsumed into the newly created Overseas Council. Without this primary source material it would have been impossible to piece together the story of the Memorial to the level of detail achieved. In addition, in appropriate circumstances and quoting directly from the material, I had the opportunity to add contemporary and authentic voices to the account.

I am told that with a book such as this it is often as difficult to decide what to leave out as to what to include. Over the three years of research I have amassed a considerable quantity of material much of which, because of space, I had to omit. To redress this situation the intention is, in time, to upload selected unpublished material onto a "blog" related to the Memorial. This will also provide an opportunity for readers of the book, and others, to add their own information and tell of their own experiences and stories of St Andrew's Church and Hospice, all of which will add new chapters to the narrative.

Two details when reading the book. Firstly, where the "Committee" is mentioned, unless otherwise stated, this is shorthand for the General Assemblies' "Joint Committee" of the Church of Scotland and the United Free Church of Scotland and their various Sub-Committees, the "Committee" responsible for the Memorial and its work. Secondly, for interest and with "online" assistance with the calculation, I have added beside some of the financial information an approximate valuation of what such amounts would be in 2014, taking inflationary factors into account.

As a novice in putting together a publication such as this, I could not have achieved it without support and assistance. My apologies to the many not listed but I am sure you will excuse me if I mention a few: the Rev. George Shand for his three years of encouragement in the project and his email that day in 2011 without which this book would not have been written; A. K. Miller for his assistance in helping me understand more fully the military background to the Palestine Campaign and the Mandate; the Rev. Tom Houston and Runa Mackay for giving me time to hear their stories of the Memorial; Chen Barnett and Gil Peled for their help with the architectural aspects of the Memorial buildings; the McLean Museum in Greenock for assistance with my research in to Ninian Hill; Tim and Sarah Holliday for background on Clifford Holliday, the Memorial architect; Mary Hager (Reid) and Melville Reid for bringing the story of the Church and Hospice to life at a difficult and dangerous time in the Memorial buildings' history; Kay McIntyre (Conradi) for meeting with me and relating her experiences with her family living in the Hospice. By no means least a special word of thanks to Sir John MacMillan who in so many ways has assisted me and offered words of guidance through this whole process for all of which I am greatly indebted.

I am grateful to many who have allowed me the use of their photographs for the book especially Joan Musgrave for her line drawing of St Andrew's for the front cover, Margaret MacGregor; George Shand, The McLean Museum, Greenock, the Holliday and Reid families and the Library of Congress for the use of photographs from the Matson Collection.

Finally I am most grateful to the Society of Friends of St Andrew's, Jerusalem, for its encouragement and support in having the book published. The final chapter of the book tells a little of the History of the Society and the work it is doing in support of St Andrew's Church and Guesthouse in their ministry today. All proceeds from the sale of this book will go to support the Society in that task. It is my hope that after reading this story of the Memorial many will also be motivated to offer their support to the work of the Society.

Walter T Dunlop.

FAITH REWARDED:
THE STORY OF ST ANDREW'S SCOTS MEMORIAL, JERUSALEM

—— CHAPTER ONE ——

The Palestine Campaign

IT IS NOT possible to relate the story of St Andrew's Church and Hospice in Jerusalem without firmly placing it in the context of the time, the events and the culture, within which the buildings were conceived.

'The Suez Canal was a vitally important supply route for the British Empire. During World War 1, troops and equipment of the Australian, New Zealand and Indian Forces passed this way en route to the Western Front, in addition to millions of tons of foodstuffs, minerals and other provisions bound for Britain and her Allies. The importance of the Canal had been recognised by the British Government long before the war, and steps were taken to provide defences with British troops stationed in Egypt.

'Germany had for many years before the war assiduously developed Turkey as an ally, which it saw as an important element of the *Drang Nacht Osten* (Drive to the East). Initially Britain set out only to defend the Canal from the Turkish troops that were massed in Palestine. However, following important victories that pushed the Turks further from the Canal, along with the helpful support of Arabs in the Hejaz and elsewhere, the British Force began to contemplate a push into Palestine. This became additionally important once the attempt on Gallipoli was a recognised failure, and Britain also needed a success in Mesopotamia. Politically, success in Palestine was believed by some to be a less costly way towards the defeat of Germany than the painful battering at the Western Front.

'From the late 1914 until mid–1915, the British Force stood on the defensive along the Suez Canal. A vital victory was gained in August 1916 at Romani near the coast, which relieved the Canal position. The British began to construct a railway and supply roads along the coastal plain at this time, both of which were to prove important when, two years later, it was necessary to provide for a larger force advancing into Palestine.' [1]

It was not until 1917 that sufficient force had been gathered, and lines of communication established, for an assault on the large Turkish forces in Palestine.

There are many resources available for those who wish to delve into the details regarding the "Palestine Campaign," shorthand for the theatre of operation which spread over today's Egypt, Israel, the Occupied Palestinian Territories, Gaza, Jordan, Saudi Arabia and Syria. General Sir George F. MacMunn wrote the following account of the 1917 campaign. The reader may find the mixture of ancient history and the battles fought in 1917 sometimes hard to follow, but his undoubted admiration for the Scottish soldier rings out with every sentence. It was this sentiment that was reflected in Edinburgh, and led to the momentous meeting of Edinburgh Presbytery of The Church of Scotland which is reported later in this chapter.

'To Scotland the campaign in Palestine must mean chiefly the Lowland Division of the Territorial Force, though the Ayr and Inverness Heavy Artillery Batteries and two battalions of the dismounted Fife and Forfar, and Ayr and Lanark Yeomanry must not be forgotten, or the many individual Scots who served in various units. But the bulk of names on the pylons are those of officers and other ranks of the 52nd Division. Its brigades were composed of Territorial Force battalions of five famous Scottish regiments of the Line – the Royal Scots Fusiliers, the Royal Scots, the King's Own Scottish Borderers, The Cameronians, and the Highland Light Infantry, to which, in substitution of a battalion sent early to France, came also a battalion of the Argyle and Sutherland Highlanders.

'To those who can remember the process whereby Great Britain awoke to the reality of war and its seriousness, and the eager dourness with which Scotland responded to the call from the earliest moment, it seems both meet and right that a Scottish Division should take a prominent part in carrying the hill up which Samson bore the gates of Gaza, and should have been the first to fight its way up the gorges of the Judaean Hills and gaze down on the Holy City from the heights of Nebi Samwil.

'The original Lowland Division, the 52nd in the order of Battle of the British Isles, first went into action against the heights of Achi Baba on the slopes of Cape Helles, and after the stirring months on the Peninsula, it was few enough of those who left their Scottish homes with the Division who found themselves recouping and re-equipping on the Sinai Desert in the spring of 1916.

'For three months the Lowland Division, under Major-General Sir Herbert Lawrence, dug itself fit again, on the banks of the Suez Canal, along with the other divisions of the Egyptian Expeditionary Force, or as it was then called, the Mediterranean Expeditionary Force. It moved forwards, when restored, to Romani, as the railway and the pipe line that brought the precious Nile water to the troops crept forward far into Sinai. In front of Romani, in what was the Delta ages-dry, of the Pelusiac channel of the Nile, up which Cleopatra in her light galleys had sped away before the heavier Roman ships, the Division entrenched a position to meet the Turkish advance, which boasted it would drive through once more to Egypt.

'In the fierce heat of August '16 the Division, with the Anzac Mounted Division, bore the brunt of the Turkish attack, and then staggered forward in the attempted pursuit of the beaten Turks. The repulse at Romani left Sir Archibald Murray free to bring his railway and pipe line steadily along the Way of the Philistines towards the Palestinian Frontier, and eventually to the gates of Gaza itself. During the First Battle of Gaza the 52nd were barely employed, but in the disappointment of the Second Battle it bore its full share endeavouring to storm the long glacis of the ridge on which the shrine of Ali El Muntar looked down into Gaza itself.

'With the failure to seize Gaza by a *coup de main*, and the impasse of the Second Battle, the campaign which freed Jerusalem from the Turk may be said to have been staged.

'July '17 saw Lord Allenby take command of the force and carry on that systematic preparation of desert front which enabled him to make his surprise attack on Beersheba in October and win the Third Battle of Gaza. Here the 52nd division assisted in the storming of the town, on the sea-coast line, and was then pushed forward as the spear point of General Bulfin's Corps in pursuit of the enemy. Crossing the Wadi Hese, south of Askelon, and wheeling to the right with their backs to the sea, the Division fought a desperate fight against a stubborn Turkish rearguard for the railway line. A determined night attack and bayonet struggle on a long ridge, known to the Army as "Sausage Hill," settled the business, and once more the Scottish troops tramped North in pursuit. The difficulties of food and water and the exhaustion of the mounted troops after their long ride to the sea from Beersheba gave the Turks some breathing space and they now attempted to form a line from the sea south of Jaffa, to the foothills of the Shephela. North of Beit Duras the 157th Brigade, after marching fourteen miles, made another determined night attack with the bayonet and then shared with the Yeomanry in their famous attack on El Maghar and adjacent villages. Pressing on against the Turkish line, which now faced seawards, at the foot of the Judaean Hills, covering the road and rail to Jerusalem, the 75th and 52nd Divisions, captured Junction Station and thereby cut the Turks in two, driving the VIIth Army eastwards up into the mountains and the VIIIth Army northwards along the coast into Sharon.

Scottish Troops on Palestine Plains.

'It was now Allenby's object to contain the latter army, and to force the VIIth out of Jerusalem. He aimed at doing this by driving through the mountains on Ramallah on the road from Nazareth to Jerusalem in the hope that he might secure the Holy City without a fight in its vicinity. But the extreme ruggedness of the spurs and valleys from the sea-ward side enabled the Turkish troops to put up a desperate resistance. The main attack up the Wadi Selman in the gorges north of the cart road to Jerusalem fell to the 52nd Division. It was a feat of endurance of which Scotland should remain proud for all time. Dressed in the cotton uniforms in which they had passed the summer and marched in the heat of the Philistine plain, the battalions found themselves called on to ascend in days of bitter driving rain, from sea level to close on 3000 feet, with little artillery support, in the teeth of a desperate resistance, with little opportunity for food and ammunition to follow them. But the race is not always to the swift, nor the battle to the strong. Shattered and reduced to skeletons, the Brigades of the 52nd captured the commanding height of Nebi Samwil and thence gazed down on the Holy City. Together with the Brigades of the 75th Division they repulsed desperate Turkish counter attacks, and then sorrowful but acquiescent, they gave place to the fresh troops which the generalship of Allenby had brought up to continue the work. Leaving many of their dead in the peaceful gardens of the monastery at El Kubeibeh, the 52nd Division withdrew, shattered but undaunted, to refit on the Coastal Plain, to gain ere long more renown at the crossing of the Auja in front of Jaffa.

'Early in December Jerusalem was evacuated by the Turks owing to the advance of General Chetwode's Army Corps, and General Allenby made his famous but unpretentious entry into the City on December 11. Though the Scottish Division took no part in this glorious occasion the success was due in no small degree to the heavy losses it had inflicted on the Turks, since it broke through their trenches at Gaza, and more especially to the stern struggles in front of Nebi Samwil and El Jib.' [2]

The Holy City had, once again, fallen to yet another conqueror. It had often gone down in blood and ruin: this time the nature of its surrender was somewhat different. On the morning of 9th December, 1917, just outside Jerusalem's Western Limits, two sergeants of the London Regiment, scouting ahead of Allenby's main force, were confronted by the Mayor of Jerusalem and a group of citizens, including its Chief of Police, waving a white flag and attempting to deliver a letter of surrender from the Ottoman Governor. The two sergeants refused to accept the letter, leaving the Mayor and his party to move on to find an officer of suitable rank who would. Written in Arabic the text of the surrender letter notes that 'Due to the severity of the siege of the City and the suffering that this peaceful country has endured from your heavy guns; and for fear that these deadly bombs will hit the holy places, we are forced to hand over to you the city through Hussain Bey al-Husseini, the Mayor of Jerusalem, hoping that you will protect Jerusalem the way we have protected it for more than five hundred years.'

Respecting the letter of surrender and in deliberate contrast to the perceived arrogance of the Kaiser's entry into Jerusalem on horseback in 1898, on the 11th December Allenby dismounted outside the City Wall and together with his officers, entered the city on foot through the Jaffa Gate out of respect for the status of Jerusalem, a Holy City, important to Judaism, Christianity and Islam. Allenby's proclamation to the citizens of Jerusalem that day continued this theme:

'To the inhabitants of Jerusalem the Blessed and the People dwelling in its Vicinity.

'The defeat inflicted upon the Turks by the troops under my command has resulted in the occupation of your city by my forces. I, therefore, here now proclaim it to be under martial law, under which form of administration it will remain so long as military considerations make necessary.

'However, lest any of you be alarmed by reason of your experience at the hands of the enemy who has retired, I hereby inform you that it is my desire that every person pursue his lawful business without fear of interruption.

'Furthermore, since your city is regarded with affection by the adherents of three of the great religions of mankind and its soil has been consecrated by the prayers and pilgrimages of multitudes of devout people of these three religions for many centuries, therefore, do I make it known to you that every sacred building, monument, holy spot, shrine, traditional site, endowment, pious bequest, or customary place of prayer of whatsoever form of the three religions, will be maintained and protected according to the existing customs and beliefs of those to whose faith they are sacred.

'Guardians have been established at Bethlehem and on Rachel's Tomb. The Tomb at Hebron has been placed under exclusive Moslem control.

'The hereditary custodians at the gates of the Holy Sepulchre have been requested to take up their accustomed duties in remembrance of the magnanimous act of the Caliph Omar, who protected that church.'

In the face of continuing setbacks in the war in other theatres, Allenby's success in the "capture" of Jerusalem was received at home with great rejoicing. The Scotsman of the 13th December notes:

'Te Deum Sung in London

'A solemn Te Deum will be sung at St Paul's Cathedral, London, this evening, as an act of Thanksgiving for the surrender of Jerusalem.

'In celebration of the event a Te Deum was sung at Westminster Catholic Cathedral last evening. The big bell, which has not been heard for three years, was set ringing on receipt of the news of the surrender.'

There is no doubt that Allenby's success was a cause for great celebration for the people of Great Britain, a long sought for military victory in a war with few, until then. But how were the implications of the conquest perceived by the great British public, still managing an Empire? A number of years after Allenby's entry into Jerusalem the Rev

William Ewing wrote a short essay on, "The Significance of our Victory in Palestine," not just from a British perspective, but also Scottish:

'Years may pass ere the full significance of our victory is realised: but a few points may be noted here. The Mohammedins (sic) in Palestine had long affected to despise the power of Great Britain. Their sense of superiority was increased by our lack of success in Gallipoli. The capture of Baghdad was regarded as more or less an accident which would soon be repaired by the splendid Yilderim force being assembled in Northern Syria. Allenby's sweeping triumph shattered their dream; and inspired them with a genuine respect for British prowess. This was important. It made them more amenable to British influence in other directions.

'The coming of the British was not simply the substitution of one alien government for another. It was nothing short of a revolution, and the introduction of Political Freedom. The Turk treated Palestine as a conquered province. Its people had no "rights," only duties, the chief of which was to furnish revenue to the Porte, and wealth to its corrupt representatives who battened on the country. Taxes and dues were collected at the point of the bayonet. Complaint of the injustice or oppression of an underling brought upon the victim the heavier hand of his superior. Agriculture, trade and industry languished. Education was neglected. The very rudiments of sanitation were unknown. Conscription, too, was a nightmare which bled the country of the best of its young men. Everywhere there were heartrending scenes as parents and relatives took farewell of lads called to service in some remote region of Arabia or elsewhere, many of whom, it was well known, would never be heard of more.

'With the British came government in the interest of the governed and recognition of the people's right, with growing capacity, to an increasing share in the management of their own affairs. They were granted freedom of speech, hitherto unknown; assurance that they would enjoy the fruit of their toil; protection against extortion and violence. Conscription was abolished. A network of primary schools spread over the country, and, with the cordial cooperation of the missionaries, higher education was provided for. Troops of experts assist the villagers in securing supplies of pure water, teach them the principles and practice of cleanliness, and guide them as to the conditions of a happier and nobler life.

'Self-determination may be very far away: but it is distinctly within the range of vision.

'The advent of the British brought also full Religious Liberty. It must be said that under the Turks a large measure of religious liberty was enjoyed. Christians and Jews were permitted their own sanctuaries, and pursued their religious exercises practically without molestation. Of course they were not allowed to forget that they were subject people, and, as compared with the Moslems, they were always at certain disadvantages. They were, however, free to profess and practice their faith.

'Difficulties arose when one desired to change his faith. With officials open to bribery it was always possible to make his path hard. Methods of prevention did not even stop short of murder. To seek to win a Moslem to the faith of Christ – to tamper with the faith of a "believer" – might be a capital offence; a "believer's" apostasy was visited with death.

'Under British aegis men are learning that a man's religious allegiance is a matter to be settled by himself: and that as far as British power and authority go, he will be protected in the exercise of his undoubted right. In the eradication of customs sanctioned by hoary tradition much patience may be required; but the good work has begun.

'The victory of our arms has led to a unique situation as regards the three great religions – Judaism, Christianity, and Islam – sprung from the one root, and nourished in soil watered by the same streams of divine revelation. No doubt their differences, and accentuated and embittered through centuries of alienation, are neither few nor small; but there are vast breadths of common ground among them, where surely some foothold may be found for a movement towards mutual understanding.

'The point here is that in Palestine Jews and Moslems are placed in juxtaposition – living their lives in each other's presence – as nowhere else in the world; and this under the dominance of a Christian power.

'The position seems to be that the Jews in their forward march stopped short of Calvary: and that the Moslems in the inspiring dawn of their day of might, passed Calvary in their stride. The problem is, how to persuade the Jews to resume the march, and the Moslems to return, until they meet where the Christians wait, under the reconciling influence of the Cross. May not this problem yet find its solution in "these holy fields"?

'The old embargo upon intelligent and orderly exploration of the land, and excavation of its ancient sites has been removed. Under reasonable regulations the work can now be carried on, freely and safely, without the old time espionage, intermeddling, and interruption. Several societies are availing themselves of the new conditions. As work proceeds at uncovering long buried city walls, fortress, temple and dwellinghouse; discovering objects of art, remains of ornaments, instruments of work, worship, and war, light is ever breaking forth upon the peoples who successively held this land, upon their character and life, their thought and occupations, during the whole period spanned by Biblical history.

'Our sorrow is touched with pride when we remember that our gallant sons, even at the cost of life, won such a victory. Their sacrifice deserves a noble monument.' [3]

So it was that on the 13th December, 1917, the day following the news of Allenby's entry into Jerusalem, the Scotsman reported on:

'A Great Event
'Presbytery of Edinburgh And Jerusalem

'The Presbytery of Edinburgh met today in the Presbytery Hall – the Rev Mr Knowles, West Coates, Moderator, presiding. The Moderator, at the outset said he thought reference should be made to the glad and glorious tidings that had reached them this week that Jerusalem was once again in Christian hands. (Applause) It might not be a great event politically or in the progress of the war, but it was a great event religiously – one of the great events of the ages. (Applause) They rejoiced that the Holy City, which had so long been in the hands of the infidel, was once again in Christian hands. They did not know what it might lead to in the future, to Palestine, to Jerusalem, to the world, but they prayed that it might mean a day had dawned of greater glory to Jerusalem than even the days of the past, that there would be a returning of God's people to Zion, a gathering in of the dispersed of Israel. (Applause)

'Scottish Joy Bells

'The Rev Dr Ogilvie, Moderator–Designate, in associating himself with the Moderator's remarks, said they did not ring bells – thank God – in Scotland for every passing success; neither did they wring their hands for every passing reverse. (Applause) They set their teeth firmly, and went on firmly to the end. When the time comes for ringing bells, no bells would ring more loudly or more joyfully than the bells of their Scottish churches. They did thank God that such a great event had taken place in Palestine. (Applause) As one who had lived in the East he could say how it would resound through every Eastern land. Politically it meant a vast deal that the Holy Places of the two great world religions of the East – Mohammedanism and Christianity – Mecca, and now

Jerusalem – were wrested from the hands of the Turks. (Applause) They did not know yet whether Scottish troops had taken part in the capture, but they did know that in the struggle which had been waged in that land no troops had played a more gallant and useful part than the Scottish troops, especially their Edinburgh troops and the men of the South country, the Kings Own Scottish Borderers. (Applause)

'Mr Ninian Hill suggested that to celebrate the occasion funds should be raised to build and endow a Scots Kirk of St Andrew, the Apostle, in the Holy City. To the Scotsmen visiting Jerusalem the absence of such a shrine was responsible for a feeling of loneliness.

'It was agreed to remit the matter to the Moderator's Committee for consideration, so that the proposal might be, if agreed upon, brought up to the General Assembly in the form of an overture.'

—— CHAPTER TWO ——

Ninian Hill

ATTENDING the 12th December, 1917, meeting of Edinburgh Presbytery as an Elder of Murrayfield Parish Church, Ninian Hill, in giving no advance notice – seemingly on the spur of the moment inspired by the great news of the day – created a vision. The development of this dream grew to become his personal crusade and dominated his life for the next twenty-nine years until his death in 1946.

Born on the 27th November, 1861, into a well-known Greenock family of considerable wealth and influence, Ninian was the second of two children, his sister, Mary, being one year older.

His father, James Ramsay Hill, by profession a master engineer and merchant, was also the owner of the Greenock Foundry Company, heavily involved in the flourishing Greenock ship building industry. The company was later absorbed into Scotts' Shipbuilding and Engineering Co., Ltd. [4]

Hill's father's family had a long history of medical general practice in the town, both his grandfather and great-grandfather much esteemed as skilful and caring physicians. His grandfather, also Ninian Hill, had studied in Edinburgh, London and Paris and was a prolific and respected author, in English and Latin, on medical matters.

Hill's mother, Mary Jane Grieve, (1838 – 1926), one of fourteen siblings, was the daughter of James Johnston Grieve (1810 – 1891) who was elected four times as Provost of Greenock and was also a Justice of the Peace of the Burgh. A Liberal politician, he represented the town in the House of Commons from 1868 to 1878. In addition to his political interest and concerns J. J. Grieve was also, for some time, the senior partner in the Greenock mercantile firm of "Baine and Johnston," a partner company with strong family and financial links to "Baine, Johnson & Co.," based in Halifax, Nova Scotia. Heavily involved in the cod fishing and sealing industries in Canada, from the 1830's through to the early 20th century, the company registered nearly three-hundred vessels, making it one of the largest shipping fleets in Canada.

Ninian was only five when his father died at the age of thirty, leaving his mother and the wider family to care for him and his sister. Given the family resources, it is reasonable to assume that their financial position was not precarious. With the intention that he be educated at Eton, Hill attended its preparatory school, "Hawtrey's," in Slough. While there, however, after an accident followed by prolonged serious illness, he continued his education at home with the help of private tutors. With health restored, he attended St Andrews University and Oxford. It was during this time he developed his interest in music and fine arts, spending time in Paris and Rome studying modern languages.

At the age of twenty-three, Ninian commissioned the construction of his ship "*Atalanta*," built in Port Glasgow by Robert Duncan & Co. Basil Lubbock in his book, "The Last of the Windjammers," [5] notes:

'In 1885 Duncan & Co. launched their last out and out clipper ship, and many say their finest. This was the Atalanta, a main skysail and double top gallant yarder, carrying 2500 tons on a net register of 1752 tons.

'All their latest ships were flat bottomed carriers. Atalanta's owner, Mr Ninian Hill, and her captain Charles McBride, who had commanded the tea clipper Normancourt previously, were immensely proud of her. Nothing was stinted by Mr Hill and McBride kept her like a yacht. On her last homeward passage she caused great admiration by sailing right up to the anchorage at the Tail of the Bank under full canvas. Here a party of officers visited her and expressed their delight in viewing such a lovely ship.

'On another occasion at Queenstown the Port Admiral and his Flag Lieutenant paid her a visit, and when the Admiral was told that she was manned by 30 men he replied that in the Royal Navy she would have 300 but they could not have kept her better.

'As regards speed she once did 950 miles in three days whilst running down her easting. On a passage from Cardiff to Singapore in 1886 she made 320 and 325 in two consecutive days.'

Engaged mostly in the Java sugar trade, by standards of the day she was held to be very fast and therefore very profitable. Hill clearly considered his status as "Shipowner" important to him at this stage of his life, as this was how he described himself and was described by others in publications of the day. Years later, in different circumstances, he described himself in the 1901 Census as "Retired Shipowner." As "Shipowner," Hill's office in Greenock was in the same building as that of his grandfather's company, "Baine and Johnston", with its direct link to the burgeoning company of similar name in Nova Scotia.

In addition to his shipping business, Hill supplemented his income with the rent from letting out the twenty-five properties he owned in the town. Of his time Hill would be considered a successful businessman, a status enhanced through public service. As his grandfather before him, he was elected in 1888, at the age of twenty-seven, as a Ward Councillor in the Burgh and, three years later, was returned unopposed until 1895. During this period he was also a Dean of Guild, 1892 to 1894, and Burgh Treasurer from 1894 to 1895.

With his business interests and public responsibilities, Hill was also associated with the work of many local religious and philanthropic societies in the town, including that of Trustee and Chairman of the Board of the Greenock Provident Bank.

The young Ninian Hill

In 1898, however, disaster struck. On the 17th November that year, the *"Atalanta"* was wrecked off the coast of Oregon with the loss of the captain and twnty-four crew. There were two survivors. A not uncommon occurrence of the time, but sadly made worse by the cause, as reported in the New York Times of the 20th November, 1898:

'Portland, Oregon, November 19. – One of the survivors of the ill fated Atalanta, the wreck of which on the Oregon coast yesterday resulted in the drowning of twenty-four men, declares that the wreck was due to the carelessness of the Captain, who paid for his folly with his life.

'The ship was racing with another vessel and was keeping closer inshore in order to get the advantage of the wind in tacking and to make a shortcut to head the other vessel off. Not seeing the light at Cape Foulweather, the Atalanta steered ahead until she struck the reef about four miles below Alsea Bay and about one mile and a half from shore with such terrific force as to snap the masts off like toothpicks, carrying away the rigging and everything on deck.'

The loss of the ship and the manner of the loss would, clearly, have had a considerable effect on Hill's life. The records note that, at the time of its sinking, the ship was valued at $50,000 and it was carrying wheat to South Africa worth $65,000 [total £1.8m]. Given the circumstances, if the insurers did not make good the loss, this event would certainly have affected his financial position.

Following this tragedy there are few records of Hill's activities until 1901 when he relocates with his mother to Edinburgh to take up the post of Honorary Secretary of the "Scottish Temperance Legislation Board" followed, in 1906, with employment as the General Secretary of the "Scottish National Society for the Prevention of Cruelty to Children." As two distinct campaigning organisations they have overlapping and related concerns regarding the society of the day and a glimpse into Hill's work with them provides some insight as to his interests, his concerns and the issues which motivate and drive him.

Hill's concerns to reform the law in Scotland regarding the opening hours of licensed premises, thereby restricting the consumption of alcohol, were revealed a number of years earlier when, in 1893, as Dean of Guild in Greenock, he seconded a motion, 'That this Council petition Parliament in favour of the "Liquor Traffic (Local Control) Bill" now before the house.' Thirteen years later, as Secretary of the "Temperance Legislation Board," Hill was now in a position to play a strategic role in the drive for reform in Scotland. A letter to the editor of the Glasgow Herald on the 22nd January, 1903, illustrates his strength of feeling on the matter:

'Lord Peel's Minority Report

'Sir,- My attention has been directed to the leader in your issue of yesterday, as it appears to call for some reply. You ask, "What has become of the formidable body created to press for legislation on the lines of the minority report of Lord Peel's Committee?" I am glad to be able to state that it continues to gain the confidence and support of the country. We have not been able to do all that we should wish but we are continually receiving fresh input of strength and influence, notwithstanding the difficulties that beset the path of the reformer.

'Lord Peel's regrettable indisposition has deprived us of his powerful advocacy and for this reason we have not been able to hold meetings in any of the large towns as we were able last year. During the summer we had a most wonderful campaign during the months of June, July, and August and very many largely attended meetings were held in the West and South of Scotland, and within the last three months we have held important public meetings in Nairn, Elgin, Peterhead, Stonehaven, Crieff, Ayr, East Wemys, Dingwall and Cromarty. These meetings have been well supported by leading citizens representing both sides of politics and by teetotallers as well as by non-teetotallers. It is just a month since the Solicitor-General made the announcement of the probability of a Licensing Bill for Scotland next session and the holidays have come in since, and we have been able to arrange a series of public meetings, beginning this week, in Dunblane, Galashiels, Port Glasgow, Kirkcaldy, Kilmarnock, Peterhead, Rothesay and Perth. Amongst those who have promised to take part are the Master of Polwarth, the Hon. and Rev. Maurice Peel, and the Provosts of Port Glasgow, Kilmarnock and Rothesay.

'At all our meetings resolutions are submitted urging the Government to introduce legislation on the lines of Lord Peel's report. We want to see every one of Lord Peel's proposals adopted *en bloc* but, failing this, we are quite ready to take them in instalments. To this end we have supported the bills for extending the power of closing public houses at 10 o'clock. We are earnestly advocating the regulation of clubs, a far more important point, to my thinking. Lord Balfour is undoubtedly in possession of all the facts regarding them. One of the most important documents relating to them was recently published by your Chief Constable. He gave a list of the alleged "bogus" clubs and it clearly showed the need, if not for licensing clubs, as has been ordained in the Transvaal, at least they are stringent regulations. One important point brought out in the list is that the bogus club flourishes in those districts where public-houses are most numerous. Clearly, then, it cannot be maintained as has been contended, that bogus clubs are the product of restriction and under-licensing.

'As regards the question of the relation of the number of public-houses and the amount of drunkenness, it has been brought out prominently in Liverpool, and Lord Balfour of Burleigh has quoted in his letter to Lord Provost Primrose that the first reason given by the Chief Constable for the remarkable reduction in the amount of crime in that city is the decrease of licensed houses. An important consideration in regard to the reduction in the number of licensed houses, and one that is often overlooked, is the improvement in the environment of the toilers of our cities that results. It seems to me that the aims of temperance legislation should not be coercion, so much as offering an improvement in the condition of life, especially in our great cities so that those who perforce are now compelled to live amid sources of temptation may have a better chance of leading sober and responsible lives. The existing licensing system is, as you say, "poisonous to our public life." For God's sake, then, let us unite and reform it.

'We believe that in so far as Lord Balfour of Burleigh sees his way to adopt the recommendations of Lord Peel's Minority Report, he will receive the enthusiastic support of this Board and of all those important sections of the country, irrespective of politics and creeds, who desire to promote the welfare of the nation.

'I am, etc., Ninian Hill, Secretary.'

This work brought him into close involvement with many of the Westminster politicians of the day, including the Lords Peel and Balfour of Burleigh, the latter being someone Hill would work closely with in time to come. Largely through the work of the Board, "The Licensing (Scotland) Act, 1903" came into being and when Hill retired as Secretary of the Board in 1904, at the time of its dissolution, Peel wrote to Hill thanking him for his personal contribution to the success of the campaign.

Hill's employment as the General Secretary of the "Scottish National Society for the Prevention of Cruelty to Children" coincided with a time of considerable change in its administration. In addition to revising the structure of the organisation to enable it to cope with growing demands, the records of the Society provide clear evidence of Hill's comprehensive knowledge and understanding of the law and the context of the issues facing the Society in its care for children. Through Hill the Society played a major role in assisting with framing the legislation contained in the "The Children Act, 1908," and, on behalf of the Society, in 1909, Hill wrote the handbook, "The Child and the State in Scotland: An Outline of the Law Relating to Children." In seeking advice, Hill's response to Society Inspectors was always clear, concise and professional, as in this letter to an Inspector in Dingwall:

'Dear Sir,

'On my return from holiday I have received your letters regarding the above named case. I think the proper way to proceed in this case is to charge the father and probably the mother with cruelty to the children under Section 12 (1). Following on conviction an application should be made to the Court under section 58 (d) for the committal of the three eldest children at any rate to Industrial Schools and an order should be made upon the parents to contribute under Section 75. In the event of an application being made for the committal of the children to Industrial Schools notice must be given to the School Board under section 74 (6). I am presuming that the (family name) have a fixed residence in Dingwall and that the School Board could not successfully plead that they are vagrants. If they are vagrants the School Board cannot be compelled to provide for the maintenance of the children. Section 75 (1) is put into operation as a matter of course but in the great majority of cases it is more or less of a form, as the contributions by parents are very uncertain. The School Board however in ordinary circumstances is bound to provide and maintain the children. Please observe that these provisions only apply to Certified Industrial Schools. You will find a list of these in the "Child and the State," page 67. Please let me know if I can give you any further information on the subject. I return the case papers.

'Yours truly, Ninian Hill, Secretary.'

--------··●·●··--------

Hill's breadth of interests and concerns are also demonstrated in his publications and contributions to a wide variety of journals and periodicals.

Hill's first publication was produced while he was living in Greenock. Published in 1898, "The Story of the Old West Kirk of Greenock, 1591 to 1898," [6] sets out to provide a history of the congregation, its culture and practices down through the years. The book also presents a well illustrated insight into Hill's detailed knowledge of the church's architecture, its pre-Raphaelite stained glass windows and related artefacts. It was at the time of the book's printing that Hill received the news of the loss of the "Atalanta" and crew, and the book is dedicated to the men who lost their lives.

In 1915 he published, "Poland and the Polish Question: Impressions and Afterthoughts." [7] In the preface Hill describes his reason for writing on the subject:

'The following pages are the outcome of a visit to Poland during the summer of 1913. What I then saw and learned led me to make a study of the history of the country and of the then existing circumstances of the Poles in Prussia, Russia, and Austria. I found the subject one of great interest and one, which by some strange oversight, has been neglected by English writers. The upheaval of Europe by the war has brought Poland once more to the attention of the public, and it is in these circumstances I venture to issue this volume. I do so in the hope that it may arouse fresh sympathy for this very gallant nation.

'In addition to the acknowledgements I have made in the course of my narrative, I desire to make grateful mention of my special indebtedness to Morfil's "Poland" in the "Story of the Nations" series, to Lelevel's "Histoire de Pologne", and, for more recent events, to the "Times".'

The book was very well received, with positive reviews in the New York Times, the Scotsman, the Daily Telegraph, and the Journal of Race Development (Vol 6, No 3, 1916). The Manchester Guardian notes that, 'Mr Hill has performed a difficult task with marked success. Not only has he given a concise and reliable account of Polish history and politics, but he has set forth the chief problems of Polish history with real judgement and unusual accuracy, handling as he does a subject on which there is practically nothing written in English.'

"The Story of the Scottish Church from the Earliest Times," was published in 1919. [8] and dedicated to the memory of Rev. Gavin Lang Pagan, B.D., Minister of St George's Parish Church, Edinburgh, 'Who at the call of his King and Country with the sanction of his Presbytery enlisted as a Private soldier and gallantly fell in action in France on 28th April, 1917.' The preface reveals Hill's deep love and concern for the Church of Scotland and its place in the development of Scotland and the Empire:

'On the occasion of a recent visit to the Grand Fleet, the Dean of the Thistle and Chapel Royal was reported in the daily press to have been asked by a naval officer apropos of the name of a patrol craft, "And who was Jenny Geddes?" The question, it is to be feared, is symptomatic of much popular ignorance concerning the national church. The following pages have been written with the object of providing the general reader with a brief sketch of the history of the Church of Scotland. For his convenience there is added in an Appendix some notes to elucidate matters of interest instead of referring to works not always readily accessible.

'It has been my earnest desire and endeavour to write nothing unfair or uncharitable to those from whose opinions on ecclesiastical matters I have been led to differ. As occasion seemed to call for it, the words of representative authorities have been quoted and references given to the works consulted. I desire to express my sincere thanks to Brigadier General, the Rev. J. A. McClyment, D.D., V.D., Principal Chaplain, Deputy Clerk of the General Assembly, for his advice and help; and also to the Society of Antiquaries of Scotland; the Rev. Norman MacLean, D.D., the Rev. Patrick M Playfair, D.D., P. McGregor Chalmers, Esq., I.A., and Thomas Liddle, Esq., for the kindness in providing me with illustrations.

'The question may be asked – "Why in the midst of a great war should we be asked to consider the subject of church history?" A sufficient answer may be given in the words of a great thinker – the late Professor Flint, who said many years ago, "The Church has done more than any other institution to make Scotland what it is." What Scotland really is has been made abundantly manifest by the war. Not less than other parts of the British Empire has it shown in all ranks and classes of society intense devotion to high ideals of righteousness and duty, and

Scotsmen have good reason to value their national church, the time and ultimate channel of their inspiration, and to cherish its history.'

Murrayfield Parish Church, Edinburgh, in which Hill was an Elder, reviewed the book in its January, 1919, Parish Supplement, noting that, 'There is no other book upon the market which is so admirably adapted to the needs of the average church member who wishes an accurate, reliable, readable account, of reasonable length, of the Genesis and development of the Scottish Church; and among clergy as well as laymen Mr Hill's volume is certain of a warm welcome.... As a congregation we may well be proud to number among us one who has performed so notable a service to the Church as a whole.'

Hill was also a prolific contributor to a variety of national and international journals, all illustrating the depth and broad sweep of his interests and knowledge. For example:

'In the "Scottish Historical Review:

'Volume 17, 1920 – "A Sidelight on the 1715," a detailed essay on the 1715 uprising, particularly in respect of the Earl of Mar's involvement and the failed French support.

'Volume 21, 1924 – a review of "The Divinity Professors in the University of Glasgow, 1640 to 1903," by the Rev. H. M. B. Reid.

'Volume 23, 1925 – a review of "Thomas Cartwright and Elizabethan Puritanism, 1535 to 1603," by the Rev. A. F. Scott Pearson.

Hill was a member of "The Church Service Society", a body whose aim was and is the promotion of traditional worship and liturgy in the church. Its chief publication, the annual "Journal", an initiative of Hill, was first published in 1929. In his introduction to this first publication, the Rt. Rev. Norman MacLean, Moderator of the General Assembly of the Church of Scotland, and by this time a friend and colleague of Hill, wrote:

'The Church of Scotland's freedom in worship can be a snare when abused. It is not a Christian service when a congregation goes through the forms of worship without confession and absolution; when the first prayer is a theological meditation; and when petitions, incongruous and interminable, jostle each other in an inchoate mass. The Church Service Society has shown that the bare and formless worship offered in the Parish churches for over two centuries was not the fruit of the Reformation and the publication of these volumes draws attention to the reverence and beauty and dignity which the worship of God requires.'

Hill edited the first two editions of the Journal and later made a number of contributions, including an article on "St Andrew's Church, Jerusalem", in 1932; and in 1938 an article, "Concerning Reverence," in which he refers to biblical foundations, considers "godly fear and awe" and its expression in deportment in church.

Later in his life, in 1945, Hill self-published "A First Communion Manual", a thirty-nine page booklet 'written primarily as an *aide-memoire* for those attending a First Communion class.' Following a set of instructions for the first communicant, culminating in their service of confirmation, Hill provides 'Some Counsels' within the booklet:

'1. Never be late on entering church. Always be in your place before the divine service begins.

'2. If you should go as a visitor to any church, always ask to be shown to a seat. If you do so, you will be sure of a welcome.

'3. When you get to your place, take off your gloves, then kneel down, or if that is impossible, bow down, and pray for a blessing on yourself, the minister, and the congregation.

'4. Every communicant should possess a Bible. If you have not one already, get a well-printed and well bound copy to last your lifetime. You should also have a "Church Hymnary"; and regard it as more than a hymn book for use in church. It is an invaluable treasury of devotional literature for private meditation and prayer.

'5. It is a laudable custom to read in your own Bible the lessons as they are read in church. It helps to keep the mind from wandering, and to impress the subject on the memory: this also applies to the text of the sermon.

'6. Don't talk in church. Here are some wise words from the "Directory"; "The Public Worship being begun, the people are wholly to attend upon it, and abstaining from all private whisperings, conferences, salutations, or doing reverence to any person present are coming in; as also from all gazing, sleeping, or other indecent behaviour which may disturb the minister or people, or hinder themselves and others in the service of God."

'7. At the end of the service, when the benediction has been pronounced, kneel down, or at least bow down, and pray. Wait in your place until the minister has retired and then leave quietly.'

On the 6th, October, 1905, a foundation stone was laid marking the construction of a new church in the Murrayfield District of Edinburgh. Although the building work had not yet been completed, on the 25th June, 1913, the Presbytery of Edinburgh gave permission to those attending worship that they could establish a parish in the area, and Murrayfield Parish Church came into being. The following year, on the 11th January, 1914, Ninian Hill was ordained as an Elder in the congregation. One month later he was elected a Trustee, the responsibilities of which included the completion of the work to the building, including fundraising. The Parish records indicate Hill's diligence in his responsibilities as an Elder and Trustee and his leadership in the Sunday school, the Boys Brigade Sunday Bible Class and the choir. In addition Hill was also an auditor of the Congregation's accounts.

During this time the war, its effect on the Congregation and people in the Parish was very much on everybody's mind. The Minute of the meeting of the Kirk Session on the 5th October, 1914, records, 'Mr Hill proposed that a "Roll of Honour" of residents in the Parish serving during the war in the King's naval and military forces should be made up, as suggested by Lord Roseberry, and that it should be hung up in the vestibule of the church. The draft of a circular to be issued on the subject was submitted. The Kirk Session heartily approved the proposal and of the circular and instructed the clerk accordingly.'

From the Kirk Session records, "Memorials," and the like, were regularly associated with Hill. On the 17th December, 1915, it is noted 'Mr Hill stated that the Murrayfield Company of the Boys Brigade proposed to present to the Church a bookstand for the Communion Table in memory of those who had fallen in the war. The Kirk Session expressed thanks to Mr Hill and the Boys Brigade for the proposed gift.'

One year later on the 15th December, 1916, Hill was appointed as Murrayfield's representative to sit on the "Roseburn (United Free Church) and Murrayfield War Saving Association." Even after the war, in 1919, Hill was appointed to the Congregation's "War Memorial Committee" which took responsibility for the resumption of the building work to the Church, which had been suspended due to the war. The Committee's remit was to proceed with the building of the Chancel, designed and supervised by Sir Robert Lorimer, and was to be dedicated as a War Memorial, 'to those of our number who have made the supreme sacrifice.'

Hill's considerable commitments to Murrayfield Church, his growing workload in developing the proposed Memorial in Jerusalem and his travels in pursuit of his many interests did not deter him from taking the decision to train for the Ministry. Following studies at Edinburgh University, he was licensed a Probationer for the Ministry in June, 1922, and on completion of the prescribed period as Assistant Minister at Greenside Parish Church, Edinburgh, was Ordained, at the age of 62, on the 11th February, 1923. The April 1923, edition of the Murrayfield Parish Church Supplement records the event:

'At the close of the evening service in St Cuthbert's on Sunday 11th February, 1923, Mr Ninian Hill was ordained to the Ministry of the Church of Scotland by the Presbytery of Edinburgh. The Rev. Norman MacLean, D.D., presided and preached the sermon. The earlier portion of the service was conducted by Dr. Fisher while lessons were read by Prof. Kennedy and Mr Rossie Brown (Minister Murrayfield Church). Dr. Strachan represented the United Free Church. After the ordination, Communion Vessels, presented by Mr Hill for the Church at Jerusalem, were dedicated in prayer.'

Through Dr. MacLean, Hill's relationship with St Cuthbert's Church was very close. On the 1st December, 1924, St Cuthbert's Kirk Session approved a proposal from the Moderator, Dr. MacLean, that due to his workload, Hill be appointed as Assistant for six months. Four and half years later Hill resigned from the appointment due to his own increasing workload in respect of the Memorial Church and Hospice in Jerusalem. However the Minute of the Kirk Session meeting on the 6th May, 1929, records the Session's '... very high appreciation of the valuable work Mr Hill had done in the Congregation and Parish. On the suggestion of the Moderator (Dr. Maclean) the Session agreed that Mr Hill's association with the Ministers of St Cuthbert's should be continued in an honorary capacity and the Clerk was instructed to send him an extract from this minute.'

Hill's workload went far beyond his work with St Cuthbert's and the Memorial in Jerusalem. As Honorary Secretary to the Church's "Committee on Chaplains of HM Forces" he visited garrisons around the country, including the new St Andrew's Garrison Church, constructed as a War Memorial, in Aldershot, and designed by Sir Robert Lorimer, the same architect involved with Hill in the completion of Murrayfield Parish Church. As a prominent member of the Church's "Committee on Psalmody and Hymns", Hill, a talented organist himself, initiated the scheme for the training of organists in Church music.

In addition to all of this, Hill still found time to travel the world, to see the church at work in India and visited China, Japan and the Middle East, all of this over and above his regular European travel to further his many interests and concerns.

In July, 1935, Hill received an Honorary Doctorate from Edinburgh University for services to the Church and Society.

Rev Dr. Ninian Hill D.D.

Three months earlier, on the 4th April, 1935, at the West Church in Inverness, Hill, at the age of 73, married Marguerite Richer, 44, from Paris, the daughter of Henri Richer and Marie Therese de Portemer. There is little recorded of Marguerite. However there is a brief character sketch in her obituary published in the Journal of the Church Service Society, following her death in June, 1971:

'Marguerite was a charming lady of simple and child-like faith in the Heavenly Father's goodness and mercy. Entwined into her life and personality were links with the whole century of different people and settings, ideas, customs, and localities. By her own very unusual whimsy and cheerfulness, she made life more exciting, gay and picturesque than it could ever have been without the unique Mrs Ninian Hill.

France and the French ethos, music and clothes, the life–boat, the church in many varied aspects, and the Church Service Society were among her enthusiasms. But her chief interest lay in the translation into stone of her beloved Ninian's version of a corner of Christian Scotland in the Holy Land.'

Of his marriage Hill said that 'God kept this best gift for the end.'

——————————••◆••——————————

Tucked away in the Minutes of the Kirk Session of Murrayfield Parish Church, there is the note of a decision which is, perhaps, key to the story of the Scots Memorial in Jerusalem. The record simply states that on the 18th May, 1917, the decision is taken that from the 1st July, that year, for the period of one year, Mr Ninian Hill will be the Congregation's representative to Edinburgh Presbytery.

For many, the formalities and procedures of a Presbytery meeting can be quite intimidating and bewildering. It takes courage and confidence to stand to make a point or propose a motion before, very often, the theological and ecclesiastical "giants" of the day. However, from what we know of Ninian Hill, the Elder, a man of varied experience, confident and articulate, held in high esteem by his peers, it is not unreasonable to assume that when he spoke, he would be listened to and words said would be carefully considered.

And so it was that the Scotsman, in reporting on the Presbytery meeting of 12th December, 1917, made the point in noting Hill's proposal to build a "Scots Kirk of St Andrew" in Jerusalem, and that it was being remitted for consideration.

—— CHAPTER THREE ——

Pursuing the Vision

ON THE 27th March, 1918, three months after Hill's made his proposal, the Presbytery of Edinburgh met and the Minute records that the Moderator 'reported on behalf of the Committee on the proposed Scots' Church at Jerusalem, that the Committee had conferred on the subject with the Business Committee of the United Free Church Presbytery of Edinburgh and that the Joint Committee were of the opinion that the erection in Jerusalem by the Scottish Churches of some suitable memorial of the recent capture of the City by the Christian Powers is worthy of the most serious consideration. Dr. Paul concluded by giving notice of an overture to the General Assembly regarding the proposed Scottish Churches Memorial in Jerusalem.'

As it had been his suggestion, Hill was invited to read to Presbytery the proposed draft overture:

'Whereas the city of Jerusalem, hallowed as the scene of the Crucifixion and Resurrection of our Lord, has again, through the blessing of God and the valour of our troops, been wrested from the Muslim after a continuous occupation of nearly seven centuries, and is now in Christian hands, and, whereas it is fitting that so memorable an event should be signalised in some worthy manner by the Christian Church in Scotland: it is humbly overtured by the Presbytery of Edinburgh to the venerable the General Assembly that the matter be remitted to a Committee appointed for the purpose, or to one of the Committees already existing with instructions to enquire into it in all its bearings, and, particularly, to consider whether the desired end would be gained by the erection in Jerusalem, when the proper time arrives, of a Scots Church befitting the sacred associations of the site, and to report to the next General Assembly; or that the Assembly should take such other action in the matter as in their wisdom may seem to them meet.'

The General Assembly considered the proposal and the positive, yet tentative, response included an instruction, 'to remit the matter it deals with to a special committee, and to report to the next General Assembly.'

Under the Convenership of Prof. A.R.S. Kennedy, the special committee met, and one of its first decisions was to invite the participation of the United Free Church of Scotland in the venture. This was on the understanding 'that if the proposed Memorial was to be truly national steps should be taken to secure, if possible, the co-operation of the United Free Church of Scotland. In its response to the invitation, "the Commission of Assembly, having heard the letter from Prof. Kennedy relative to a proposal to erect a Scottish Memorial at Jerusalem, cordially expressed general approval of the proposal contained therein, and, at the same time, would cherish the hope that ways may be found whereby it will be possible to include in the movement Presbyterian Churches other than those in Scotland, that thereby a large Presbyterian Memorial may be founded in Jerusalem."'

The "joint" special committee was formed and met just once, on the 13th January, 1919, to consider the proposed Memorial and each reported to their respective General Assemblies with the recommendation:

'1. That the Memorial should be, as originally proposed, Scottish and national, inasmuch as the end in view is to give "visible and permanent" expression to the Scottish people's gratitude to God for the deliverance of Jerusalem, and to their grateful remembrance of the brave men of Scottish birth who have given their lives for the liberation of the Holy City and the Holy Land.

'2. That the said Memorial should combine a Church with an Institute for Biblical Study, and might bear some such title as "The Scots Kirk and College in Jerusalem."

'3. The Sub-Committee estimate the sum required for the erection of such a memorial, and for its necessary endowment, at approximately £30,000.'

Continuing with an explanation to the General Assemblies, 'your Committee would indicate briefly the reasons which have led them to adopt a combined Church and School of Biblical Study as the most appropriate form of the proposed memorial. In the first place, they consider that no memorial would meet the wishes of the Scottish people that did not include a Church for the worship of God according to the custom of our fathers. The building contemplated would be of modest dimensions, but both without and within it must be worthy alike of our country and of its sacred site. In a suitable place the names might be inscribed of all Scottish men and women who have died in the course of the British Army's operations in Palestine.

'The case for the erection of a Church as part, at least, of a Scottish Churches Memorial, could not be more effectively presented than it is in a letter which was written, quite independently of the present movement, to a friend in Edinburgh, by Judge Scott, President of the Court of Appeal in Jerusalem under the British administration.

'In addition, it may be urged that the provision in Jerusalem of 'a house of prayer,' in which Presbyterians of 'all nations' could unite in common worship, is a legitimate desire on the part of those to whom other forms of worship are unfamiliar and unsatisfying.

'The objection, that the addition of another church to the many already existing in Jerusalem is uncalled for, is met in large part by the Committee's proposal to combine therewith a permanent institution for the promotion of sacred learning. To this part of the memorial, indeed, your Committee attach special importance. They contemplate the establishment, with a sufficient endowment, of an institution resembling the old-time Scots Colleges on the Continent.

'In this 'School of the Prophets' ministers, missionaries, students of divinity, and other members of our Churches would have a unique opportunity, under the guidance of a competent director, of studying the Old and New Testaments in the city of the prophets and apostles. From Jerusalem as a centre they would be able to investigate the sacred sites and antiquities of Palestine, and to study at first hand the life, languages, and customs of the East.

'The "Scots College" in Jerusalem would also be a rallying-point for all visitors from the home land, and would, it is hoped, be taken advantage of by our Presbyterian brethren from other lands.

'Your Committee are convinced that an institution on these lines would appeal to the sympathy and generosity of the Scottish people, both rich and poor, for whom the city of Jerusalem holds so many hallowed associations. Nor will it be denied that a course of study, such as that outlined above, would add materially to the equipment of our ministers for their sacred office. To live and work, even for a short period, amid the scenes where our Saviour Himself lived, and taught, and suffered, could not fail to be a source of lifelong inspiration to those who are called to be preachers of His Holy Gospel.'

The 'coincidental' letter from Judge Scott, after a description of the part played by Scottish soldiers in General Allenby's campaign, continues:

'What of the cost? Scattered throughout the length and breadth of the land, from Dan to Beersheba, from the sea to Jordan and beyond, are lonely Scottish graves. Many relatives will wish to visit these, will wish to see the land for which their dear ones fought, to visit Jerusalem, where the greatest of all sacrifices was made, and to worship where the Redeemer of mankind died. Will they not wish to worship according to the rites of 'the church of their fathers,' and, in the city where it was instituted, to "keep the feast" after the manner in which they have been accustomed so to do? Will not all Scotsmen, then, irrespective of Church divisions, band themselves together to build a Church in honour of our Master, and as a fitting Memorial for all those heroic Scotsmen who died in the waterless deserts, in the battlefields of Gaza, round about Jaffa, among the mountains of Judaea, and right on to Damascus?

'It is all twice holy ground. Once our Lord walked there; now sons, fathers, husbands, brothers, sweethearts lie there till the resurrection.... They gave much, yea all that was dear to them. Surely then all Scots – both men and women – will give a little, that a lasting and most fitting Memorial may be set up for them in the place where our Lord was crucified!'

With this the records note that:

'The General Assembly approved generally of the Report, re-appoint the Committee with power to add to their number, and authorise them, in co-operation with the corresponding Committee of the United Free Church of Scotland, to take all such measures as may seem best adapted to promote the end in view, and report to the next General Assembly.' (1920).

Significantly, this new Committee was constituted under the authority of the respective General Assemblies but was not responsible to any other Board or Council of the Churches and while this had distinct advantages it did create difficulties. This "independent" status was somewhat enhanced by the General Assemblies in permitting it 'to take all such measures as may seem best adapted to promote the end in view.' Not exactly *carte blanche* but certainly wide ranging authority to facilitate its work in establishing the Memorial.

The decision to proceed with the Memorial was well recorded in the press of the day. The Scotsman in its report on the Church of Scotland General Assembly, on the 26th May, 1919, quoted Lord Scott Dixon in his support of the proposed Memorial stating that '...he was glad the Scottish people were beginning to awaken to their responsibilities in this matter. It was not only fitting but necessary that their Presbyterian

Churches should have a recognised place of worship in the Holy City, where almost every other religious community was represented. It was all to the good that in setting about this memorial church they were to be associated with their brethren of the United Free Church. To his mind it was of happy augury that this common church should be started by the Church of Scotland and the United Free Church. It seemed to him that that was the beginning at Jerusalem in a very proper manner. (Applause).'

Through the years of the work of the Committee seeking to build the Memorial, the press, especially the Scotsman in Edinburgh, gave considerable publicity and support to the scheme. To mark the second anniversary of General Allenby's entrance into Jerusalem, the Scotsman, on the 11th December, 1919, gave space to the Rev. Dr. Norman MacLean, by this time a member of the Committee, to write on the event. The article, here reproduced in full, was later printed as a booklet for publicity and fundraising purposes. Written a year after the end of the war, with events, including the victory celebrations, still fresh in the memory, the reader today may find the language a little extravagant:

Jerusalem Redeemed

'Now and again it happens that eternity projects itself into the midst of the ephemeral and wearisome deliberations of a court of the Church, and it is always unexpectedly that the stars thus shine forth. It was so at a meeting of the Presbytery of Edinburgh shortly after the deliverance of Jerusalem. A motion was made expressing thankfulness that the shame of seven centuries was ended. The right things were said, and the Presbytery was to pass on to its schedules when an elder got up in a back seat – and the eternal stars began to shine. He was not accustomed to public speech; he had difficulty in controlling his voice; but the emotion that brought him to his feet found the words for its utterance. This, said he, was the greatest event in the history of the world since Titus captured the Holy City; to realise its significance the event must be viewed in the light of that surging emotion that set six million of the youth and chivalry of Europe in motion towards Palestine in the Middle Ages to deliver the Holy Sepulchre from the Mohammedans. The greatest of the Scottish Kings, Robert Bruce, had vowed himself to that cause; and Douglas, with a handful of followers, set forth bearing the heart of Bruce in a golden casket to lay it in the Sepulchre of the Redeemer ... While the elder's sentences gathered strength, a strange thing happened to a member of the Presbytery who had been aforetime wearied. Something cracked inside his head, and he became conscious in an instant of what this thing meant, how the Realm Unseen the hosts of crusaders and saints rejoiced over the accomplishment at last of what they had died for so long ago; and he heard "The shout of them that triumph, the song of them that feast."

'That Presbytery hall was suddenly transformed into a shrine of the soul, filled with the melodies of heaven. And the elder moved that the Presbytery at once take steps to build a Scottish church in Jerusalem as a thank offering to God. The boldness of the proposal was disconcerting. The members wanted to get on with their day's work. But the elder got his motion referred to a Committee; the Committee overtured the Assembly; the Assembly appointed a Committee; the United Free Church Assembly did the same; and now the two great Scottish Churches have united their forces and the elder who galvanised a weary Presbytery into life by first proposing the great undertaking is the joint-secretary of the United Committee......

'In the last five years there was no event so great as the delivery of Jerusalem from the bondage of the Turk. That bondage had lasted so long that Christians had got inured to its shame. To the cause of Christianity, the possession of its own holy places will be a great re-enforcement. And no result of the deliverance could appeal more to the Scottish race than this proposal to build a Scots Church and College in the Holy City. Of the scheme the College is an essential part. In other days there were Scots Colleges in Paris and Rome, and there the Scottish priesthood learned a wider outlook than their isolated land could give. But these were lost; and the clergy of the Scottish churches have lost greatly through their losing touch with other lands. The day is doubtless coming when the Church of Scotland – reunited again – will provide that every minister shall have a term in the Scots College of Jerusalem. There in the atmosphere of the East they will realise that Christianity is not a matter of Western syllogisms, but of Eastern imagery. Amid the very scenes of the world's redemption they will be taught to read the story anew until reverence and devotion fill the heart. A term in the Scots College at Jerusalem, where history would be taught on the scene of its greatest triumphs and tragedies, and where devotion would be learned in Gethsemane, would bring the breath of a new life to the Scottish pulpits. And the Scottish pilgrim to Jerusalem would find a new goal to their pilgrimage in the Scots College where trained teachers would interpret the golden past to them. When the Lord's day came students and pilgrims would meet in the Scots Church and sing together, 'T'was on that night when doomed to know,' with the upper chamber and Calvary there beside them; and they would remember and thank God for the white crosses that gleam over the world that brought again salvation and peace; and when they come back home, life would be ever fuller and richer because there they had breathed the very air out of which Christianity came. All this is no idle dream. For the world has been made into one neighbourhood by engine and airplane. Jerusalem is only eight hours by rail from Port Said. As things now are in the Hebrides, it is quicker to travel from London to Jerusalem than to Bernera in Lewis! The day when the Black Watch set guards on the Holy Sepulchre was the first of many days – when Scotsman will learn again to go on pilgrimage. And there must be for them a Scots Church in Jerusalem.... The two great Scottish Churches are united in this. They ask £50,000 that this vision may be realised. For such a work Scotland would find £100,000. At heart the Scot is a visionary; but he is more than a visionary. He ever knits the vision to the task, and carries the task to glorious completion... Who will be the first to give £1000?

Norman Maclean.'

The article prompted many responses from the public, including the single donation of £1000 [£49,500] towards the construction of the Memorial.

It was also matched by an equally enthusiastic response to the Scotsman written by Rabbi Dr. Salis Daiches, on behalf of the Jewish Community in Edinburgh. He 'begged leave to join in the expression of joy and thankfulness which the epoch-making event that we commemorate has evoked not only in the hearts of millions of Christians but in the hearts of the scattered remnants of Judah all the world over who have hailed the conquest of the Holy Land by General Allenby and his troops as a sign of the coming of a new era and the beginning of the realisation of our hopes and prayers of the ages.' He then marked the contrast between the British approach and that of the previous barbarous regime and looked forward to 'the restoration of the Holy Land to its pristine glory by the people who first made the land holy and glorious.' With many references to the shared heritage of the Christian and Jewish faiths he sees a future where 'The Jews of the world, restored as a nation in the land of the patriarchs and prophets will be glad to see great temples, houses of worship and seats of learning erected in the Holy City by the religious communities of the world.' The support that he offered for the projected church and centre of learning also provided a platform for him to air the aspirations of the Jews for the homeland promised in the Balfour Declaration.

Unsurprisingly, not everyone was in favour of the scheme to build the Memorial. The press, as well as reporting on the decision to proceed with the Memorial also became the battleground for those against and those for the proposal. At its first meeting, in October 1919, the Committee took the decision to raise the appeal to fund the project from £30,000 to £50,000 [£2.5m], in part to increase the endowment to fund the ongoing cost of the School for Biblical Study, once in place. This led to months of correspondence in the newspapers. On the 27th March, 1920, "El Kuds" writes in the letter page of the Scotsman in response to earlier correspondence from Hill:

'Sir, – I have read the letters from your correspondents 'C.' and 'J. E. L.,' and the rejoinder from Mr N. Hill regarding the proposed Scottish memorial in Jerusalem, and I beg to present my views on the subject. The decision of the General Assemblies to erect a church and college or hostel would appear to have been rather hasty and ill-considered. I first read of the decision whilst in Jerusalem, and, looking round me at the multiplicity of religious buildings, I could not help thinking that the money would be ill spent in adding one more to their number.

'Somewhere I have read that the proposed memorial is to occupy a "commanding" site. Are Mr Hill and his committee aware that the Jerusalem municipality has become so impressed with the necessity for the regulation of building operations in and around Jerusalem that they have had a plan of the city and its environs prepared by Mr Maclean, of Alexandria, showing: –

'(a) The Holy City within whose walls no additional new buildings would be permitted to be erected;

'(b) The area immediately outwith the walls where new buildings might with permission be erected;

'(c)The area beyond (b) where new buildings could be erected in conformity with the proposed street plan?

'Surely it is not proposed to add, even if permission were granted, another building to those already on the Mount of Olives. The Russian Church, the Russian Hospice, and the German Hospice, etc., are horrible examples of the disfigurement of a sacred site. Mount Zion is overcrowded already, and the only other "commanding" site near the city would be somewhere between the Jaffa Gate and the station, to the west of the Hebron Road and East of the station road, not a particularly salubrious spot, as many could testify.

'Another point I have not seen explained is where the congregation of the church and the students for the college or hostel are to come from. The Church of England followers in Jerusalem are numerically much stronger than the Scottish churches are ever likely to be, and yet they muster fewer than one hundred communicants, not all of British extraction. Students of the topography of Palestine and Jerusalem, in my opinion, could, with more profit and no bodily danger, peruse at home here the works of the learned authors named in the concluding paragraph of Mr Hill's letter.

'Further, Palestine has certainly been liberated from the Turk, but it has still to be decided which nation is to administer it. Probably it is not well known that the vote of the people themselves was not in favour of Britain having the mandate. In view of uncertainty on this and other points the Scottish Church members would be wise to withhold their money. If, however, they have money to spare for church work abroad let them give it freely to their missions already in Palestine. Hebron, Nazareth, and Tiberias could do with as many thousand pounds as Scotland cares to send, and it would be spent more in the Master's service than on any stone and lime edifice in Jerusalem.

'No one who has travelled Palestine and endeavoured to find out from the people themselves the worth of the missionaries' work at the stations named above or that of other workers at certain other places in the Holy Land could fail to be convinced that it is through the medical and educational work that any hope of reaching the Muslim population lies. The Scots whose graves dotted along 'the Way of the Philistines' from Kantara and Rumani to Gaza and from Gaza to Jaffa, the Mount of Olives, and beyond, need no memorial beyond that already being erected in Jerusalem. Rather let us who remain endeavour to be worthy of their sacrifice.

– I am, etc., El Kuds.'

To which Hill responds four days later:

'Sir, – I shall be obliged if you will allow me to assure "El Kuds" that the Joint Committee have ample information as to the conditions prevailing in Jerusalem, and that the proposal to celebrate the liberation of the Holy City by the erection of a worthy memorial was fully considered by various bodies during more than a year before it was unanimously adopted by both General Assemblies.

'"El Kuds" writes: – "Somewhere I have read that the proposed memorial is to occupy a commanding site ……. Surely it is not proposed to add another building to those already on the Mount of Olives." Your correspondent's memory, or rather lack of memory, has entirely misled him. The Joint Committee have no such ambitious aims, and certainly have never contemplated building on the Mount of Olives. They hope to obtain in due time a convenient and suitable site where Scotsmen and Scotswomen may meet under a common roof for study guided by a competent director, and where they can worship according to the custom of their fathers. It is true that there are already many churches in Jerusalem, but the sad fact remains that their doors are barred against us who are regarded as heretics and schismatics. This is not a pleasant position in which to find oneself, and it is surely not an unreasonable proposal to provide for the spiritual and intellectual needs of those of our own country when visiting the Holy Land. It may interest others besides "El Kuds" to learn that two days ago I received a donation of £100 for the memorial from a Scotsman residing in Jerusalem. Another contributor wrote recently: – "For such an object Scotsmen would willingly give £100,000."

'As regards "El Kuds"' reference to the Jewish missions, he may rest assured that their interests are safe in the hands of our conveners – the Rev. Prof. A.R.S. Kennedy and W.M. Macgregor; our vice convener, the Rev. Dr. W. Ewing, M.C.; and my joint hon. secretary, the Rev. J. Mcdonald Webster, whose absence from home deprives me of his assistance in addressing you.

– I am, etc., Ninian Hill, Hon Secretary.'

Not persuaded by this, "El Kuds" replies eight days later:

'Sir, – Mr Hill's letter of the 31st ult. does not greatly increase our information re the memorial. Certainly I am assured by him that the Committee in charge have ample information as to local conditions in Jerusalem, and that it is not proposed to erect the memorial on a "commanding site," as I read in either "The Egyptian Gazette" or "The Palestine News."

'From the tone of Mr Hill's letters he does not appear to realise that through the medium of your correspondence columns he is being permitted to reach a greater number of Church members than he would in writing to either 'Life and Work' or "The U.F.C. Record," and that much fuller details are desired by many. Even in the "Record" of the Church of which I am a member I can find no mention of the memorial in the issues from August, 1919, to March, 1920, inclusive.

'Mr Hill says "the doors of the Jerusalem churches are barred against us, who are regarded as heretics and schismatics." If this statement is intended in the figurative sense it is calculated to mislead those who have never visited the Holy City; if intended literally, it is untrue.

'I cannot conceive of any place where entrance into churches is freer than in Jerusalem. At any hour of the day it is possible to enter most of them for meditation or prayer, and St George's (Church of England) is no exception. I have worshiped many times in it. The German Protestant Church of the Redeemer is likewise open. Greek, Latin, and Armenian places of worship are not "barred" either.

In the "Record" of November last on page 239, there is a delightful little paragraph which goes to prove that "Barring-out" in Palestine is non-existent. I do not require to be assured that the interests of our Jewish missions are safe in the capable hands of the gentlemen named by Mr Hill, but it is undoubtedly a fact that to repair wars' ravages in Palestine and Syria, without allowing for any forward movement, much money is still required. Paragraph 2 of the full-page advertisement which appeared in the "Record" for several months, and various statements which have been made from time to time in the same magazine, would certainly have led me to think so had I not already first–hand information on the point.

'Mr Hill states that the subject has been fully considered. That being so, I submit that the members of the two Churches concerned are entitled to know before subscribing –

'(1) What is the (approximate) resident Scotch population of Jerusalem?

'(2) What is the estimated number of Scotch visitors per annum to Jerusalem?

'(3) Who are to be the students of the college, and what is to be studied?

'(4) Can the exact functions of the hostel be detailed?

'To found a British School of Archaeology in Jerusalem £20,000 is considered sufficient, but the members of the Scottish Churches are asked to subscribe more than double this amount for an object about which they have been told little or nothing. – I am, etc., El Kuds.'

Concerned about the real reason he perceives as to why the memorial is to be constructed in Jerusalem, "H" writes to the Scotsman on the 6th April, 1920:

'Sir, – Will you kindly allow me to add my protest to those which have already appeared in your columns against the proposed building?

'A few years ago I was in Jerusalem with some friends, and we were all amazed to see so many churches and missions. Scottish, English, American, French, and German, and almost every sector was represented, all aiming at the conversion of the Jews, which is truly a hopeless task. The only result of the keen competition for converts was, we were informed, to add to the huge army of beggars and hangers–on at missions. Likely converts receive many material as well as spiritual comforts, but, as soon as the former begin to diminish because they will not abjure the Jewish religion, they cease to attend that church or mission and attach themselves to another, where the same process and the same results follow, to be repeated again and again.

'When there are so many and such deserving calls on the charitable for money to feed, clothe, and help the countless sufferers in our own and other lands, let one and all contribute liberally to such real practical Christianity, instead of wasting £50,000 to gratify the whim of a few enthusiastic members of the Church of Scotland. Jerusalem can do without more churches and missions until our competing sects are fewer in number and the notion to build another church, where there are already more than enough, has passed away.

– I am, etc., H.'

Objections to the proposed Memorial did not stop at the level of funds appealed for. Prompted by a letter in the Scotsman from "Anglican" decrying the need for a Scots Kirk in Jerusalem when there is already British representation in the city with the presence of the Anglican Church, J.K.M. Oswald writes on the 27th December, 1919:

'Sir, – The suggestion of "Anglican" in your issue of 25th inst. is almost amusingly characteristic of the prevalent mind in the section of the body ecclesiastical to which he belongs.

'That one of the State Churches of Great Britain – the Church of England – should have a place of worship in Jerusalem is, of course, very proper and desirable for many reasons; but that the other – the Church of Scotland – should propose to erect another building in order to supply its own dear form of worship to sojourners and dwellers there is, it would appear, to offend the spirit and hurt the cause of 'the primal unity.' But is it so? Suppose the latter church had had priority of erection in the Holy City, would "Anglican," I wonder, have urged that the English should not erect another, lest, by doing so, it should imperil the Christian unity he professes to desire? I leave the question with him.

'The jibe at 'the fancy religions in our island home' and 'the outward trappings' of Christianity sounds strange, to say the least of it, from the mouth of a champion of the Church of England and of the "primal unity."

'In all fairness, I submit, both Presbyterianism and Episcopacy, or, say, both State Churches in our Empire, should be represented in Jerusalem, in order that both, dwelling and working and communicating together on equal terms, might co-operate in the effort to realise, not perhaps the primal unity (for that may never be), but the larger, grander unity which every man truly in touch with 'the very heart of Christianity' longs to see realised in our days.

– I am, etc., J.K.M. Oswald.'

But not all correspondence was confrontational. The proposal to build a Memorial in Jerusalem was celebrated in poetry by J. McKean and printed in the Scotsman in December, 1919:

The Scots Kirk at Jerusalem

A' ower the world in antrin spots,
Far frae Land's End or John o' Groats,
You're sure to find some wanderin' Scots
Whaur danger's brewin',
Wha very soon tak' off their coats
When something's doing.

Much in the world's been made an' marred,
And much o' Scotsmen has been heard
Since their forebears were bodyguard
To Pontius Pilate.
They've done good work wi' pen an' sword,
Wi' trowel an' mallet.

Thus after mony a hundred year,
When great events again appear,
They guard again wi' gun and spear
The Holy City,
An' scenes their hamefolk much revere
In sacred ditty.

There build a kirk where you can a'
For worship oft together draw,
An' thank for mercies great an' sma'
The King o' Kings,
Wha still exerts His sovereign law
Ower earthly things.

Whose power excels the strongest force
O' cannon, chariot, foot, or horse;
Wha often turns them frae their course
In fearfu' rabble,
An soon consumes them up like gorse
Or burnin' stubble.

———••●••———

From the beginning the task facing the "Committee on the Scottish Churches Memorial in Jerusalem," as it was initially called, later the "Committee on the Scots Memorial, Jerusalem (St Andrews Church and Hospice)," was not underestimated. There was no support from any of the Boards or Councils of either Church, except for the use of a room and banking facilities in each. With no previous experience of how to develop and manage such a project it seems that the priority was to bring on board as many people with as much influence and status as they could in order, not only to establish its own status as a Committee of the respective General Assemblies, but also to influence opinion and support for the project, and spread the work load which lay ahead. Within a few years the Committee grew to seventy- four in number and was a mix of Ex-Moderators, Principals and Professors from Theological Colleges, Knights of the Realm and Lords of the Manor, including at one time,

Lord Balfour of Burleigh. The proportion of ordained members to lay varied from year to year, as did the numbers on the Committee.

What was constant, however, was the fact that membership was male. This prompted a letter from Frances Balfour to the Scotsman on the 2nd January, 1920:

> 'Sir, – The appeal for the Scottish Churches Memorial in Jerusalem has been issued by a Joint Committee of both Scottish Presbyterian Churches, 36 for the Auld Kirk, and 38 for the United Free Church. On neither of these Committees does the name of a woman appear. Women are appealed to under the general term of 'others.' They are asked to hold sales of work, to arrange meetings in the drawing rooms, and to raise funds, in the allocation of which they are allowed neither interest nor responsibility. This scheme is one avowedly based on sentiment. Are Scottish Churchwomen without sentiment? Have they no 'rights' in the story of Palestine, and in a city where a mother saw her Son die? Have women not served with the Scottish troops, and suffered loss of health, and life, in their crusade? Some of us within the Scottish Church are waiting for the day which removes 'sex disqualifications' from the life and work and the responsibilities of the Churches in our native land.
>
> – I am, etc., Frances Balfour.'

Frances Balfour, the daughter of George Douglas Campbell, the eighth Duke of Argyll and sister-in-law to Arthur Balfour – of the Balfour Declaration of 1917 – was a celebrated supporter of women's suffrage. In 1896 she became President of the Central Society for Women's Suffrage, a position she held for eighteen years. Through her political connections, Lady Frances was well placed to try and influence leading members of the House of Commons. Frances and her sister-in-law, Betty Balfour, tried hard to persuade Arthur Balfour, Prime Minister from 1902 to 1905, to support Women's Suffrage with little success.

Despite its numbers, attendance at the "Joint" meetings, sometimes meeting only two or three times per year was very poor, latterly normally with around fifteen to twenty in attendance. In due course and work increased the majority of the detailed business was carried out by a variety of "Executive" Committees, with membership selected from the "Joint" Committee. These sub-committees were established with specific remits and covered such areas as "Fundraising", "Property" and "Chaplaincy". Meeting regularly and very often acting without prior reference to the full Committee it is no surprise that numbers attending the "Joint" Committee fell away when it became clear that very often their role was simply to ratify decisions already taken and even acted on.

As time went on and serious consideration was being given to possible sites and property options for the Memorial, it became clear that there was a need for establishing a Committee in Jerusalem. On Hill's advice this "Local Advisory Committee" was made up of members of the Scots community in Jerusalem, all with a Presbyterian background and all holding senior appointments within the British administration in the region.

The "Joint Committee" ceased to exist as such when on the 2nd October, 1929, the Church of Scotland and the United Free Church of Scotland came together under the name of the Church of Scotland and the Committee continued as a single body reporting to the one General Assembly.

-------------------- ··●●·· --------------------

In the early 1960's the Church of Scotland began to consider rationalising its Committee structure in respect of its work "overseas." In a rapidly changing world with shifting geopolitical circumstances, many Committees found their work either diminishing or expanding, and often overlapping with the work of others. This was the case with the "Memorial Committee," the "Jewish Mission Committee" and the "Colonial and Continental Committee." In 1964 all Committees with overseas remits united under a newly formed "Overseas Council," within which the "Committee on the Church and Israel" would "exercise all the functions and powers of the Committee of the Scots Memorial, Jerusalem." Twenty years later the "Board of World Mission and Unity" replaced the "Overseas Council", followed in 1994 by the "Board of World Mission". This was replaced by the "World Mission Council" in 2005 and is, today, the successor to the independent General Assemblies' Committee established in 1919 to develop the Memorial.

—— CHAPTER FOUR ——
Raising The Funds

FROM THE OUTSET the greatest challenge for the Joint Committee was to raise the funds required to secure a site to construct the Memorial or purchase property for the purpose. With no assistance from any of the Boards or Councils of either Church the Committee was left to its own resources to mount a fundraising campaign. This was a task not made any easier by the environment in which the target of £50,000 was to be raised. As a result of World War I, the economic situation in Great Britain, indeed globally, was catastrophic. This was encouraged, to some extent, by the prevailing attitude highlighted by the publicity for the British World War I propaganda film "For the Empire" which carried the slogan, "Damn the cost. We must win the war." The resultant debts accrued by all of the major combatants stalked the post-war economic world. In Britain industrial unrest and unemployment was rife. Inflation, hovering between 15% and 20%, dramatically increased the cost of living. The First World War abruptly ended a period of relative economic prosperity, replacing it with two decades of economic misery.

On the second anniversary of Allenby's entry into Jerusalem, 11th December 1919, the fundraising appeal was inaugurated with great publicity and with a Service of Worship at St Giles' Cathedral in Edinburgh. This was immediately followed by a public meeting hosted by Edinburgh's Lord Provost in the nearby City Chambers. In subsequent years a variety of initiatives were put in place to publicise and raise funds towards the enterprise, for example:

- a committee was formed to seek contributions from Military Units and individuals connected with the Palestine Campaign;

- regional fundraising committees were formed and public meetings were arranged in towns and cities throughout Scotland as well as in London and Liverpool with speakers from the Edinburgh Committee providing presentations;

- the Usher Hall in Edinburgh and other notable venues in Scotland were used for the presentation of lectures with Lantern Slides on related topics, for example, "With Allenby in the Holy Land";

- approaches were made to "St Andrew and other Scottish and patriotic societies in foreign lands";

- appeals to Sunday Schools and young people's societies;

- a Committee member, Sir John Cowan, hosted a successful "lunch" meeting for "50 gentlemen" in the Caledonian Station Hotel in Edinburgh, reported on in the Scotsman;

- encouraged by this there followed a number of "luncheon" and "drawing room" meetings throughout the country hosted in people's private houses;

- many articles were written for and advertisements placed in the press, including the Church of Scotland's "Life and Work"; the United Free Church "Record" and the Bible Society's "Quarterly."

In addition, a considerable amount of publicity material was produced for distribution, some of it more than a simple leaflet. A number of different booklets were produced throughout the many years of fundraising. One notable eight page illustrated booklet entitled "Scotland's National Memorial in Jerusalem," had its front cover designed by A. E. Haswell Miller. The artist was born in 1887 and won the M. C. serving with 7th (Blythswood) Battalion of the Highland Light Infantry and became well known for his paintings of military figures in their various uniforms.

Appeal booklet cover

Despite a considerable amount of publicity and effort, by the end of 1922, four years into the appeal, only £5,100 had been raised, 10% of the target. In July, 1923, in acknowledging the need to put more energy into fundraising, the Committee decided to employ an "Organising Secretary." In August Captain Duncan Campbell from Cambuslang was appointed, initially for six months, at a salary of £400 per year. At the end of January 1924, Captain Campbell's appointment was terminated when it became clear that his salary outweighed donations received.

In parallel with the fundraising, the Committee was also exploring the purchase of property or a site for the Memorial. By 1925 the Committee, feeling a bit under pressure by the length of time being taken to fulfil the vision, was giving serious consideration to a number of properties and sites. In March that year, the Committee agreed to put in an offer of £13,000 to purchase Bute House in Jerusalem (owned by Lady Margaret Macrae, daughter of the 3rd Marques of Bute), despite the fact that it had by that time raised only £7,600. Recognising that, perhaps, one of the reasons for the slow response to the fundraising was the ambitious target, the Committee also reduced the appeal and set a new target of £12,000 which, with the funds it already had, would provide for remodelling and refurbishing the property, as necessary.

Frustration developed when the offer to purchase Bute House was turned down and no progress was being made in respect of the other sites. At its meeting on the 18th December, 1925, in exasperation, the Committee 'unanimously agreed that the whole question of purchasing a suitable site and or property be remitted with full powers to the Property Sub-Committee and if they should see fit, authorise Mr Hill to proceed to Jerusalem and in consultation with the Local Committee come to a decision in the matter.'

Hill was duly despatched to Jerusalem and four months later, in April, 1926, a site was purchased at which point the Committee took stock of its financial position. The figures produced by the Architect indicated that based on the cost of the site and projected cost of buildings, fees, etc., there would be a shortfall of £8,219. However, having got over the hurdle of securing a site, the Committee set about making good the shortfall with renewed vigour and enthusiasm. The target was again revised, from £12,000 to £10,000, leaving a small inbuilt contingency. The Committee reviewed its strategy and decided to re-form local fundraising committees in Scotland; appoint a new Organising Secretary; organise a Bazaar and sale of work – ("no raffles and no whist drives"); hold flag days; ask the General Assemblies to support "special" collections; invite congregations and church societies to contribute £10 [£530] for a chair to be placed in the church; ask Sunday Schools and Bible Class to donate £1 and £2 to purchase a stone for the building, and all this to be supported with new publicity material, including a revised eight page booklet.

A typical example of the publicity material of the time would be that of the appeal for contributions towards the cost of chairs in the church:

'Dear Sir or Madam,

'We are in urgent need of funds to build a Memorial Church in Jerusalem on the fine site described in the accompanying pamphlet and we earnestly ask your help in the following manner.

'The church will be seated with chairs and it is proposed that in consideration of the contribution of £10 in response to this appeal, the name of the place where the money was subscribed will be engraved on a metal plate and be affixed on the chair. Familiar Scottish names thus affixed to the chairs will add much interest to the Memorial Church in Jerusalem.

'Friends in a limited number of places are being asked to help in this manner, and we should be greatly obliged if you could secure the services of someone who would undertake to collect £10 in your neighbourhood, so that a chair might be inscribed appropriately.

'All interested, of whatever denomination, are invited to contribute, and donations from Ladies' Work Parties, Bible Classes, Sunday Schools or other associations will be welcomed.'

In October, 1926, Mrs Isobel MacRae, formerly General Secretary of the Y.W.C.A. in Jerusalem, was appointed as the new Organising Secretary with a salary of £200 per year. This appointment of Mrs MacRae proved to be significant in the story of the Memorial reaching beyond that of Organising Secretary.

In addition to organising and monitoring the work of the local fundraising committees with their own "sales of works," the major task for Mrs MacRae was organising the arrangements for the upcoming Bazaar to be held in the Music Hall in George Street, Edinburgh, on the 2nd and 3rd December, 1927. In the period leading up to the Bazaar, and beyond, there was no lengths to which Mrs MacRae and the Committee would not go to add to the funds. Again, various appeals were sent out for "£1 or more", for example:

'To all Ministers and Kirk Sessions of both Churches.

'Rev. and Dear Sir,

'We beg to ask that you will do us the favour of laying the accompanying pamphlet before your Kirk Session when they are allocating funds to the various schemes of the Church. It describes the purpose and progress of the movement for the erection of a Memorial Church and Hospice in the Holy City, and we appeal for

A DONATION OF £1

'or more to enable us to proceed with the building. A limited number of chairs in the Church will be inscribed with the name of any town, village or rural parish, for a sum of £10.

THE GENERAL ASSEMBLY

'**renew their earnest recommendation** that on suitable occasions, such as the Christian festivals of Easter and Christmas, or St Andrew's Day, the attention of Congregations and Sunday Schools be drawn to the historic significance of the Holy City, and that, **whenever possible, a contribution be given** to the Building Fund of the Scottish Churches' Memorial in Jerusalem.'

Other appeals included:

- to Scottish peers for "£1,500 [£80,000] to meet the cost of the Chancel of the Chapel";

- to "The Great Priory of Scotland" of "The Order of the Temple" seeking permission to approach its various Preceptories (Districts) with a view to making an appeal on behalf of the Memorial;

- to name rooms in the hospice "for the donation of £300";

- to have the North and South transept stained glass windows named the Bethlehem and Nazareth Windows in return for a donation of £150;

- for funding of furniture, for example – dining room and common room chairs, £5 each; bookcases, £20; single room furniture, £40; double room furniture, £50.

At its meeting on the 11th January, 1928, the Committee noted that an appeal had been made 'to a fund which had been collected about twenty years ago towards building a hospital in the Lebanon Hills, an object which was now impossible of achievement, and that in these circumstances an application had been made to the Trustees concerned asking them to pay over the money for the Memorial. It was agreed that in the event of the Trustees consenting to do so the Committee would guarantee them, by a policy of insurance, against any claim which might arise in the future.' This request was unsuccessful.

The Bazaar was, of course, the major fundraising event of the time. Many influential individuals were recruited to promote this key event. In addition to the Moderators of the two Churches hosting the Bazaar, plus the Moderator of The Free Church of Scotland, a formidable list of Dukes and Duchesses and Lords and Ladies were included in the list of over sixty Patrons. The Committee succeeded in securing considerable press publicity for the two-day event which was considered to have been a great success in raising just short of £3,000 [£160,000].

Mrs MacRae's report to the Committee on the 2nd March, 1928, provides insight not only into the work behind organising the Bazaar but also her work with the local fundraising committees:

'For the most part 1927 was taken up with preparations for the Bazaar held in Edinburgh on December 2nd and 3rd. The preliminary arrangements were of necessity slow and laborious, as there was no existing organisation to set in motion to form a starting point. Each individual had to be brought in separately and this involved a considerable amount of visiting. By the early summer plans were sufficiently advanced to enable the Bazaar committee to organise three preliminary efforts to raise money towards the expenses.

'During September a room was secured in 121 George Street and from that time preparations proceeded unceasingly. Mention should be made of the invaluable service rendered by Miss Dorothy Ewing who for two months came regularly to the office and bore a considerable share of the burden of work.

'The Bazaar realised almost £3000. The General Fund benefited and will benefit, however, to a much greater extent, as many contributions were sent direct to the Church Offices and there is a marked increase of interest throughout the country which can also be traced to the Bazaar.

'At the same time systematic attempts have been made to interest large towns. This has not been easy as in every case it was found that some effort had been made within the last year or two and people were somewhat reluctant to rouse themselves to a fresh endeavour. However, local committees have been formed in Glasgow, Aberdeen, Dundee and Inverness.

'Glasgow. Has been difficult and various ways were tried without much success. The situation is very hopeful now, as Dr. Boyd Scott had undertaken to convene the committee which is representative of the churches, businessmen and men who served in the Palestine campaign. A strong effort is being made to get Lord Allenby to visit Glasgow, and give a lecture and be present at a luncheon.

'Aberdeen. Early in May some days were spent in Aberdeen and as a result of a strong committee was got together with Principal Sir G.A.Smith as Chairman and Mr George Angus Mitchell as Secretary. This committee hoped to raise sufficient money to build the library and their first effort takes place this month. Principal Smith has issued an appeal to the Women's Committee, convened by Lady Simpson, who has organised a Cafe Chantant for March 3rd. Most of the necessary advertising, posters, leaflets, etc., for this has been done from 121 George Street.

'Inverness. Two days were spent in Inverness in May, and the Rev. Donald MacLeod agreed to act as Chairman of the committee. Inverness, however, lay dormant until last month when it was wakened up by a letter, in response to which Mr MacLeod reports that his committee will make some effort, which will probably coincide with the visit of the Moderator in May.

'Dundee. The local committee was formed in June with the Rev. D.B. Nicol and Rev. A.J. Forrest as Joint Secretaries. A public meeting was held in December which was addressed by the Joint Conveners of your Committee. About £100 was raised and a considerable amount of interest was aroused. At a meeting of the local committee in February it was decided to make another effort, probably a garden fete in summer and a play in the autumn.

'Helensburgh. Early in April it was arranged that Joint Conveners should visit Helensburgh, preach on the Sunday and address a drawing room meeting on the Monday. The effort was very successful, £300 being received as a result.

'Plans are also in train for a joint effort between Galashiels and Melrose to furnish one or two bedrooms. Visits to Dalry, Ayrshire, and Ayr have been arranged, and correspondence with other centres in the Borders and in the North is going on with a view to getting a number of the country towns to undertake to furnish at least one room each.

'Through the kindness of Lord Alness introductions to influential men in London have been secured, and these will be followed up after Easter.

'If the response, reasonably to be expected, is received to these efforts which this year will be spread throughout the country by the end of 1928 we should be well on the way to complete the sum required.

'Isobel MacRae'

On the 2nd March, 1928, the Committee, once again, reviewed the financial position as at the end of 1927 noting that, after expenses, the fund had a balance of £10,495. With this information the Committee agreed 'to proceed with the erection of the Memorial building,' despite having no knowledge as to the financial implications of that decision.

Designs were developed by the Architect, tender documents were sent out and returned on the 28th November, 1928. The contract with the Main Contractor was signed in December, 1928, with the design for the buildings not yet complete and a considerable amount of construction detailing still to be resolved. It was not until June, 1929, six months later, when a clearer, yet still incomplete, picture of the financial situation emerged. This revealed that there was a projected shortfall of available funds in excess of £5,000, and this did not, even then, take into account a number of uncosted aspects of the work, e.g., the floor to the church, windows, electric lighting and Architect's fees. (If, at this time, a more accurate cost projection had been carried out, the Committee would have been made aware that the shortfall was more than double the amount they thought it was, nearer to £12,000! [£660,000])

Apart from seeking the support of the May 1930 General Assembly for a general appeal to congregations, there was very little specific attempt to "close" the shortfall until, one month later, when funds ran out! At its meeting in June, five months before the Church and Hospice were due to be opened on St Andrew's Day, 1930, the Committee noted that in response to a request from the Local Committee for £4,000 to make an interim payment to contractors, the only funds available, £2,500, were remitted and that 'it had become necessary to arrange an overdraft from the "General Finance Committee"' of the Church.

A memorandum was sent, setting out the position of the "Memorial Scheme", as requested by the Finance Committee, which included the following information:

a) the history of the project, including a brief summary of the key stages of the development.

b) a breakdown of the income and expenditure for the 11 years of the fund, from 1919 to 1929:

Total revenue from Contributions and Legacies received during the years

1919		£2,698 7 7
1920		1,235 5 3
1921		759 15 11
1922		473 18 10
1923		1,962 6 6
1924		515 10 7
1925		583 13 4
1926		1,727 16 10
1927	Including Bazaar in Edinburgh	4 713 - 1
1928		2,145 14 6
1929		2,067 2 10
Total =		£18,882 12 3
Total Expenditure, including Printing, Postage, Chaplaincies, Bursary, Organisers' salaries and Outlays,		£3,440 3 11
Less Interest received & Profit on Investment		3,188 9 8
Net cost for eleven years =		£ 261 14 3

c) an estimate of the cost of the works, as at October, 1929 with the deficit at that time of £5,199. The memorandum noted 'It is not possible as yet to give a definite and final estimate of the financial position as inclusive contracts are unusual if not unknown in Palestine. Further, the circumstances of the case present peculiar difficulties. The Committee is charged with the duty of erecting buildings at a distance of some 2,000 miles, and is dependent upon the supervision of a Local Committee of very capable and keenly interested Government officials whose official duties have been greatly increased in consequence of the riots of last August.'

d) A note as to how the overdraft will be paid off:

'The sources from which the debt will be liquidated are: –

'1. Contributions at home, including the response to the appeal to be made on St Andrew's Day, 30th November, as recommended by the General Assembly, and results of work of the Organising Secretary which have yet to fructify.

'2. Profit on the working of the Hospice. The money expended on the Hospice is to be regarded as an investment which should yield a satisfactory income. Mrs Isobel MacRae, who has been appointed as Lady Warden, was for four years General Secretary of the Y.W.C.A. in Jerusalem and lived in, and, from time to time had charge of their Hostel. In the Y.W.C.A. report for 1928, on page 12, the hostel is valued at £8,000. Page 11 shows that they have an overdraft of £1,957 at 7% from Barclays Bank. The surplus of profit as stated on page 9 in two sums equal £450. The Hostel was not originally built for the purpose and is a very commonplace building in an unattractive situation. Our Hospice has more accommodation and is much superior in every way. Under what amounts to the same management it should give not less satisfactory financial results.'

e) Finally, collections in the church and donations from visitors in Jerusalem.'

With the submission of the memorandum there followed a flurry of intense activity. This began with the Finance Committee's prompt response advising that it was 'out with their power to comply with the request' but 'it was thought desirable that the position might be investigated further' between the two Committees. At the subsequent meeting it was pointed out to representatives of the Finance Committee that it had had the use of the Memorial Committee's money during the past eleven years to finance the work of other Committees of the Church. However 'after a full and frank discussion lasting about one hour the conference terminated without any finding being arrived at.'

In response to an approach to the Senior Clerks of the General Assembly on the matter by the Committee Convener, he received the following response from the Rev. James Harvey:

'Dear Dr. Maclean,

'I am in receipt of your letter of the 9th instant regarding the situation in Jerusalem. Many thanks for so kindly giving me the details of the Scheme as to liabilities and receipts. I had some idea as to how things stood, but I was not aware there was such an actual deficit. The position of the Finance Committee in the matter is quite intelligible. While successive Assemblies have given their blessing to the Scheme they have never committed the Church to financial liability in the matter, and I suspect that is the reason why the Finance Committee could not see their way to give such a large overdraft without the direct sanction of the Assembly. On the other hand, <u>something must certainly be done</u> in the interests of the prestige of the Church, and it should not be beyond our powers to extricate the Committee from this untoward situation. I notice that the matter comes up again before the Finance Committee on Wednesday, the 16th, and perhaps by that time some way out may be discovered.

'With all kind regards.

'Yours sincerely,

'James Harvey.'

Within a few days of the "full and frank" meeting a way forward was proposed by the Finance Committee suggesting that 'If the Memorial Committee could during the next fortnight obtain guarantees for the amount required to finance the enterprise.... and if the Finance Committee were satisfied with the guarantees of security to be offered, it would mean that the Memorial Committee would obtain (through the Finance Committee) accommodation on much more favourable terms than they could get from an ordinary Bank.'

Subsequent to this and at its meeting on the 8th July, 1930, (five months before the opening of the Church and Hospice, with the contractors still working and unpaid!) the Committee was advised that the Convener, Dr. Norman Maclean, 'was in communication with a number of friends in an endeavour to obtain guarantors and donations and that he and Mr Hill had each resolved to guarantee £1,000 [£55,000] and the donor who had promised £500 for the marble panelling and gold mosaic in the Apse had agreed to waive these purposes and that the sum be applied for general purposes.'

On the 15th July, 1930, a letter was sent to the Finance Committee from Ninian Hill confirming that, at that date, an estimated £10,000 was still required to complete the works and that with a hoped-for overdraft of £3800 based on raised security and cash in hand, or promised, amounting to £1,688, the balance will be raised by an ongoing appeal. The following day, the Finance Committee met and agreed to allow the Memorial Committee to overdraw £3,800 on its account with a clear instruction that they 'would use their utmost endeavour to raise, without delay, in cash the whole sum which may be necessary to meet their obligations which they have incurred with the Memorial.'

Once again appeal letters were drafted and distributed; seven-hundred to former subscribers; two-thousand two-hundred to branches of the Women's Guild; two-hundred and sixty-six to Presbyteries, and 'forty-seven appeals were being issued to Continental, Indian and other Chaplains and also to Church of Scotland Churches in England.' In addition an appeal was made to the "Pilgrim Trust" in London for a grant of £36,000, not only to cover the cost of the completion of the Hospice as an "Institute for Biblical Study" but also to provide an endowment of £15,000 for funding the Director of Studies, £10,000 for scholarships for students and £3,000 to purchase a small house and garden to the rear of the Hospice for the Director of Studies. This request was unsuccessful.

To ease the pressure on the Committee the Main Contractor agreed that, in the event of the work being completed and funds still being due to him, he 'would be prepared to accept deferred payments extending over two years at the charge of six and three-quarter percent per annum.'

By the end of 1930, the debt on the project stood at £7,300, including the overdraft of £3,800. With a combination of continuing fundraising and income from the Hospice being operated as a "guesthouse" the debt was finally written off in November 1935, five years after the opening of the Memorial.

However, at this point the Committee was faced with two challenges, one continuing and one new. The first was to progress, with renewed vigour, the appeal for an endowment fund to initiate and secure the future of the Hospice as the "Institute for Biblical Studies." The second was to raise funds towards the purchase of land adjoining the church and hospice in order to secure the amenity of the property. (See Chapter 5)

The Committee had great difficulty securing funds to meet both needs. The endowment fund did, however, reach the amount of £12,300 by September 1960. Nevertheless, with no sign of the "Institute" coming to fruition and the financial demands on the Church and Hospice ever growing, over a period of time the funds were re-directed to pay for running costs, development costs and ongoing repairs, including making good damage caused to the property arising from the "Six Day War" in 1967. The pressure to raise capital for additional land ceased when, in 1952, the Committee leased rather than purchased the land.

Over the years the Memorial, the Church and the Hospice, has endured a fragile existence financially. The past fifty years have required a continuous input of funds for a number of extensive upgrading and remodelling projects in the Hospice/Guesthouse, including a major bedroom extension. In the beginning driven by their overwhelming commitment to the vision and purpose of the Memorial, Ninian Hill and many others overcame immense financial obstacles in order to make it a reality. Today the needs are different but that financial challenge continues.

—— CHAPTER FIVE ——

Securing The Site

FOR A CHURCH or a "foreign enterprise" attempting to purchase land in Israel or Palestine today, it would be nigh impossible. However, for the Committee in Edinburgh charged with bringing the Memorial into existence the very idea of such a purchase in a "foreign land" was not an issue. The Empire had been enlarged. Palestine was now under the authority of a British administration many of whose administrators, particularly at senior level, were either members of or associated with the Church of Scotland.

More of a problem for the Committee was the probable cost of securing a site. At its first meeting on the 20th October, 1919, following approval by both General Assemblies to proceed with the scheme, the main business of the Committee was taken up with consideration of a site. The meeting was addressed by Judge Scott from Jerusalem and Dr. Alexander Paterson from Hebron, both of whom cautioned Committee members on the rapidly increasing cost of land and construction work in the country generally and in Jerusalem particularly. However this news did not appear to have blunted the Committee's enthusiasm to secure a site or property at this stage, even though they had no funds. At the meeting it was agreed to enquire about purchasing the site of the "Hospital of St John's of Jerusalem" belonging to the "German Lutheran Church." In addition Scott and Paterson were given the task of identifying alternative suitable sites or buildings for the Memorial.

From the records it is clear that the Committee, over the following years, spent a considerable amount of time exploring a variety of ideas and proposals, not helped by the growing strength and confidence within the Jewish community. The Committee recognised this and in June 1920, decided that 'In view of the adverse attitudes taken up by the Zionists to all sales of land to any but Jews, it was agreed that Prof. Kennedy (Chairman of the Committee) should make enquiries as to the best manner of approaching the Foreign Office in order to obtain facilities for obtaining a site.'

The site on which the Church and Hospice/Guesthouse sits today was purchased in August 1926, over seven years from the time when the decision was taken to proceed with the scheme. In that period the Committee deliberated on a considerable number of proposals, with only a few being serious contenders.

At its meeting in April, 1922, the Committee noted an appeal by a Mrs Todd Osborne to raise funds to establish a "Soldiers' Home in Jerusalem." Questions were raised as to how this Home might impact on the proposed Memorial. It was agreed to find out more 'as to the progress and prospects of the scheme,' but do nothing in the meantime.

A remarkable Glasgow lady, Mrs Alice Todd Osborne, had spent many years developing Soldiers' Homes in the Mediterranean, and had a particular interest in setting one up in Jerusalem in the belief that there would be a long term garrison in the City. She was known to the Committee, in particular to Lord MacLay who represented the Free Church on the Committee and was also a trustee of Mrs Todd Osborne's charity. (For more background on Mrs Alice Todd Osborne and her work see Appendix [1])

In her search for premises for the Jerusalem Soldiers' Home, she identified a plot alongside what eventually became the site of the Memorial, though the Soldiers' Home was never built. Plans to work together to produce a scaled down version of the Soldiers' Home alongside the Memorial were given detailed consideration both in Edinburgh and by the Local Committee. Dr. John McQueen reported in a letter dated the 7th November, 1923, confirming its location to the east of the railway station, noting 'It is I should think the finest in Jerusalem. Personally although I had often been inside the walls I had not realised how fine the view was. From the highest point looking north-east across the Kidron and Siloam Valleys one sees the Mount of Olives with the Garden of Gethsemane at the foot. Following round towards the West is the Mosque of Omar (Temple Area), the Old City, its walls standing out clearly, Zion Hill, David's Tower, the Jaffa Gate, the Russian Buildings, Ratisbonne, "Herod's Tomb," the German Colony and, Southwards, the hills and the road to Bethlehem. From a few yards further up the hill one can look right across the Jordan Valley to the Hills of Moab and get a glimpse of the Dead Sea.'

Readers who are familiar with the site upon which the Scots Memorial Church and Guesthouse sit today and who have had the pleasure of being able to view the panorama from the roof of the building will recognise the Local Committee's description as it could reasonably be used to describe the view from the plot purchased three years later upon which the Memorial was built! The Todd Osborne site is, in fact, the area of undeveloped land to the south of and adjacent to the Memorial site, known today as Bible Hill.

Dr. McQueen's letter supporting the proposal to build the Memorial on the Todd Osborne site continues, 'We think you can reasonably expect people living in hotels and hospices in the town to go to church there. To visitors the return fare from the town of 20 PT (four shillings) for a carriage would be a small item, or in the spring when most of them come to Jerusalem the heat is not sufficient to make the walk a deterrent. The site is convenient for British residents in the German and Greek Colonies. It's impossible to say whether we will continue to stay in the German houses there but there is no doubt in our mind that the bulk of the British people who are to be permanently here will stay in this area. It surrounds the sports club and in addition it is we think the pleasantest quarter of the town. The site will be well suited for study and sightseeing. The climate, as I well know, is particularly good on that Hill. There are less mosquitoes there than anywhere else and although somewhat windy in the winter it is rarely very hot. We whose homes are here and whose business is more with the present than with the past Jerusalem are apt to become immune to the impressions which the spectacle of the city arouses in the visitor for the first time. But we are impressed. How much more so will be the student who after his years of labour in Scotland first sees the city in the spring time of the year from a Scottish Hostel standing where we stood.'

Having had such a positive meeting with Mrs Todd Osborne and Lord Maclay and a very encouraging report from the Local Committee, it was agreed 'without reserve' to pursue the matter with Mrs Todd Osborne. However, after such encouraging potential as to a site for the Memorial hopes were dashed when it was reported by the Local Committee on the 9th June, 1924 'that Mrs Todd Osborne had expressed herself to members of the Local Committee in Jerusalem in decidedly adverse terms to the proposal that the Memorial should occupy the site gifted to the Soldiers' Home.' There the matter ended, or so the Committee thought. Two years later, in 1926, on conclusion of the purchase of the site for the Memorial, the Committee was advised that Lord Maclay had once again approached the Executive Committee in Edinburgh 'regarding the late Mrs Todd Osborne's ground which he proposed to hand over to the Committee for the purposes of the Memorial. After consulting the Local Committee in Jerusalem it was found that the circumstances now were such that they could not entertain the proposal, the reasons being,

'1. they had already accepted the Patriarchate's offer of a site at the price stated;

'2. Mrs Todd Osborne's ground was gifted by the Patriarch to her for the purpose of erecting a Soldiers' Home;

'3. the Local Committee advised (a) that it was unlikely that the Commission on the Finances of the Patriarchate would alter the deed of gift so as to sanction the use of the ground for any other purpose, (b) that the legality of the gift itself was being questioned and (c) that the acceptance of Lord Maclay's offer would probably lead to protracted litigation with the Patriarchate.

'4. the Memorial site was preferable as regards accessibility, the nature of the foundations and supply of stone.'

While the "on–off" discussions on the Todd Osborne site were taking place the Committees in Edinburgh and in Jerusalem were also spending a considerable amount of time deliberating on, as the records indicate, eight sites and properties. These included the German Archaeological Institute, with fourteen rooms, in the Christian Quarter of the Old City adjoining the Lutheran Church; land near St George's Anglican Cathedral, situated in today's East Jerusalem; land adjoining St John's Ophthalmic Hospital at its first site on the Bethlehem Road, and a house under construction next to the Wadi Joz, a district to the north of the Old City and near to the Department of Antiquities. The Committee considered this last property to be promising since it required only £1,500 to complete the construction and 'there is room for a Chapel.'

However these options were not pursued with any great vigour mainly because in parallel with considering the Todd Osborne site they were also juggling negotiations on options it considered more serious. At its meeting on the 5th March, 1925, the Committee considered its Property Sub-Committee's report on progress on investigations into two properties:

'1. It is desirable to recall that the General Assemblies in May, 1919, approved of the proposal that the Memorial should "combine a Church within an Institute for Biblical Study under some such title as the 'Scots' Church and College in Jerusalem.'" The Committee has always kept in view the twofold character of the Memorial – the old-time idea of a Scots College or Hostel with the Chapel attached. Without pronouncing on the relative importance or urgency of a

Chapel or Hostel it goes without saying that the Chapel must be specially built for the purpose of a Memorial, and that though of small dimensions it must be worthy of its object. No necessity, however, to build arises as regards a hostel, provided a suitable house, with sufficient ground on which to erect a Chapel can be obtained.

'2. After making exhaustive enquiries when in Jerusalem Dr Ewing reported on a number of properties for the purposes of the Memorial. On full consideration the choice has since become limited to (a) Bute House and ground, and (b) a vacant site on the new George V. Avenue which, failing Bute House, has since been recommended by the Local Committee.

'3. Bute House belongs to Lady Margaret Macrae and is occupied as the French Consulate at a rent of £500 per annum on a lease expiring in June, 1925. It contains about 18 bedrooms and there is ample space in the garden on which to erect a Chapel. Pending the erection of the Chapel, Divine Service could be held in the principal public room. The house is well built and has a dignified appearance. The property adjoins the Russian Compound, faces the Public Gardens off the Jaffa Road, and lies about seven minutes' walk northwards from the Jaffa Gate. It is most conveniently situated in the neighbourhood of the hotels, hospices, government offices, shops and Archaeological schools. When Dr Ewing was in Jerusalem a year ago it was stated that the property might be bought for £8,000. In consequence of the request of a firm offer the Bute Trustees sent their Agent to Jerusalem to enquire as to its probable value with the result that some local competition ensued, and it now appears unlikely that the property can be acquired for less than £12,000.

'4. George V. Avenue, which has just been opened for traffic, is described as the broadest and likely to become one of the best roads of the City. It commences on the Jaffa Road about a kilometre west of the Post Office, and curves southwards, and joins onto the re-constructed road to the Station and German Colony. A site 100 x 200 feet = 4,000 pics. could probably be acquired at P.T.80 = £3,200.

'5. It is not possible at this stage to make any definite estimate of the financial requirements of the two propositions but the following considerations may be mentioned: –

'(a) Bute House.

On purchasing this property we should acquire a central site of sufficient size on which a commodious hostel with cisterns is already built and the total cost of the Memorial might amount to:

Bute house and grounds	£12,000	
Furnishing	2,000	
Chapel	5,000	£19,000
(b) George V. Avenue.		
Cost of Site and enclosing it	£ 4,000	
Chapel, as above	5,000	
Hostel	8,000	
Furnishing	2,000	£19,000

'6. The total funds on hand now amount to about £7,750

'7. In conclusion the subcommittee is impressed with the need of the Memorial materialising without delay. They believe that by the acquisition of a property or a site in Jerusalem the raising of further funds will best be facilitated.

'They recommend: –

'(a) That an offer of £12,000 be made for Bute House;

'(b) In the event of that offer not being accepted, that a site in George V. Avenue be acquired at a cost of about £3,500, and the question of proceeding to erect the Memorial Chapel at once should be considered;

'(c) And that an appeal for £12,000 be issued.'

In the event the offer was raised to £13,000 and, as noted in the previous Chapter, was turned down and, in frustration, Ninian Hill was sent to Jerusalem to finally locate and negotiate a site for the Memorial.

With this authority, Hill arrived in Jerusalem on the 12th February, 1926, and a few days later, on the 23rd February, Hill, with representatives from the Local Committee and Mr Clifford Holliday, an architect based in Jerusalem, inspected various sites around Jerusalem. They continued the following day, this time accompanied by a representative of the Greek Orthodox Patriarchate. Among sites visited was Harariah Hill, close to St John's Ophthalmic Hospital, and which, according to the Patriarch's representative, 'might be obtained for about P.T100 per square pic.' The group expressed their interest in the site and met with the Patriarch on the 2nd March following which he offered to sell the site for P.T125 per square pic. Eventually a compromise was reached and on the 13th April Hill sent a telegram to the Committee in

Edinburgh, 'Local Committee approves site lowest price 112piasters per pic equals £1.14.03 sterling per square yard total cost probably £3,700 shall we accept cable reply.'

Two days later, Hill received the response 'secure site at figure named.' The purchase of the site was registered with the Land Registry on the 6th October, 1926.

Both Committees, in Edinburgh and Jerusalem, had spent seven years exploring possibilities and negotiating on a variety of properties and sites with no success. In the end, borne out of frustration, with focus and determination it had taken only two months to identify, negotiate and secure a site. However there was a consequence to the haste in which the site was purchased.

Situated on the brow of the Harariah Hill with a commanding view over the Hinnom Valley and the Old City to the east and north, the irregular shaped site had no direct access to any main road. In order to keep costs down the area of land purchased was kept to a minimum and was, virtually, an "island" with the only access being a pedestrian "right of way" of about one-hundred yards west of the site to the road leading to the railway station from the City. To the south was the Todd Osborne site.

The limitations on the site became apparent when, during the construction of the building Hill noted in his report following a visit in 1929, 'The back of the Hospice comes to about fifteen feet from our boundary and it is desirable when funds permit to acquire additional ground. I ascertained at the Patriarchate that it can be obtained, probably at a lower rate than previously paid.'

Not only was the need for additional land becoming an issue at this early stage, even before the Church and Hospice was up and running, Hill also noted that additional accommodation would be helpful. He indicated that 'a small house of four rooms and basement on the adjoining ground may be rented at £50 per annum, and the Local Committee recommends taking it on a lease for three years with the option to purchase at an agreed price.' The Committee agreed.

Hill's concerns over the restricted size of the site were not immediately recognised as being important. The Committee's main concern was the establishment of the Church and Hospice as functioning resources meeting their objectives as originally envisaged. It was not until 1935, once the debt relating to the construction of the buildings had been paid off, that the fear of a potential sale or lease of adjacent land to another party was fully recognised as potentially inhibiting the work of the Church and Hospice. At its meeting in November 1935, the Committee acknowledged the need to preserve the amenity of the property 'by purchasing certain pieces of ground in the immediate vicinity and also a house.' It was calculated that this might cost upwards of £20,000. [£1.25m]

Continuing to discuss the matter, with nothing being acted upon, the Committee confirmed six months later, 'the absolute necessity of getting the land.' Persistent approaches to the Patriarchate over the following three years bore no fruit until October 1938. At this point, while it was made very clear to the Committee that there would be no opportunity whatsoever of being sold any of the property on the site adjacent to the "railway station" road, an offer was made to sell land closer to the Church and Hospice. However, the offer was such that a) it was at a price which the Committee could not afford, and b) the area on offer did not protect either the pedestrian "right of way" or secure the rented house. However there were two items of good news which came out of that discussion. The first was an agreement to grant "first refusal" on the land if the Patriarchate was to change its mind and dispose of the property through sale or lease.

The second was a proposal from the Patriarchate to transfer the current pedestrian "right of way" to a new alignment with vehicular access from the north-west corner of the site. This road would be seven metres wide, there would be no cost to the Committee for the land on which the road would sit and the cost of construction would be shared equally by the Church and the Patriarchate which would retain equal right of access. Both the Committee in Edinburgh and, by this time, the Kirk Session in Jerusalem agreed to the realignment of the "right of way" on the condition that the Church would be 'permitted to erect at the entrance from the main road pillars or an archway,' thereby providing an informal boundary to the Memorial site.

New access drive from main road

Welcome as it was, the proposal did not remove the feeling of vulnerability to the Memorial of any sale of land between it and the "railway station" road. This fear reduced when the Committee Convener noted on the 7th October, 1938, that 'in view of the present impossibility of purchasing the land fronting the road he had interviewed the Town Planning Adviser who assured him that building developments on this land were subject to strict controls and that if representations were made at the appropriate time to the District Town Planning Committee, the Kirk Session could rest assured that before permits are granted for buildings, the question of their effect on the amenities of the Memorial buildings and the approach would receive careful consideration and all reasonable restrictions enforced to preserve these amenities.' With this assurance the Committee returned to considering the purchase of the land closer to the Church and Hospice. However, with the advent of World War II it was decided to take no further action 'until the war should come to an end. The price of land may probably be lowered by the economic conditions.'

In November 1944, the Committee revived the attempt to purchase the land next to the "railway station" road, which included the house continuing to be leased and used as the manse. In the intervening war years, Palestine and Jerusalem in particular, had become a hub of activity for the Army and St Andrew's. The Hospice had gained a reputation as a welcoming and caring centre for military personnel, especially those with a Scots or Presbyterian background. Sunday Services were very well attended and the Hospice was often full to capacity.

With its work flourishing the perceived need was to develop further, this confirmed in a letter from the Committee to the Kirk Session in

Jerusalem, dated November 1944, regarding the proposed purchase of land, 'It might be well to recall a little of the past. The purposes for which we propose to acquire additional land are: –

'1. To preserve the amenities of the Memorial

'2. For future developments which may take the form of building a manse, extra Hospice accommodation, construction of a church hall, provision of garages and servants quarters.'

In later correspondence a "canteen" was added to the list of developments.

The whole matter of the surrounding land came to a head, however, in July 1952. The Committee was advised of developments within the Patriarchate which precipitated an offer of not a sale but a lease of the land to the Church. It was reported to the Committee, 'that the question of leasing the land around the Memorial had suddenly become urgent and that this was due to an approach made to the proprietors of the land by a Jewish organisation. The Patriarchate were hard pressed to find money to pay heavy taxes in Israel and were obliged, therefore, to consent to lease the land, though they would not, for political reasons, sell it. Since the Committee held an option, the Patriarchate had offered the lease to the Committee in the first place.' The Committee suddenly had the opportunity now to secure what it had been seeking for over twenty years, not so much the space to build a manse, a church hall or a canteen, but the surrounding space to protect its interests.

However it was not to be that easy. The Committee considered that it could not afford the annual rent for the whole of the area on offer, which included the house next to the "railway station" road. With the pressure on not to lose this opportunity of protection, and with the aim to reduce the size of the lease and therefore its financial commitment, the Committee proposed to the Patriarchate that the Committee should be permitted to sublease the house and its surrounding land to the British Foreign Office which, at the time, was looking for property to rent as a Consulate for people living in West Jerusalem. Following discussion, instead of a lease and a sublease, two separate leases were created with the Church leasing three dunams (three-thousand square metres) for a period of seventy-four years, until 2026, and the remainder of the area with the house leased to the Foreign Office.

While the Church of Scotland continues with its lease, the Foreign Office no longer leases the building and surrounding land to the rear of the Guesthouse, which has reverted to the Patriarchate.

The Committee were inspired when they chose the site for the Memorial, but they did not realise how fortunate this was to prove in future years. Of particular importance has been the area known as Giv'at HaTanakh (Bible Hill). This is the land immediately to the south of the Memorial on which Mrs Todd Osborne had planned to build the Soldiers' Home. The hill takes its curious name from its association with the passage in the Book of Joshua delineating the territory between the Biblical tribal allotments of Judah and Benjamin (Ch.15 v 8), 'The boundary then passed through the Valley of Hinnom, along the southern shoulder of Jebus (where the city of Jerusalem is located), then west to the top of the mountain above the Valley of Hinnom, and on up to the northern end of the Valley of Rephaim.' (Living Bible). It is the watershed between the Ninnom Valley, where the springs form the headwaters of streams feeding into the Dead Sea, and Emek Raphaim whose streams flow into the Mediterranean. With the death of Mrs Todd Osborne the area was given back to the Patriarchate and is now leased to The Jewish National Fund and has been designated Urban Nature Site No 11. It is notable for the many varieties of wild flower which grow there as well as being unique as the only peak where development has not been permitted.

One body which had plans for the site is the "Israel Society for Biblical Research." Established in 1950 the Society seeks to promote and encourage Bible study and research within the Jewish community worldwide. In its early days it was supported and encouraged in its work by many of the country's leaders, including Prime Minister David Ben Gurion and Presidents Ephraim Katzir and Shalman Shazar.

Inspired by Jerusalem as a home for the three major monotheistic religions, in the mid-1960's the Society began to develop the concept of an extensive building complex to be situated on this open space adjacent to the Memorial. The scheme which was developed included the construction of a major conference centre designed to hold over two-thousand people, together with a library containing all translations of the Bible in all languages with other related material. This central building was to be surrounded by four "hubs" each dedicated to "The Bible and Judaism," "The Bible and Islam," "The Bible and Christianity" and "The History of Jerusalem." With car parking and ancillary buildings the plan for the scheme would have covered the area of Bible Hill and the central building of the complex would have dwarfed the Memorial's tower. To date the development has been prevented through lack of funds. It would still have to gain planning permission and other approvals.

––––––––––––––––•–•–●–•–•–––––––––––––

To the east of the Memorial site, between it and the Menachem Begin Heritage Centre lies an area with major biblical significance. Ketef Hinnom ("The Shoulder of Hinnom") was the subject of an archaeological dig carried out by Gabriel Barkay between 1975 and 1996 under the auspices of the Institute of Archaeology of Tel Aviv University and the Israel Exploration Society. (A brief description of the work carried out and discoveries made is set out in Appendix [2])

The series of excavations revealed an astonishing number and variety of artefacts which have not only provided us with a deeper appreciation of life in Jerusalem two-thousand, five hundred years ago, they have also made an enormous contribution to our understanding of the development of the text of the Hebrew Bible.

––––––––––––––––•–•–●–•–•–––––––––––––

From its inception a major element in Hill's vision for the Memorial, and that of the Committee, was the incorporation of an "Institute of Biblical Studies" for students from Scotland, a dream unfulfilled. It is sad to think that in selecting the site they did for the Memorial they had no knowledge that, no more than fifty yards from the door of the Hospice, secrets would later be revealed making the site one of the major resources of study for Biblical scholars worldwide.

———— CHAPTER SIX ————

Realising The Dream

TODAY, ANY organisation, including the Church, embarking on such an exciting enterprise as the construction of a new building complex, requiring the investment of considerable resources of time, energy and funding, may require years of preparation and innumerable committee and subcommittee meetings. In most cases systems will be in place to ensure an efficient decision making process with prescribed levels of accountability.

With the design and construction of the Memorial in Jerusalem the records indicate a less than structured or planned process. With no financial plan, no certainty of income and no reliable day-to-day information being produced as to the cost of the works, it is no surprise that towards the end of the project, after years of toil, one gets a real sense of everyone's frustration at the lack of progress. In the end the opening and dedication of the Memorial was performed without the work to the buildings being complete and owing the Contractor funds the Committee did not have. There is no doubt that, faced with realities in the pursuit of the dream, the construction of the Memorial is a clear testament to the faith and dogged commitment of many in both Committees, particularly Ninian Hill, the dominant power behind the whole scheme.

In the earlier chapter, reading of his background and achievements, there is no doubt that Hill was a man of formidable intellect, including a wide and varied interest in the arts and classical architecture. There are a number of instances where it is obvious that this was a knowledge he put to good use, for example, in the completion of the apse of Murrayfield Church in Edinburgh, dedicated as a War Memorial, and also in his writing on the history of the Old West Kirk in Greenock and his book on the history of the Church of Scotland. While it is widely acknowledged that Hill initiated the very idea of the Memorial in Jerusalem, what is probably less known is the extent to which Hill influenced and very often took the initiative deciding not only the size and scale of the buildings, but also the concept, design and details. It is not unreasonable to assume from the records that as a leading member of the Committee in Edinburgh, with his drive and commitment and knowledge of church architecture, the Committee gave way to him, certainly at the early stage of the process. In a later memorandum to the Committee on an issue of design Hill reminded them that they had given him full powers in 1926 and in 1929 and 'I decided to have the church designed by Mr A.C. Holliday as an early Christian Basilica. This style is well described and illustrated in Sir Banister Fletcher's 'History of Architecture'. In 1928 I made a careful study of the churches of this period, Centuries IV – IX, in Rome.'

With the Committees or, arguably, Hill as the client the other key person in any properly organised construction project is, of course, the Architect. In the case of the Memorial this was Albert Clifford Holliday, BArch, A.R.I.B.A. (1897-1960). A graduate of Liverpool University in Architecture and Civic Design, Holliday, with his wife, Eunice, travelled to Palestine in 1922 to take up the position of Civic Adviser to the City of Jerusalem. He was the successor to Charles Robert Ashbee, an Architect and designer in the "Arts and Crafts" movement and who, because of his reputation, had been appointed by Ronald Storrs, the first Governor of Jerusalem, to develop what became known as the "Pro–Jerusalem Society", a cross-community body whose aim was 'the preservation and advancement of the interests of Jerusalem, its district and inhabitants; more especially: –

'1. The protection of and the addition to the amenities of Jerusalem and its district.

'2. The provision and maintenance of parks, gardens, and open spaces in Jerusalem and its district.

'3. The establishment in the district of Jerusalem of Museums, Libraries, Art Galleries, Exhibitions, Musical and Dramatic Centres, or other institutions of similar nature for the benefit of the public.

'4 The protection and preservation, with the consent of the Government, of the antiquities in the district of Jerusalem.

'5. The encouragement in the district of Jerusalem of arts, handicrafts, and industries in consonance with the general objects of the Society.

'6. The administration of any immovable property in the district of Jerusalem which is acquired by the society is entrusted to it by any person or corporation with a view to securing the improvement of the property and the welfare of its tenants of occupants.

'7. To co-operate with the Department of Education, Agriculture, Public Health, Public Works, so far as may be in harmony with the general objects of the Society.' [9]

It was in this positive environment of constructive development within the City of Jerusalem and the surrounding district that Holliday took up his responsibilities. As a young man of twenty-four and just out of university, on the one hand this must have filled him with fearful trepidation, but on the other he would have acknowledged the incredible opportunities such an appointment offered for the development of his skills in architecture and urban planning. From his arrival in Palestine in 1922 until his departure in 1936 it is clear that, from the portfolio of work entrusted to him, he had built up an impressive reputation in a region of the world ripe for development. In 1927 he went into "private practice" serving also as Town Planning Adviser to the Palestine Government. In these various capacities, he was central to many major planning proposals, including the master plan (1926 – 1930) of Jerusalem, the restoration of the walls and gates of the Old City and, together with Patrick Abercrombie, a regional plan (1933 – 1936) for Haifa Bay for the Jewish National Fund. His work in Jerusalem was traditional, responding sensitively to local climate, materials and culture, e.g., Barclays Bank and the 'Khan' of St John's Ophthalmic Hospital (1929 – 1930). With the Jewish architect Richard Kauffmann, he planned the Reclamation Area (1929 – 1931) in Haifa, and later, between 1933 and 1937, he set the architectural guidelines for its development.

Clifford Holliday, Architect

Holliday's son, Tim, who was the first child baptised in the new St Andrew's Church on the 7th December, 1930, writes of his father, 'As a man my father was restless, dynamic and excitable. His approach to design was intuitive and imaginative rather than intellectual. He would however research thoroughly if this was necessary. He thought history and the tradition of vernacular buildings important. He appreciated and loved beautiful things: Jerusalem pottery, Persian rugs, paintings, local crafts, simple, honestly built churches and dwellings.

'Clifford Holliday came from a family of hard – headed businessmen. He was destined as the eldest son to take over the firm. Some time in his 'teens' he told his parents that he wanted to be an artist. They were horrified. A compromise was reached: he would study architecture. After seeing action in France during the First World War when he was wounded he became a student at the School of Architecture at Liverpool University. He was twenty-four when he came to work in Jerusalem. His appointment as Civic Adviser to the city brought him into contact the Military Governor, Ronald Storrs. I think this crucial. Storrs was a very cultured and enlightened boss.

'As a boy I used to watch my father sketch plans and layouts of buildings. His pencil would fly about with great speed going over outlines again and again until they were quite black. The more measured drawings that attended to detail and scale, done with using T-squares and French curves, for the attention of builders and contractors, were, it seemed to me, done with a kind of magical flair. He seemed to be a master of his trade and was always happy when he was designing. He was more of an artist than a technical expert. If he was caught in a web of administration and regulation he would become morose and depressed. Once, when I was about seven or eight years old he found me constructing an elaborate building with toy bricks. My father said, "Don't make it symmetrical!" "Symmetrical" was a word he often used in a derogatory way. I know what he meant. He didn't like the over formal, oversimplified view of academic order. It was my first lesson in architecture.

'The Church was, amongst the numerous schemes father carried out in various places about the world, probably his favourite piece of work. I remember he had a large photo of it in his office when he was Professor of Town Planning at Manchester University. It was also, I believe on the cover of an exhibition catalogue that was issued in connection with works by ex-students of the Liverpool School of Architecture.'

There is no record of why Hill selected Holliday for the Memorial Architect. What is known is that by 1926 when Hill was in need of an Architect, Holliday had already developed his reputation within Jerusalem. In addition with his work for the Government of Palestine Holliday's name will have been well-known to members of the Local Committee, most of whom held senior positions within the Local Authority and Government.

———————————————————

A problem that Hill and the Committees had was the cost of the site which had been offered by the Patriarchate for the Memorial. At thirty-four shillings per square yard it was considered still to be expensive. Clearly the aim was to purchase only what they needed and therefore keep the purchase cost down to a minimum. The Committee had the funds for the site but no funds for the building at this stage. The need to determine the extent of land required led to a meeting in Holliday's home in April 1926 where Hill and the Local Committee sat with the Architect and set out the brief for the project. It was agreed that '…. the Hospice should contain the following; – entrance hall with secretary's office adjoining, cloakroom, common room, library, dining room, service room, kitchen, two servants' bedrooms and lavatory; fifteen bedrooms of which eight single and seven double bedded, linen press, bathrooms and WC's.

'For the Chapel it was agreed that it should be seated with fifty chairs normally with ample crusher for utilisation when the occasion required. Some difference of opinion was expressed as to whether a square or oblong ground plan was preferable and Mr Holliday agreed to consider the matter and report thereon later.'

Holliday was instructed to prepare sketch plans based on the brief and ascertain the area of land required. One month later, in May, at the Local Committee, Holliday produced sketch plans and a plaster model of the proposed Church and Hospice which were 'greatly admired, were approved and Mr Holliday was congratulated on the success of his labours.' The plans and the model were put on show one month later for the 'Scottish Community' in Jerusalem.

THE PROJECTED CHURCH AND HOSPICE

The plaster model

At this same meeting, Holliday also produced provisional costs for the work, with the Hospice calculated at £7,500 and the Church, £3,500. This total of £11,000 excluded the cost of furnishings and fees. With this the Committee was able to determine what it thought would be the overall cost of the project and establish the shortfall to be fundraised:

i.Cost of site	£ 3,726	
ii.Cost of Registration of Site	£ 132	
iii.Buildings	£11,000	
iv.Architect's Fees	£ 1,020	
v.Furnishings	£ 1,200	
	£17,078	[£905,000]
Amount of Funds to Hand	£ 8,859	
Balance Required	£ 8,219	[£435,000]

However, with sparse information regarding the overall design and accompanying details, it is not surprising that the cost of the building work was well underestimated and that the shortfall turned out to be a much greater figure than envisaged. But that would become an issue for the future.

What now gripped the Committee's imagination was a report that the Prince of Wales was due to visit the Holy Land in the Spring of 1927 to attend the dedication of the new War Cemetery on Mount Scopus. It was agreed to approach the Secretary of State for Scotland with the request that the Prince would lay the foundation stone for the Memorial. Recognising that this was only six months away, instructions were given to the Local Committee and the Architect to make arrangements for this hoped for great honour. However the timing was such that the plans for the new building were at no stage for anyone to know where the foundation stone might be best laid. A pragmatic resolution to the matter appreciated that before any foundation could be built, upon which a foundation stone could be laid, one very practical provision had to be made for the storage of water for the Hospice once in operation. It was essential that a cistern had to be dug to store this water and with few architectural design constraints, it could be prepared quite quickly. Instructions were given to the Architect by the Committee in Edinburgh to prepare tenders for the preparation of the site and for the construction of the cistern, "preferably below the church"! As it transpired, the Prince of Wales could not attend the dedication of the War Cemetery and, therefore, also lay the Memorial foundation stone. However it was discovered that Lord Allenby was to attend the Mount Scopus dedication in the afternoon of the 7th May, 1927, and was asked if he would lay the Memorial foundation stone, which he did in the morning prior to the Mount Scopus dedication. Both events were widely reported in the Press. The London Times notes:

'The Palestine Campaign – Memorials unveiled in Jerusalem 'Jerusalem, May 7.

'To-day has been a day of memorable ceremonies in the history of the Holy City. It began with a simple and impressive service in the War Cemetery conducted by Dr. Rennie MacInnes, Anglican Bishop in Jerusalem, assisted by Dr. Semple, at which Field-Marshall Lord Plumer, the British High Commissioner, and his staff were present.

'Later in the morning Field Marshal Lord Allenby laid the foundation stone of the Scottish War Memorial. Dr. Christie, of the United Free Church of Scotland, assisted by Dr. Semple and by Mr. McGowan, of the Presbyterian Church of Australia, conducted the service in the presence of Bishop MacInnes, the Syrian Coptic, Greek Orthodox, and Armenian Bishops, and a large number of Palestinian notables.

'Mr S.G. Kermack, the Government Advocate, in an explanatory speech, said that the Memorial was intended to commemorate the liberation of Jerusalem and the Holy Land, the Scots who fell in the Palestine Campaign, and, as these Scots soldiers would not have wished it otherwise, their Imperial comrades who fought and fell by their side.

'Lord Allenby paid a tribute to the valour of the Scottish troops and said that under his command had been an entirely Scottish Division, the

52nd, which was second to none and which came from the trenches at Gaza straight to the heights overlooking Jerusalem, and took and retained them against attacks and counter-attacks until the main body arrived and the city fell.

'The Memorial, which is being erected by the Church of Scotland and the United Free Church, will take the form of a hostel where divinity students can pursue their religious studies and a chapel where residents and visitors can worship according to the Scottish ritual. The design is due to Mr A.C. Holliday, Civic Adviser to the Jerusalem Municipality, and the general type is Eastern, to harmonize with the surroundings. The site is on the brow of the hill on the western side of the Bethlehem road, overlooking the Valley of Hinnom, with behind it the Holy City and beyond the mountains of Moab.

'Cemetery Memorial

'The most important ceremony of all, the unveiling of the memorial in the War Cemetery, followed in the afternoon. The countryside was black with humanity climbing Mount Scopus, and on the road was a ceaseless stream of cars, cabs, and all manner of vehicles ......'

The laying of the stone, coinciding with Allenby's visit, was an opportunity grasped. It was a symbolic act and good for publicity. However it was temporary! The stone was removed from its resting place not only because it would have to be repositioned to a more appropriate place in the building once the plans were finalised and construction work begun (twenty months later at the end of 1928), it was also moved for safekeeping following a major earthquake in the area. For Hill, the stone turned out to be an object of great consternation.

Many years later, in 1934, after it must have been preying on his mind, Hill wrote a memorandum to both the Committee in Edinburgh and also, by then, the Kirk Session in Jerusalem:

'In 1927 an Order of Service for the Ceremony (for the laying of the foundation stone) and an inscription for the stone were carefully prepared and sent to Jerusalem to the Architect; also a silver trowel. A serious earthquake occurred shortly after the ceremony and further progress became impossible – the stone being a slab about 6 inches thick from King Solomon's Quarries was removed to a place of safety.

'In 1929 I found on arriving in Jerusalem that the inscription had been altered. These changes were –

'1. The words "Scottish Churches Memorial" headed the inscription.

'2. The Christian Cross in a conventionalised form which should have headed the inscription was omitted. A St Andrew's Cross in a shield was added under the new heading.

'3. The dates were stated in a different and unsatisfactory manner thus, – "9 Dec 1917" changed to "Dec 9, 1917"

'I felt much disappointed at these changes but after mature consideration with Mr Holliday I came most reluctantly to the conclusion that it was not practicable even if it were desirable to tamper with the stone laid by Lord Allenby.

'Ninian Hill, 11ᵗʰ June 1934.'

In the meantime while the foundation stone rested, work continued with preparing the plans for the Church and Hospice, despite the Architect having no formal contract. Instead there existed a "gentleman's agreement" which was only formalised in January 1928, nearly two years after Holliday's first meeting with Hill and the Local Committee.

Today, communication has improved considerably with the use of electronic media. In the 1920's communicating internationally by post was not only frustrating but also, very often, confusing, especially in trying to express concepts and details. When it was not possible for face-to-face interaction the recourse was to attempt to spell out in print what you are seeking to achieve. An example of this is Hill's long letter to the Architect of the 3rd January, 1928, at a time when the plans were still being developed. Although not an architect himself the level of detail in which Hill tries to make clear his design objectives for the Memorial provides a clear example of Hill's depth of knowledge and his meticulous attention to every element of the building:

'Dear Mr Holliday,

'I am sending you a number of photographs, sketches and letters regarding various items in the interior of the church for your consideration and report. An informal but general approval has been given to my proposals which have been shaped and reshaped as I have found out how not to do it, and benefited by criticism and advice. My conclusions at present are as follows: –

'I.GROUND PLAN: A tracing of your plan is enclosed showing in red ink what is proposed. (a) the Chancel is raised two steps above the level of the floor at the Nave. The steps, with the tread of 2 feet are so placed as to give more room on the floor of the Nave and to reduce the floor space of the Chancel which is unnecessarily large and which otherwise might appear empty and bare. The Prayer Desk, i.e. chair and book board are placed in the centre of the bay directly opposite the organ. The walls of the Chancel should be of marble but treated in a different manner from the Apse. (b) The Sanctuary is raised two steps above the Chancel floor and the Table is placed on a third step which should be about two feet broad in front and a few inches on either side as shown in the plan and in the Westminster Cathedral guide facing page 25.

'Around the Apse is a plain marble bench without any division marking off the seats. The presiding minister's seat in the centre will, however, have arms and a back, and should be raised a few inches above the bench. It should be of quite simple design (see photo of S.Sabina). A footstool will be required at this seat, and a small platform behind the Table for use when celebrating. (c) It is proposed to pave the Apse with marble from Iona. See letter and sketches from Messrs Galbraith & Winton. The plan without the crosses is preferred. Iona marble is not to be had in large pieces, and as the quarry is closed the stock is limited. Please send me a tracing of the floor of the Apse as now arranged, so that I can instruct Messrs Galbraith & Winton accordingly.

'II. THE TABLE: I have abandoned the proposal to make the Table and Pulpit of bleached oak because I feel that marble is the proper material in such a church as we are building, and also because I find the bleached oak in the Thistle Chapel, erected just twenty years ago, is already becoming discoloured in places. When I was in London last autumn I was advised to consult Messrs Burke & Co. who had executed some very fine mosaic and marble work in St Columba's (Church of Scotland) London. I enclose two letters from them and also sketch of a Table in white marble with mosaic inlay based on a photograph I gave them of an altar in Rome, but with the Chi-Rho monogram from a sarcophagus in Ravenna. The drawing of the columns is not very happy but I think Burke's know how to make them which is the main thing. The dimensions as sketched are – width 5 ft: breadth 2 ft: and height 3 ft. Please advise these are approved.

'III. THE CONCH OR SEMI-DOME: This will be lined with plain gold mosaic. See Messrs Burke's letter. I have now given up the idea of having a band of Celtic design just above the marble as the whole scale is so small. The method of doing the mosaic work is simple. Burke's place cubes on the floor face up, then cover them with strongly gummed paper to which they adhere. The sheets of paper are packed up and sent off. They are then pasted onto to the prepared surface of the semi-dome, as if the place were being papered. When dry and properly set, the paper backing is damped and scraped off leaving the gold mosaic showing. Burke's will give directions for preparing the ground to receive the mosaic.

(The method proposed of affixing the mosaic was on further consideration disapproved – it should be done by hand – each tesserae separately).

'IV. THE WALLS OF THE APSE: It is proposed that these should be lined with marble as shown in the photograph of S.Sabina and in the Westminster Cathedral guide facing pages 25, 33 and 40. I also refer to the rough sketch and notes which I made after visiting the Cathedral. It is desirable that we should have a plain Latin Cross somewhere in the Apse, and I think it would come in appropriately if the central panel of the marble above the Minister's seat were extended a little as on page 25 so as to provide a suitable setting for a gold cross. It will also be an advantage to break the line.

The treatment of the Apse as here proposed has also the recommendation of simplicity. It does not require either columns or cornice. I assume that suitable marbles are obtainable in Palestine.

'V. THE WALLS OF THE CHANCEL: These should be lined with marble but not in the same manner as the Apse.

'VI. THE PULPIT: The accompanying photograph of an ambon in S.Maria in Cosmedin has been much admired and it is desired to adapt it for the purpose of a Pulpit. The rough sketch shows how this might be done and the ground plan shows where it should be placed. Since I made the sketch, I am inclined to think that the stair should be turned and enter from the first step of the Chancel. This would reduce the number of steps by one. It is not desirable to have a Pulpit higher than necessary for the people in the back of the Church to see the preacher. I suggest a height of 2 ft or 2½ ft from the floor of the Pulpit. A seat in the Pulpit is not needed and I think 3 ft clear inside would be sufficiently wide by 3 ft inside height. There would be the usual brass book board. Please advise if such a Pulpit could be satisfactorily made in Jerusalem, or whether it should be made here and sent out for erection. The four pilasters and the little cornice present the only difficulty that I can see.

'VII. LECTERN: A marble Lectern will probably be most suitable, but until the sight position has been found from experience, it will be best to use a simple bookstand of wood. I have marked in pencil on the ground plan where I think it will probably be placed.

'VIII. THE PRAYER DESK: This is simply a seat and bookstand and such can, I think, only be of bleached oak, made here and sent out along with the temporary Lectern.

'IX. THE WINDOWS: You will remember that we agreed to take the windows in St. Anne's as our model. I suggest that in the centre south transept window we might have an opening in the form of a star (of Bethlehem), and a Maltese Cross in the corresponding north window. I would try and get special donations for these windows. The star and cross (not too large) would be filled in with clear crystallised glass; the other openings with translucent blue glass. This would give a glow of rich colour, but I'm not sure that it would give sufficient light. The windows are so small it may be difficult to arrange for a border of say very slightly blue glass to let in the light and contrast with the darker blue of the rest of the window. The west circular window, which should open to give ventilation, would be treated differently, and I suggest as in the Westminster Cathedral, i.e. small round knotted glasses in a metal frame. I don't know the makes but that can no doubt be ascertained. Such a window would let in a flood of somewhat diffused light.

'X. THE CORBELS: I have been considering what, if any, devices should be carved on the twelve corbels. I am advised that it would be safer to leave them alone. I suggest that we should only deal with the two corbels in the Chancel, one bearing the St Andrew Cross and the other the Cross Keys of St Andrew's brother, St Peter.

'XI. We must have a "Burning Bush" somewhere and I think the most appropriate place would be in a panel over the door in the porch of the Hospice. Also I think we might have a bas-relief of St. Andrew in a panel over the Church door in the outside of the tower. I could get both of these designed and executed by the artist who did such work in the Memorial in the Castle here.

Please let me have a plan of the porch and of the tower, and show how you think such as I have suggested might be carried out.

'XII. THE 52ⁿᵈ DIVISION: are going to provide for a monument in the Church and have got a very beautiful and suitable design for one in alabaster designed by Messrs Gawthorpe & Co., London, which it is proposed to place in the centre of the south bay directly opposite the door on entering. It is of a simple but dignified Renaissance style which will harmonise well with the interior. Photo enclosed of monument to be adapted to the purpose. It was necessary to get a design in order to secure the support of the 52ⁿᵈ Division Club.

'XIII THE CHURCH BELL: I enclose a letter from Messrs. Taylor, Loughborough, who are to supply a bell as estimated. You will notice what they say about the girders and advise me as you think best. The bell rope, I think, should descend to the porch so that it can be rung there. There will be a small Memorial Bronze tablet in the porch recording the gift of "St Brides Bell".

'XIV THE FONT: I would have liked to have had our font of Aberdeen granite, but I fear owing to the weight it is impracticable. How would a block from King Solomon's Quarry serve? There is no need for any drainage.

'XV THE VESTRY: Should we not have a small built in safe for the Communion Plate?

'These are the various matters which I think now require attention, and I shall be glad to learn what you think after you have considered them.

'With kind regards

'Yours very truly,

'Ninian Hill.'

Holliday's response to this was slow in coming and in March the Committee expressed its concern accordingly. However to move the matter forward, at Hill's suggestion it was agreed that once the plans were received they should be passed on to Sir Robert Lorimer to review and if he is satisfied with them Holliday should be instructed to invite tenders for the work and proceed with the construction. Despite Hill's close association with Lorimer he turned down the invitation noting that he was unfamiliar with the environment and the context of the proposed Memorial!

Holliday's outline proposals, once they arrived, were agreed to but with much of the detail carefully set out in Hill's January letter, frustratingly, still to be considered. Matters came to a head in September 1928, when, at a "conference" held in Hill's home in Edinburgh and with two members of the Local Committee in Jerusalem in attendance, 'Regret was expressed at the delay in commencing building operations and Messrs Miller and Turnbull (from Jerusalem) undertook to urge on Mr Holliday the importance of hastening on matters so that, if possible, the Church and Hospice might be opened and dedicated on St Andrew's Day, 1929.' - in fourteen months time! It was also agreed that, despite the lack of final plans for the buildings, tenders for the work should be secured and the Local Committee should review them and report.

In the meantime, the Committee in Edinburgh, which had been seeking to appoint a Clerk of Works to supervise the upcoming building work, had received a letter from Captain E.H. Pearcey, M.B.E., R.E. (Retired), 'who had acted as Clerk of Works for the War Memorial at Aldershot, expressing his willingness to act as such for the Memorial buildings in Jerusalem.' It was agreed to appoint him on a salary of £40 per month, plus travel costs, and that he should 'enter on his duties towards the end of October so as to assist in the adjustment of the contract.'

In October the specification for the works was drawn up by Holliday, which included the following:

'1. GENERAL DESCRIPTION OF THE BUILDING:

'The church is placed on the brow of the cliff with the main axis East and West and the Hospice is planned on a lower plateau to the north. The size of the church is twenty eight metres by nine and half metres, comprising: a vaulted nave, a domed central space, a chancel and an apse. In addition, there is a tower with stack rooms, an entrance porch, vestry and a chair store. A wide external stairway gives access from the Hospice garden to the Church. The Hospice comprises: an entrance porch, vestibule, hall, common room, dining room, library, wardens room, office, cloak rooms, kitchen service, fifteen principal bedrooms, bath rooms, linen rooms and servants' rooms. There is an internal staircase from the common room to the Church. Constructionally, the outer walls are of Kalkoule stone★ with a concrete backing, and the interior skeleton: columns, beams, slabs, domes and vaults, are of reinforced concrete. Internal partitions are of coke breeze, expanded metal and hollow tiles. The special fittings and appointments will be arranged under separate contracts, the main items being: marble and tile work, parquet floors, woodwork, steel windows, electric light and drainage. The hot water system will be installed in the cellar to supply the kitchen and bath rooms. The heating of the Church and bedrooms will be by electric radiators. The drainage disposal will be a septic tank and percolation pit. Water supply will be from a large cistern under the kitchen and connection will be made to the Municipal main.'

(* Quarried from the Mount of Olives)

Nine tenders were received for the work and were considered by the Local Committee, Holliday and Pearcey on the 28th November, 1928, as follows:

'1. Mr. Arfad Gut of Tel Aviv	LP.14,722.009 mils
'2. Mr. Selim Aboussouan, Jerusalem	LP. 7,938.440 mils
'3. Messrs. Rutans & Sons, Jerusalem	LP. 14,699.042 mils
'4. Fth. Levnott & Co., Jerusalem	LP. 10,820.543 mils
'5. Mr. Geo. Shiber, Jerusalem	LP. 11,024.219 mils
'6. Mr. Jeries Ishak, Jerusalem	LP. 10,673.996 mils
'7. Mr. Pauerle, Jerusalem	LP. 11,155.074 mils
'8. Mr. Gurovitz, Tel Aviv	LP. 11,548.262 mils
'9. Messrs. De Farro & Co., Jerusalem	LP. 10,457.298 mils'

It was noted that the lowest tender was submitted by Mr Aboussouan. However the Architect and one member of the Local Committee stated that, 'they did not think it was possible for any Contractor to carry out the work according to the schedule at the figure quoted, and that they were unable to recommend Mr Aboussouan as a suitable Contractor. He had not been on the list of approved Contractors originally invited to tender and had only been allowed to do so after a great deal of pressure had been brought to bear on several members of the Committee.' Instead, De Farro's tender was accepted and the contract was signed on the 5th December, 1928, and work commenced – despite, at that time, insufficient detail regarding the works and insufficient funds to complete the works!

The outcome of the tendering process was reported to the Committee in Edinburgh one month later noting, "the work to be started immediately and the whole to be finished by St Andrew's Day, 1929, under penalty of £10 per day. This was approved" – as if the Committee could do otherwise by this time. In addition, neither the date for completion of the works or the financial penalty, as noted in the Committee minute, were included in the signed contract with the Contractor!

With a Contractor and work on the project underway, there was still the matter of deciding the details, which led to a spate of correspondence between Edinburgh and Jerusalem. Remarkably, many of the issues raised by Hill in his detailed letter of 3rd January, 1928, a year ago, had still not been fully addressed. Hill sent a reminder on the 7th January, 1929, and the Local Committee met with the Architect on the 9th February, 1929, to respond, as minuted:

'1. GROUND PLAN:

'A detailed drawing was submitted by Mr Holliday showing the arrangements in the Chancel and Apse, the position of the Communion Table, seating in Apse, Steps, Organ, Pulpit, Lectern and Prayer Desk and was approved in principle

'2. APSE PAVING:

'The Committee were not impressed with the design submitted by Messrs Galbraith, Winton & Co., and it was suggested that this firm be asked to send available sizes of marble slabs and fresh designs will be prepared by Mr Holliday.

'3. COMMUNION TABLE, PULPIT, FONT:

'The Committee were of the opinion that these should be of stone and not marble. It was felt that the simpler form of Communion Table would be more in keeping with the design of the Church. The Committee favoured making the Communion Table, Pulpit and Font of similar stone to that of the pulpit in Christ Church.

'4. SEMI-DOME & APSE (interior decoration):

'The Committee would much prefer to see the interior treatment as simple as possible, preferably the white stone walls and plaster ceiling as contracted for.

'5. WINDOWS:

'Mr Holliday was asked to send the sizes of all windows in the Church and the Committee at home might guide as to designs.

'6. SHIELDS (Corbels):

'The Committee were of the opinion that these shields were originally intended for the Regimental Crests of our Scottish Regiments. There is sufficient space for 50 Badges, Crosses, etc., and this could be executed in Jerusalem as good work of this description can be done locally.

'7. 52nd DIVISION MEMORIAL:

'The design submitted did not commend itself to the Committee. It was considered too elaborate and as most of us were connected with the 52nd Division during the War we feel that a simple Bronze Tablet would be a more fitting memorial.

'8. BELL: approved.

'9. SAFE: approved.'

Then on the 8th March, after receiving from Holliday a set of updated plans for the scheme, with only nine months until the anticipated date of opening, Hill writes:

'Dear Mr Holliday,

'It was with the utmost regret that the Committee sent you the following cable on 6th March: "Plans received. Committee disallows changed form of arch in Church. Must adhere approved plan. Confirm Hill's letter re Chancel Apse. Maclean Ewing Conveners."

'It is evident that there has been a serious misunderstanding somewhere. We had not the slightest idea that you were contemplating any change on the plans which were approved last summer and which have elicited on all hand nothing but approval and admiration; the only modification which is desired was with regard to the entrance and that you agreed to. It was an intense disappointment to find that you have entirely altered the character of the interior of the Church.

'The classical tradition, the vertical lines and rounded arches have been departed from, and the ultramodern form of arch which is repeated again and again strikes a note which is alien to our traditions and the whole edifice – you may perhaps remember that you tried the effect of such arches in the Hospice in one of your first sketches and that we both agreed in condemning them and in deciding on the round arch. You have retained it in the Hospice, why change it in the Church?

'It will no doubt cause delay and expense to return to the approved plan but we look to you confidently to do your utmost to minimise these. We have made many sacrifices these past eleven years, and we must see the thing through at whatever cost.

'Let me add that we approve of the enlarged vestibule and entrance to the Church, the vestry, the dome and the large single like windows in the transepts as in the new plans.

'But we do not approve also of the enlarged Chancel. You must have noticed, in my letter of 7th January, that I made a proposal to reduce the apparent size. We do not need to provide space for surpliced choirs as in an Episcopal Church. We only need space for the organ on one side and a Minister's seat on the other as in my sketch plan. It is true that the increase is only two feet, but the whole scale is so small that it becomes important. The new plan of the Apse compares very unfavourably with the former plan. It lacks breadth of treatment and loses dignity. The three little windows which look well enough in the exterior are mere toys, reminiscent of the Dolls House style of the little English Church at Port Said. The Apse is far too small for windows and unquestionably we ought to follow the model of the smaller Italian Basilicas as exemplified in Westminster Cathedral, admittedly, a work of genius, and have a plain gold mosaic Conch for the cost of which we have promised a donation.

'Yours, Ninian Hill.'

...... and on the same day, the 8th March, having received the telegram Hill refers to, Holliday writes,

'Dear Mr Hill,

'I was very surprised to receive your telegram yesterday.

'I am at a loss to know what the Committee's views are on the alterations suggested; it may be that the plans are not properly understood by your Committee. The sections appear complicated as various parts are shown in half sections only. The general lines of the original architectural treatment have been kept; of course, you must allow for various modifications in making final drawings, there are many points to consider both aesthetic and constructional. The groin of the vault does not give a correct picture in a scale drawing, it is simply a cross vault. I was complimenting myself on the successful treatment of the whole interior; in my opinion, the working drawings have turned out much better than expected, and I am sure the result will be a simple and dignified design. There is nothing that is not in keeping with the exterior treatment and the kind of work one expects to find in Palestine. It should be clearly understood that any drastic alteration now will make great difficulties, all the quantities have been got out and are included in the tender with De Farro. In addition, there are very complicated calculations for the dome and reinforced concrete vault, perhaps it is not realised how much work and thought has been put into this building; nothing has been spared and I have done my best to meet the requirements of the two Committees.

'Are you coming to Palestine this summer? Many details could be discussed; your advice on the actual "Finish" would be very useful.

'The actual construction of the Church will not, I am sure, begin for three months. At present we are only striking the formwork of the foundations and basement of the Hostel, all the first floor must be built before the Church can begin.

'Regarding the suggestions you sent, they were brought before the Local Committee; I understand that Mr Turnbull has sent to you the minutes. I am forwarding some detail drawing showing the proposals for the Apse. You will see that everything is kept as simple and severe as possible. The Local Committee are very anxious not to have a display of marble or other ornamental work. In addition to the drawings I am sending you later an abstract of the quantities as priced out by Mr De Farro; as there is only one copy, the one I send is made specially for you; Mr Turnbull thinks you will be interested in local prices.

'You ask about the staircase from the Hostel to the Church, this is clearly shown on the drawing I sent you. There has been one further modification, the Municipality require two entrances to the Church, I have therefore arranged for an entrance through a small vestibule adjacent the vestry. Should you require any further details or explanations, I shall be very happy to send them. Please excuse my seeming neglect in not answering your letter before this, but I'm sure you will understand how busy we have been to get the work started.

In conclusion I feel I must say how well Captain Pearcey is doing his job as Clerk of Works. He is an excellent man and I have no hesitation in saying that the work done so far is the best I've seen in Palestine.

'With kind regards to yourself and Miss Hill

'Yours very sincerely,

'A.C. Holliday.'

It is clear that the exchange of correspondence and the seeming disregard for his ideas on the design of the Church is beginning to get a bit too much for Hill who, taking time out from his holidays in Brighton, writes a week later to the Local Committee in Jerusalem:

'Dear Mr Turnbull,

'I have to thank you for your letter of 7th inst. enclosing Minutes of three Committee meetings and extracts of your cashbook all of which I am forwarding to the Committee in Edinburgh.

'First of all I wish to express what I know they will all feel and that is our appreciation of your unstinting interest and labours on behalf of the scheme which is so dear to our hearts and for which we have laboured so long.

'I note that Mr Holliday is writing me in reply to my letter of the 8th January regarding the furnishings of the church. My first thought was to await his letter before writing you on the subject, but as I feel very uncertain when the letter will come, I think it better to write now. I trust that Mr Holliday has some satisfactory explanation to offer regarding his departure from the approved plan of the Church. It must have been apparent if he paid any attention to my letter of the 7th January that we were at cross purposes and yet I see from your Minutes that on 9th February he submitted to your Committee a detailed plan showing arrangements for the Chancel and Apse. What the nature of his plan is we do not know, or whether he has altered the Chancel and Apse in accordance with the approved plan and my tracing. Obviously such are matters in which Ministers, whose office it is to conduct Public Worship, are the proper persons to consult. For our Committee I can assure you that they do greatly value the advice of the Local Committee, but it is the Joint Committee which is responsible to the General Assembly and to the subscribers and I don't understand why Mr Holliday did not send us a tracing of his plan. If you will refer to my letter of 7th January his advice was asked for on various matters mentioned and we are still awaiting his reply. I hope we have always treated Mr Holliday with the utmost consideration and respect; it has at any rate been my constant endeavour to do so, but I think I should state quite frankly that his unbusinesslike lack of attention is creating a regrettable impression. It is three years since we acquired the site and Mr Holliday has apparently thrown the plans of the Church into the melting pot. It is simply deplorable.

'I now wish to submit some observations on the recommendations of your Committee. The way to approach the subject of the internal treatment of the Church is along the lines we have already followed. We agreed in the very beginning that our Memorial must be one worthy of the occasion, and that the building should be of an eastern character and harmonious with the environment. We have been most heartily congratulated on that decision, and up to the present it has been adhered to and must be continued. An Eastern style in reference to the Church can only mean the Byzantine style and the approved plans have been recognised at once as Byzantine. Now the characteristics of Church decoration in that style are marble and gold mosaic; just as in Gothic it is sculptured stone in stained glass. The consideration of any of the classic examples of Gothic and Byzantine Cathedrals will make this quite clear and it is to such standards we must adhere if we are to avoid adverse criticism

'The proposals contained in my letter were made after prolonged study and with the approval of Dr Arnold Hamilton who has made a special study in Greece of Byzantine Architecture, and Dr Wotherspoon who is a recognised authority on ecclesiology. Further the proposals were based as I stated on what may be regarded as classic examples, and I don't think that we can be seriously questioned though the details are of course subject to modification. It comes to this then that I think we must adopt marble and gold mosaic. With regard to the Table I have no wish to press for the two spiral columns with gold mosaic inlay. Such columns are I think very beautiful and they indicate the Table aspect, but they are not essential and (as donor) I am willing to omit them in deference to the opinion of your Committee. A "Burning Bush" would be out of place on the front of the Table and I can think of no more appropriate device for the Communion Table in Eastern Christendom than the Chi-Rho symbol. The photo I sent of the Ambon was greatly admired for its simplicity but it is not the only simple type of pulpit, and if only Mr Holliday will say what he recommends without further delay you may be sure that the Committee will give it most prompt and careful consideration.

'Strong objection has been taken to Military crests and badges in the House of the Prince of Peace and I think quite rightly.

'I withdraw what I wrote about the windows in respect of the change of size made in the new plans which is approved.

'The matter of the 52nd Division Memorial lies in the hands of the Dinner Club. I am sorry you have not seen the finished drawing of the proposed monument which has been greatly admired. Do you think a bronze tablet would be adequate?

'Yours sincerely,

'Ninian Hill.'

And a few days later, on the 22nd March, Hill, as the Church of Scotland Honorary Secretary on the Edinburgh Committee, wrote to his United Free Church of Scotland counterpart on the Committee, the Rev. John Philip:

'Dear Mr Philip,

'I send you a letter and four plans received this morning from Mr Holliday. I think the most important thing to tell you is how difficult, if not indeed impossible, it will be to arrange matters satisfactorily by correspondence. Our Local Committee seem to be suffering from what I understand is called "an inferiority complex" while perhaps we may be thought to be the victims of "a superiority complex", but I think if we had a talk together we might settle matters to our mutual satisfaction and advantage. Curiously enough I wrote to Dr. MacLean yesterday before receiving Holliday's letter suggesting that it might be well for us to take a run out and I am willing to go say early in May when I can get a Summer Fare passage. Only to do any good I must, as was the case of looking for a site, have full powers.

'I was very glad to learn that work has not actually begun on the Church so that it will be a simple matter to adhere to the approved grand plan for the Chancel and Apse. I can't understand why they wanted to enlarge the Chancel and reduce the Apse.

'As regards the plans sent - the Circular Window in the west gable and the window in the Gauseph are all right - I have already expressed my opinion of the little windows in the Apse and the plan shows which we objected to viz, – no vertical lines and no round arch. The Table is curious and impossible – when in this wide world was anything ever seen like it. Perhaps Holliday thinks it is Presbyterian!

We go on Monday to Paris where our address, 'till further notice will be c/o Thomas Cook & Sons, Ltd.

'Kindest regards,

'Yours very truly,

'Ninian Hill.'

Mr Philip agreed to the proposal and, with 'full powers,' Hill travelled to Jerusalem to resolve matters! In October, having spent April and May in Jerusalem, Hill reported on progress to the Committee, as minuted:

'In consequence of the receipt from Mr Holliday, Architect, of new detailed plans for the Church and Hospice showing considerable variation from those of the church which had been approved in the summer of 1928: and various questions on matters of detail having arisen which it would have been difficult to settle satisfactorily by correspondence – it was arranged that I should proceed to Jerusalem to confer with the Architect and Local Committee and was given full powers to do what appeared to be best as advised by Mr Philip in his letter of 26 March, 1929.

'On arrival in Jerusalem on Friday, 19th April, I was met at the station by Dr. McQueen, Mr Turnbull, Mr Holliday and Capt. Pearcey. I found the basement of the Hospice just about completed and that the foundations of the Church had been laid in concrete. Further work on the Church would not be undertaken until the Hospice should reach the level of the Church. On Monday, 22nd April, I met Lord Dean of Guild Forrest of Edinburgh, brother of our missionary at Jaffa, in Mr Holliday's office. The Dean had visited our site and expressed his entire satisfaction both of the stone and concrete work.

'THE CHURCH. The Dean warmly approved of the interior walls being of stone, beyond this he expressed no opinion as to the relative merits of the old and new plans except agreeing that vertical lines gave an impression of height. Mr Holliday explained that in changing the plans he had endeavoured to introduce a Palestinian character with low sprung, elliptical, pointed arches of Crusading origin, and that he had regarded it as a matter on which his clients would have allowed him a free hand. I pointed out that these Palestinian elements were absent in the Hospice and I urged the propriety of adhering to the vertical lines and rounded arches of the approved design. He readily agreed to revert to the approved plan, which was subsequently slightly modified in detail, and admitted that the Palestinian character might be regarded as a corruption rather than a development of classical forms. In the course of working out the plans it was found necessary to heighten the walls slightly to allow sufficient light by means of clerestory windows, and in order to comply with the building regulations it was necessary to have an additional exit to the Church. Otherwise the revised plans adhere to the plans approved in 1928.

'THE HOSPICE. It was intimated that the Public Health Department insisted upon Hospices having a laundry, and as the only space available was intended for a garage it had to be placed there. The extra cost is estimated at £180.

'Much consideration was given to the question of fuel, and after examining a Petrol gas plant, Dr. McQueen, Mr Turnbull and Capt. Pearcey, recommended its adoption for cooking and the geysers in the bathrooms. – Estimated cost probably £260.

'Careful consideration was also given to the electric light installation, and on Mr Tweedie Millar's strong recommendation it has been found advisable, and indeed necessary, to have steel tubing. – The cost is estimated at £550.

'Accompanied by Mr Turnbull and Mr Tweedie Millar, I visited Messrs. Goralsky & Krenitzi's furniture factory in Jaffa and found that excellent furniture can be obtained there at moderate prices. Mr Heron, chief storekeeper of the Government Hospitals Department, to whom I was introduced by Dr. McQueen, gave me much valuable information about furnishings generally. I found on enquiry at the Governate that goods for a Church are admitted free of duty, but this exemption does not apply to Hospices which are placed on the same footing as Hotels.

'FINANCIAL POSITION. The financial position is somewhat obscure owing to the prevailing system of separate contracts for the different tradesmen's work. Mr Holliday's estimate is as follows:

ESTIMATE:-

De Farro's contract	£10,500
Electric Lighting	550
Metal work, windows, etc.	850
Plumbing, drainage, etc.	650
Joinery.	500
Flooring- Hospice only.	1,600
Painting	260
Laundry	180
Petrol gas plant.	260

Hospice furnishings	1,000	
Chairs for Church (140 @ £1)	140	
Organ (£270 plus freight, etc)	300	
Clerk of Works (12 months @ £40 and passage home)	600	
	17,390	[£950,000]
Funds available	12,191	
Deficit	5,199	[£285,000]

PLUS: Architect's Fees; Enclosure, parapet and railings; Church floor, windows

and electric lighting.

NOTE: It is hoped to reduce the cost estimated for flooring and plumbing.

'ARCHITECT'S FEES. The sum of £810 has been paid and a further sum of £313 as requested by Mr Holliday. In his account two items refer to the rejected plans for the Church. (1) 2% on £7000 = £140. Mr Holliday states that under the RIBA Schedule the rate would be 4% as on abandoned work and he reduces it 2%. It is however open to question whether the circumstances warrant the rejected plans being described as abandoned work. Mr Holliday stated that he had made the reduction as he felt he was partly, but not altogether, to blame for the misunderstanding which had arisen and which he attributed to his clients being 2000 miles distant. (2) Bill of quantities 2% on £5000 being part of De Farro's contract. This represents the time occupied by his staff on the plans and constituted an actual loss to him in cash.

'COMPLETION OF WORKS. It was quite evident when I arrived that no one had any expectation of the building being ready for occupation by St Andrew's Day (1929), and after a faint hope being expressed that it might be possible in February, when I left it was thought that Easter, 1930, would be the earliest date for opening. As to that Mr Holliday promised to give us six months notice and to advise us definitely early in October.

'CONCLUDING REMARKS. The residential suburbs of Jerusalem are steadily developing as anticipated, in our direction, and there is a marked improvement in the means of access through tarred roads and motor omnibus services. Mr Holliday is keenly interested in the work and my relations with him and with the Local Committee were of the most harmonious nature. In Capt. Pearcey we have a most diligent and efficient Master of Works. In design, material and craftsmanship we shall have buildings which in these respects will compare favourably with any in Jerusalem. I cannot express myself too highly regarding the valuable and most willing services rendered by Mr Turnbull, Dr MacQueen and Mr Tweedie Millar. Other members of the Local Committee were absent on furlough.

'I left Jerusalem on the 2nd June, 1929, after a stay of a little more than six weeks.'

At this stage there were two major concerns for the Committees. The first was to reconcile the fact that the comparable cost of undertaking the building work as envisaged in May, 1926 had, by October 1929, increased by some £5,000 [£270,000] - with still a considerable amount of work as yet to be costed and a continuing shortfall of funds.

Of course the second concern was the struggle to complete the works. The project had by now taken ten years to get to this point. It was a matter of pride and reputation which drove all concerned to complete the works. As a sign that progress was being made, it was agreed, come what may, to hold an Easter Service in 1930, with a pilgrimage from Scotland and a Dedication Service to be held later in the year on St Andrew's Day. As it transpired the Church was not ready for the Easter Service and it did not happen. From correspondence it is clear that patience was running out!

In one of her many letters home to England, Eunice, Clifford Holliday's wife, writes on the 15th July that year, following a visit to Port Said to attend the funeral of Holliday's father who died on his way back to England after a visit to Holliday and his family in Jerusalem, 'We got back here on Friday morning feeling rather limp. There are some nice letters waiting for Cliff, but these wretched Scottish Memorial people are the limit. There is not a word of sympathy from any of them. All they do is simply pester Cliff for work he has not been able to do. Really, some people are hard.' However a slightly different tone is noted when, on the 20th November, ten days before St Andrews Day, Eunice writes, 'Cliff is spending all his time on the Scottish Memorial. It is to be opened a week on Sunday, St Andrew's Day. Mr Hill arrived this week. He was the man we stayed with in Edinburgh. He is to be the resident Minister for the first year. He is a nice old man, we like him very much. He is going to Christen Timothy.' [10]

However, despite the hive of activity, by St Andrew's Day and the Dedication of the Memorial, the work was still not finished. It took until the end of January, 1931, before the work was considered complete and the Final Account could be compiled by Capt. Pearcey and agreed with

De Farro and the other contractors and suppliers. At this point Captain Pearcey's own contract of employment came to an end.

Memorial from across the Hinnom Valley

St Andrew's from Jaffa Gate

St Andrew's towards Jaffa Gate

The Final Account for the construction work, fees, etc., amounted to £24,416 (See Appendix [3]), more than double the £12,020 estimated in May, 1926. On agreeing the Final Account the outstanding amount due to De Farro, the Main Contractor, was £1,743 [£99,200], funds the Committee did not have. De Farro agreed to be paid in instalments over two years, with interest at the rate of 6.75% per annum.

Captain Pearcey's key role in the design and construction of the Church and Hospice was acknowledged in a letter to him from the Local Committee dated the 27th January, 1931:

'Dear Captain Pearcey,

'The time has arrived when your engagement as Clerk of Works of the Scottish Churches' Memorial in Jerusalem is about to terminate on the completion of the building of the St Andrew's Church and Hospice. The Local Committee in parting with you on your return home desire to express to you and to place on record their high appreciation of your services and the pleasure it has been to be associated with you in the important work which has been entrusted to us. Since your arrival here in December 1928 you have given the most careful and unremitting attention to your duties, never having taken a day's respite from your labour even on Sundays. When the riots of August 1929 broke out you at once enrolled in the Emergency Defence Corps and rendered important service in maintaining the public peace.

'We rejoice in thinking that you will be able to look back upon your labours, which have been most wholehearted, in the erection of this beautiful Scottish Memorial in the Holy City with the utmost satisfaction. That it has been so well and faithfully built is in no small measure due to your expert knowledge and careful supervision.

'We thank you most heartily and wish you a happy return home.

'Ninian Hill; T. Tweedie Millar; J. N. Turnbull; Isobel MacRae.'

Captain Pearcey, Clerk of Works

There is little doubt that the Church as we know it today is as a result of Hill's steadfast pursuit of his idea of what it should look like, 'a Memorial worthy of the occasion.' His well documented determination and commitment to the task gave him leverage amongst his peers to be given the authority to make decisions without recourse. However he did not always get his own way and this troubled him. In his view, to complete the vision, some outstanding details required to be attended to. In December, 1938, as Vice Convener of the Committee, he sent a memorandum to his Committee in Edinburgh and to the Kirk Session in Jerusalem:

'In October, 1937, Mrs Ritchie, Greenhill, Brompton Terrace, Perth, and her sister, Mrs Dewar, offered about £100 for a Memorial to their sister, Miss Ella Smart, to be placed in the Church, and they agreed that it should take the form of covering the conch, or semi-dome, of the Apse with gold mosaic as originally planned.

'Owing to the financial crisis of the Committee in 1930, drastic economies had to be effected, the projected marble lining of the Apse and the mosaic were sacrificed and, with the donors consent, the sum of £500 provided for these and other embellishments was given to the general funds. The opportunity now offers to redeem in a measure the misfortunes of the past.

'Until 1933 the surface of the walls and conch of the Apse was of bare plaster which contrasted most unfavourably with the fine stone of the rest of the interior. To improve matters I then provided a beautiful velour curtain to cover the walls and tinted the conch with distemper to approximate the shade of gold.

'The Kirk Session have found it difficult to approve of the proposed mosaic and have considered various other ways of decorating the Apse permanently. Their suggestions, though suitable enough in a Gothic building, were not in harmony with the style of our church to which it is most important to adhere. Ultimately they have thought it would be best "to let well alone".

'Given full powers by the Committee in 1926 and in 1929, I decided to have the Church designed by Mr A.C. Holliday as an early Christian basilica. This style is well described and illustrated in Sir Banister Fletcher's "History of Architecture". Among other characteristics noted are, – domed surfaces are covered with mosaic and backgrounds of gold. In 1928 I made a careful study of the churches of this period, centuries IV – IX, in Rome, and have recently discussed the subject with Dr. Douglas Strachan, who recently visited the Church, and who, with his brother, Mr Alexander Strachan, filled the windows with stained glass.

'Dr Strachan expressed himself emphatically in favour of the proposed gold mosaic.

'I therefore recommend most strongly that the temporary distempered surface be replaced permanently by one inch squares of gold glass tesserae (mosaic) as originally planned and approved by the Committee. If they, however, feel any doubt on the subject, I beg they will consult the Professor of Fine Art in the University.

'Ninian Hill.'

Church interior

Once again, and to Hill's dismay, both the Committee and the Kirk Session resolved not to proceed with his request. But that was not the end of the story! As Convener of the Committee Hill's last attendance was in January, 1944, at which meeting he gave notice of his intention to resign at the General Assembly in May that year, due to ill health. Still smarting from not getting his own way on the Church design detail, his parting shot was an impressive one thousand word self funded publication once again addressed to the Committee and the Kirk Session in Jerusalem:

'Memorandum

by Dr Ninian Hill, Convener, for the information of the Members of Committee and the Kirk Session of Jerusalem.

'PRIVATE AND CONFIDENTIAL

'I desire to leave on record my views on two uncompleted features of the Church and the Hospice in the hope that the Committee and the Kirk Session will be so kind as to give them due consideration when suitable circumstances arise.

'1 ST ANDREWS CHURCH. During the summer of 1930, it should be recalled, very drastic steps had to be taken to save all unnecessary expenditure in completing the buildings owing to the difficulties experienced in obtaining an overdraft. Among the works abandoned or deferred was that of completing the apse by lining the wall with marble panelling and covering the conch or semi-dome with gold mosaic. The apse was accordingly left with an unsightly expanse of rough concrete which contrasted very unfavourably with the fine white stone walls of the interior of the Church.

'To remedy matters somewhat I provided in 1933, in consultation with Mr Holliday, our Architect and with the approval of the Local Committee, a silk velour curtain of a beautiful old golden colour to cover the wall, and I tinted the conch with yellow distemper. The appearance of the interior of the church was thereby greatly improved and has met with general approval. It must, however be admitted that in such a Church a curtain and distemper can only be regarded as a temporary expedient, and it is important that the apse should be completed in a worthy manner and in accordance with the architectural style of the building as soon as circumstances permit. The layout of the apse, the Holy Table, "throne" and bench, also the geometrical tracery of the windows are distinctive features of Early Christian basilicas such as abound in Italy dating from the sixth to tenth centuries. These differ in such distinctive respects as mentioned from Norman apses, and still more from French Gothic apses and windows of later date which are more generally known in this country. The dome resting on pendentives is a Byzantine feature introduced by Mr Holliday on his own initiative with happy results.

'No plan showing how Mr Holliday proposed to panel the wall of the apse is known to exist, but he approved of following the example of the basilica of St Sabina in Rome. In that event there would be a central vertical or upright panel over the throne flanked by three or four similar panels on either side. It is useful for the throne to have a back. This would correspond with the back of the chair at the Prayer Desk, but the medallion should bear an emblem of our Lord, for which the Chi-Rho monogram would, in Jerusalem, be most appropriate.

'It is to be regretted that the instructions of the Committee to make the Table of marble (for which a special donation had been offered) were ignored and that it was made of stone. The panels of marble from Iona were, however, embedded in the stonework and constitute an interesting and beautiful feature. In these circumstances I think the decision to cover the wall of the apse entirely with marble should be reconsidered and modified. Had the Table been made of marble, marble would have been the appropriate material for the wall, but, failing a reconstruction of the Table which I fear cannot be contemplated, it appears to me that the wall of the apse should be treated in the same manner as the Table. Accordingly, I think the upright framework of the panels of the apse should be made of artificial stone similar to that of frieze, and that the panels be either of Iona marble or Aberdeen red granite – polished or unpolished.

'As regards the conch, Sir Banister Fletcher in his "History of Architecture," 7th Edition, p. 202, writes regarding Early Christian basilicas, "The Vista was rounded off by an apse lined with marble slabs and crowned with the semi-dome encrusted with glittering golden mosaics." When the matter was considered by the Joint Committee, gold tesserae of various sizes, obtained by Mr Holliday from Salviati (of Venice) in London, were submitted, it was thought that those of 1 inch square would be most suitable. These were to be placed in position by hand on a bed of white cement, with a small margin of about 1/16 inch between each. It was reserved for further consideration whether or not there should be immediately above the stone frieze a band of about 18 inches in depth of coloured mosaic in a Celtic design with the central panel bearing an emblem of our Lord.

'It was not found possible to estimate the cost of the proposed mosaic, the marble panelling and the marble Table but it was thought that the sum of £500, which I gave and had intended to use for this and other similar purposes, was sufficient to cover the cost twice over. The chief expense, it was said, would not be the gold tesserae but the time spent in placing each piece in position by hand. Unfortunately the sum in question had to go to help to keep the building operations agoing and is no longer available.

'Two large photographs of the basilica of St Sabina referred to and a number of other more or less relevant materials will be found in the archives of the Committee in the custody of the Hon. Secretary.

'2. ST ANDREWS HOSPICE. One other matter I wish to leave on record. It was proposed to insert over the front door of the Hospice a sculptured representation of the Burning Bush with the date 1930. The Local Committee disapproved, and for a few years the space prepared remained empty and unsightly. Without any intimation they then had the space filled in with a plain stone. I still think it is desirable, more especially in a foreign country, that a Church of Scotland institution such as the Hospice should bear a distinctive emblem, and that the date is one to be had in remembrance. I therefore hope that on reconsideration the omission may be rectified.

'In conclusion, while humbly acknowledging the good hand of God upon our labours in the past, I feel confident that He will provide the funds necessary to complete our noble basilica in a worthy manner and A. M. G. D. ["A La Mayor Gloria De Dios" – "To the Greater Glory Of God"]

'Ninian Hill, DD, Convener, 15th May, 1944.'

For Hill, this puts the record right – "this is how I would have wanted the finished product and I leave it to you to finish it for me". A few days later the General Assembly acknowledged his resignation as Convener of the Committee, noting with gratitude his twenty six years of faithful endeavour on the Committee, and although he continued as a member of the Committee he attended no further meetings and died two years later, in 1946. Hill's hopes regarding the completion of the work to the apse and the provision of the Burning Bush at the entrance to the Hospice/Guesthouse, as his last communication to the Committee and to the Kirk Session, remain unfulfilled.

The Church and Hospice/Guesthouse continued to benefit from ongoing development and maintenance, as funds permitted. Particular pressure came on the Church in making good the damage caused to the property as a result of the 1948 Israeli "War of Independence" and later in June, 1967, during the "Six-day War". With its location and exposure, the property was very much on the firing line and vulnerable to attack from all sides. Evidence of the conflicts remains to this day with chipped stonework and bullet holes scarring the external face of the buildings.

While very little has been done to the physical appearance of the Church, the Hospice today is now a Guesthouse and the difference is more than in the name. Changing attitudes and expectations of visitors and guests has meant that changes were inevitable through the years. Modern health and safety regulations and Local Authority statutes have also played a part.

Some elements of the upgrading to the Guesthouse may be surprising. For example it took nearly sixty years, from when the facility was opened, to provide en-suite bedrooms. The effect of this was to reduce the number of bedrooms, a loss made good sometime later with the addition of six bedrooms to the rear of the building.

A further development, slightly controversial at the time, was the enclosing of the veranda to the front of the Guesthouse thereby providing both a more useful public lounge space and a greater level of comfort, especially in the winter.

Developing and maintaining these unique buildings, Church and Guesthouse, is a constant challenge. Whether it be the upgrading of the kitchen facilities or the renewal of the electrical and water supply services the key concern is to ensure the highest possible level of stewardship of "a Memorial worthy of the occasion," - and a lasting reminder of the dedication of the Committees in Edinburgh and Jerusalem, of the talented Architect and, above all, of the vision, inspiration and persistence in overcoming the many difficulties shown by Ninian Hill.

(For more information on the design detailing of the Church and Hospice see Appendix [4])

—— CHAPTER SEVEN ——

A Living Memorial

THE PROVISION of worship services and pastoral care to the Scots and Presbyterian communities in Jerusalem by the Church of Scotland began many years before the completion of the building work to the Memorial in 1930. In 1922 the Committee decided that there were good reasons to send a "Chaplain" to Jerusalem. In addition to providing worship in the Presbyterian tradition it would not only allow an opportunity to gauge the potential of a worshipping community once a Memorial had been built but also explore where it might be sited.

Dr. Norman Maclean of St Cuthbert's Parish Church in Edinburgh and a member of the Memorial Committee accepted this 'temporary Chaplaincy or scholarship.' In addition Ninian Hill offered, at his own expense, to accompany him, 'to assist in any possible way,' and this was accepted by the Committee. So it was, on the 18th March, 1923, the ministry of the Church of Scotland began in the Old City of Jerusalem, in the Lutheran Church of the Redeemer, as recorded in the Scotsman of the 20th March:

'Within a stone's throw of the Church of the Holy Sepulchre lies the site of the ancient home of the crusading Knights Hospitallers of St John of Jerusalem. A ruined church and cloister were all that remained on it when the Sultan presented it in 1869 to Prince Frederick William of Prussia. Since then the church has been rebuilt in the style of German 12th century architecture, and it is now a noble edifice, known as the Church of the Redeemer. By the courtesy of the Lutheran authorities, a goodly company of Scottish residents and visitors, as well as of Presbyterians from other lands, assembled therein on Sunday, 18th March, for the first of a series of services authorised by the General Assemblies, which it has been arranged to hold during the season.

'The service was conducted by the Rev. Dr. Norman Maclean, of St Cuthbert's, assisted by the Rev. William Ross, Fountainhall U.F. Church, Edinburgh; the Rev. D.S. Stiven, Maclean Scholar, St Andrews; and the Rev. Ninian Hill, joint honorary secretary of the Scottish Churches' Memorial in Jerusalem.

'Dr. Maclean preached an impressive sermon from the text, "Seeing we also are compassed about with so great a cloud of witnesses," which he aptly illustrated by some of the sacred memories connected with the Holy City. Those present will not readily forget the singing in such circumstances of the psalms and paraphrases to the old tunes. A large proportion of the congregation attended the celebration of Holy Communion. The collection was on behalf of the Scots College Hostel and Chapel which it is hoped to establish in Jerusalem, and for which the need is very evident, and even urgent.

'The following day the ministers had the honour of being received by His Beatitude the Armenian Patriarch, and expressed to him the sympathy of the Scottish Church in the cruel persecutions and massacre suffered by the Christians of his country. They learned that no fewer than 800 orphaned children are being maintained in Jerusalem.

'In reply, the Patriarch acknowledged with gratitude the sympathy of the people of Scotland and the gifts they had contributed to relieve the distress. Before leaving, His Beatitude bestowed the Patriarchal benediction upon his visitors.'

Maclean and Hill remained in Jerusalem for two months conducting worship, including the first baptism of their ministry on the 1st April. It was a time for getting to know the Scots' community and it was also when the "Local Advisory Committee" was established. Between this first visit and the opening of the Memorial seven years later a number of Church of Scotland and United Free Church ministers already in Palestine, in Jaffa, Tiberias, Safed, Hebron and Haifa, assisted with the Chaplaincy conducting worship for those choosing to attend a Presbyterian form of worship in Jerusalem. Services continued to be held in the Lutheran Church of the Redeemer, the Anglican St George's Cathedral and Christ Church in the Old City. Pastoral care was also offered to those who wished.

It was during this period, in 1927, that the Foundation Stone of the Memorial was laid. With no-one present from the Committee in Edinburgh it fell to the "local" Clergy to make all the necessary arrangements. The service was conducted by the Rev. W.M. Christie, Tiberias, assisted by the Rev. Principal Semple, of the Scots College in Safed.

As the date for the opening of the Memorial grew close the Committee in Edinburgh decided that Ninian Hill should be its first Chaplain, for one year, and set out the 'the arrangements for the administration of Church and Hospice,' making clear the relationship between the Chaplain and the recently appointed Lady Warden of the Hospice:

'1. The Chaplain will be responsible for the conduct of all religious services, both in the Chapel and the Hospice, including lectures and tuition.

'2. The Chaplain and the Kirk Session will be responsible for the upkeep of the buildings.

'3. The Lady in Charge of the Hospice to be designated Lady Warden.

'4. The Lady Warden to have full control over the domestic arrangements of the Hospice.

'5. The remuneration of the Lady Warden to be at the rate of £200 [£12,000] per annum with full board and laundry. Six weeks holiday to be allowed each year; with additional six weeks every third year. Passage home and back to be paid by the Committee every two years.

'6. The Lady Warden will submit to the Home Committee the scale of charges for the guests.

'7. The Lady Warden will submit to the Kirk Session her accounts monthly for transmission to the Home Committee.

'8. The engagement of the Lady Warden in the first instance to be for three-years: but terminable, at any time, on six months notice on either side. The Committee will be responsible for passage home.'

At the outset the Committee was clear that the Chaplain had a distinct role from that relating to the management of the Hospice. The Committee also assumes the creation of a Kirk Session, which did not come into being until four years later, in 1934. The salary for the Lady Warden is set out in the document. However it was not necessary to do so in the case of Hill who, in accepting the decision of the Committee to take up the post of Chaplain confirmed that he required no salary on this or any other occasion when he ministered in Jerusalem.

In making the appointment of Chaplain and acknowledging that Hill's generosity could not be assumed in succeeding appointments the Committee approached the Colonial and Continental Committee of the Church of Scotland asking that it take over responsibility for the Chaplaincy. This was turned down resulting in the Memorial Committee remaining responsible for the recruitment and funding of future Chaplains/Ministers until it was incorporated into the Overseas

Council in 1964. Until 1964 the terminology, "Chaplain" and "Minister" were interchangeable in the Committee records.

Thirteen years from that evening meeting of Edinburgh Presbytery in 1917, when Hill stood and put forward the very idea of the construction of the Memorial in Jerusalem the great day came when the vision was no longer a dream but a reality. The January 1931, edition of the Church's Life and Work records the occasion:

'Scotland and her national Church is at last worthily represented in the mother–city of our faith. On a commanding site overlooking the road to Bethlehem and almost within a stone's throw of the place where, according to tradition, the first meeting for Christian worship was held (Acts1 v 23), now stands the Church of St Andrew, with the Hospice for the reception of Scottish students and pilgrims to the Holy City.

'To one standing outside the Jaffa Gate looking southwards the most outstanding feature in the landscape is a noble pile of buildings with a conspicuous bell tower, gleaming white in the winter sunshine. It is the Scottish Churches' Memorial, raised to commemorate the liberation of Palestine from Turkish misrule, and in memory of the men of Scottish birth and blood who made the supreme sacrifice in the campaigns of 1917 and 1918.

'The form for the service of dedication was drawn up by the honorary minister, the Rev. Ninian Hill, by whom the movement was initiated, and to whom, more than to any other, it is due that the scheme for the combined Church and Hospice has been brought to a successful completion. Mr Hill conducted the devotional part of the service while the scripture lessons were read by the Rev. W.M. Christie, D.D., Haifa and Principal the Rev. S.H. Semple, B.D., of the Scots College, Safed. The prayer of dedication was offered by the Rev. Prof. A.R.S. Kennedy, D.D., of Edinburgh University representing the General Assembly's Committee. The prayer contained the following petition:

"Hear us, we beseech thee, as in all humility and joyful assurance we now dedicate this place to Thy service in honour of Thy Servant St Andrew, Apostle and Martyr, in commemoration of the deliverance of this Holy City and of the sacrifice of so many of our country-men."

'Mr Hill also preached the sermon, taking as his text the words of Joshua 4 v 21, "What mean these stones?" The little church was filled to its utmost capacity by a congregation of worshippers from all parts of

Palestine, including His Excellency the High Commissioner Sir John Chancellor, G.C.M.G., G.C.V.O., the Chief Secretary, the Anglican Bishop and the Archdeacon of Jerusalem, the O.C., H.M Forces in Palestine and many other prominent representatives of the public life in the city.

'Mention must be made of the church's indebtedness to the Local Committee and especially to Mr Tweedie Millar and Mr J.M. Trimble, the Chairman and Secretary respectively, for their unwearied efforts in furtherance of the scheme. Grateful thanks are also due to the Right Rev. Bishop MacInnis, who, with an all too rare catholicity granted the use of the Chapel in St George's Cathedral for occasional Presbyterian services, and to the Rev. M.L. Maxwell of Christ Church for a like hospitality.'

———————————————··●··———————————————

With the Church and Hospice now a reality the Committee's attention was directed to the development of St Andrew's as a worshipping and witnessing Congregation. The first task was to form a Kirk Session and in February 1931, the Committee was told that it was outside their powers to consider the matter. It had been the intention to select a number of members of the Church in Jerusalem that they 'might be ordained to the eldership during a furlough at home and so be qualified to act in Jerusalem.'

To overcome this setback, Hill, while still in Jerusalem, met with the members of the Congregation on the 4th March, 1931, three months after the opening of the Memorial, to form a Committee to take the place of the Kirk Session. With Hill elected as Chair of the Committee its main role was to support of Mrs MacRae, the Lady Warden, to monitor her accounts and, in its early days, complete the outstanding construction work to the Church and Hospice.

In addition to these many practical needs the new Local Committee, with the Chaplain, was involved with nurturing a growing Congregation. In his letter of the 2nd July, 1932, to the Committee in Edinburgh, the Rev. Dr. William Ewing notes, 'I had three baptisms in the Church last Sunday morning. One of the three was the son of Dr Harkness, who is a member of the Local Committee. If all goes well we should soon have another baptism: so you see we are laying the foundations of a Church.' With signs of hope the congregation also had its tragedies. In the same letter Ewing related the news of the death of the wife of Mr Tweedie Millar, a member of the Church's Local Committee. Their house had been broken into and both Mr and Mrs Tweedie Millar were attacked and stabbed with Mrs Tweedie Millar killed out right and Mr Tweedie Millar severely injured. Such incidents were not rare but greatly affected the relatively small congregation. Mrs Tweedie Millar was buried in the "Zion (English) Cemetery."

The second tragedy happened three weeks after writing his letter, when Mr Ewing died suddenly and was buried in the same cemetery. Dr. Ewing had been Joint Convener of the Committee in Edinburgh and had taken the opportunity to be Chaplain in Jerusalem having had been a missionary at one time in Tiberias and then Minister of "St Catherine's in Grange" in Edinburgh. Ewing, like many of his peers who served the Church in Palestine had a strong military connection. Two years after his death, with subscriptions having been raised in Scotland a Memorial stone was placed in the cemetery in Jerusalem. Of this occasion "The Church News" reported:

'On Sunday, 7th April, in the English Cemetery, Jerusalem, in the presence of His Excellency the High Commissioner, Lieut.-General Sir Arthur Wauchope, and a large number of friends, a gravestone erected by public subscription was dedicated to the memory of the late Rev. William Ewing M.C., D.D. The service was conducted by the Rev. William Ross, B.D., assisted by the Rev. G.L.B. Sloan, M.A., of Tiberias.

'General Sir Arthur Wauchope said that ever since the death of Dr. Ewing some two years ago it had been greatly felt, both in Palestine and in Scotland, that a Memorial to him and his work should be erected in the cemetery where his body now lay. Under the guidance of Dr. Maclean in Scotland and of Mr Ross in Jerusalem, funds had been collected, and that day they were gathered round this grave with its Celtic Cross in affectionate remembrance of the former and well-beloved Minister, Dr. William Ewing.

"Surely very many years will pass before the memory of Dr. Ewing will begin to fade" said Sir Arthur Wauchope "He combined in himself so many qualities of the highest order, a scholar of distinction, a writer of valuable works, a preacher, thoughtful, moving and inspiring – all who knew Dr Ewing recognised in him a man of fearless and outstanding character. Well do I remember the first time I met him. It was in Iraq on the field of battle. My regiment on that day was in reserve. 'Where are the Seaforth Highlanders?' was his first question, for he was Chaplain at the time to that regiment. 'In the forefront of the battle,' was my answer, 'and that is a dangerous place for any man to go to now.' 'If it be a dangerous place,' he replied, 'there may be many wounded and many who need my aid.' He turned his horse and pressed forward. Before sundown he had given that aid, though he himself was wounded before his work was done.

"Today we pay tribute to the Rev. William Ewing. Many have known him far longer and more intimately than I. But for me he will always stand out as a man faithful and fearless at all times and in all places; prompted by his great heart and his most Christian spirit, he was a man ever ready to give help where help is most needed."

'As his nearest neighbour in the ministry in Edinburgh, Mr Ross spoke of him as a gallant servant of his Church and country, as a great hearted, generous friend.

'The stone is the work of Messrs Stewart McGlashan and Sons (Ltd), Edinburgh. It is a large Celtic Cross. In sculpture and in lettering it is one of the finest memorial stones in Palestine.'

The 15th November, 1933, was the first of two momentous days in the history of the congregation. The first was when the Commission of the General Assembly authorised the election of elders and the constitution of the Kirk Session:

'At Edinburgh the fifteenth day of November in the year one-thousand, nine-hundred and thirty-three, which day the Commission of the General Assembly of the Church of Scotland being met and duly constituted: –

'The Commission received a report from the General Administration Committee under a remit from the General Assembly in the case of the Petition from the Minister and Communicants at St Andrew's Church, Jerusalem, craving authority to form a Kirk Session and to have as Moderator of the Kirk Session the Minister officiating there as Chaplain, which was given in by the Very Rev. Dr James Harvey, Vice-Convener.

'It was moved, seconded and agreed, –

'That the Commission authorise the Election of Elders and the Constitution of a Kirk Session in the Congregation of St Andrew's, Jerusalem, and the appointment as Moderator of the Kirk Session so constituted of the Minister of the Church of Scotland officiating as Chaplain there for the time being under the authority of the Committee of the General Assembly on the Scots' Memorial, Jerusalem;

That the Commission remit to the Committee on the Scots' Memorial, Jerusalem, in consultation with the Presbytery of Edinburgh, to make the necessary arrangements to this end; and further, that the Commission appoint and declare that the Minister of the Congregation for the time being acting as Moderator of the Kirk Session be a Member of the Presbytery of Edinburgh during the term of his office, and that the Kirk Session and Congregation of St Andrew's, Jerusalem, be meanwhile under the jurisdiction of the Presbytery of Edinburgh, pending further legislation as to the status of the congregation and the relation of the said St Andrew's Church, Jerusalem, to the property and funds of the Church of Scotland.'

At its meeting on the 23rd November, 1933, the Committee 'resolved to ask the Presbytery to appoint as Assessors, the Rev. G.L.B. Sloan, Tiberias; the Rev. S.H. Semple, Safed; the Rev. Dr. W.M. Christie, Haifa; the Duke of Montrose; Sir Ian Colquhoun; Lord Polwarth and Dr. G.F. Barbour, and appoint the first Sunday in March for the ordination of Elders in St Andrew's Church, Jerusalem,' an event reported in the Scotsman newspaper:

'On Sunday, 4th March, a service was held in St Andrew's Church, Jerusalem, which cannot but appeal to the imagination of Scotsmen throughout the world. For that day in the Church the first Kirk Session in Palestine was constituted, by the authority of the General Assembly and in accordance with the regulations of the Presbytery of Edinburgh.

'The congregation at that service was representative not only of Scotland but of the Empire. The pilgrimage which was initiated by the Duke of Montrose brought many Scots to the city. Contingents of Scots came from Haifa, from Galilee, from Jaffa, and all parts of Palestine. The Bishop of Jerusalem represented the Church of England, Sir Henry Lunn represented the Methodist Church in England, a Presbyterian Minister from Toronto represented Canada. Colonel Anderson, commanding the British troops in Palestine, was there with his officers and a detachment of men. Lord Polwarth represented the Borders, and Dr Freeland Barbour the Central Highlands. The Highland chiefs were represented by Colonel Cameron of Lochiel, and the Western Isles were represented by the Honourable Mrs Maclean and Mrs Duncan MacRae, the Lady Warden. The capital of the Highlands was there in the person of the Rev. Donald Macleod, and Glasgow was represented by Colonel Norman MacLeod and Mr Ballantyne, elders. Most remarkable of all was a contingent of Royal Scots Fusiliers, commanded by Major McGregor Whitton, that came forty miles from Sarafend.

'The church proved too small for the great company of Scots who sought to share in the historic service. On that day the congregation in the Holy City was a microcosm of Scotland.

'It is only in circumstances such as these that the religious fervour of the Scots finds full expression. The service began with the "Old Hundred," and it is strange how words so familiar can come with new meaning. As a great volume of praise ascended the words rang out, "His truth at all times firmly stood, and shall from age to age endure," they sounded as a challenge. There flashed on the mind the memory of all that the City of Jerusalem has done for the world, and the thought that no prophecy of its future can seem impossible. The prayers were offered by the Rev. D.L. Cattanach, the Chaplain; the lessons were read by Principal S.H. Semple, of Safed College, and it fell to Dr. Norman Maclean to preach the sermon and set apart the elders.

'Thereafter seven men took their place before the Communion Table, and the service of ordination began. It is fitting to record the names. They are John Turnbull, paymaster to the police; Thomas Griffiths, accountant; Joseph Harkness, assistant director of public health; Adam Rankin, medical officer, Jaffa; John Shepherd, irrigation officer; James Stubbs, director of lands; and Sir Arthur Wauchope, High Commissioner for Palestine. The congregation stood (as the habit of Scots once was) while the prayer of ordination was offered. Thereafter the elders took their seats in the Apse; the 2nd Paraphrase was sung; and so the first Kirk Session of the Church of Scotland was constituted in Jerusalem. After the service of ordination, there was a celebration of Holy Communion for which almost all of the congregation waited.

'If it be true that Scotland "has no need of history apart from the Scottish Church," then it is of all things the most fitting that Scotland should have her own shrine, her own altar in that city whence her life sprang. The Church of St Andrew, with its duly regulated court, is but a symbol of the debt that never can be repaid. And that the Scottish race should have seven men, holding such responsible posts in Jerusalem, is in itself a great symbol of the place occupied by Scotsmen in the building up and the administration of the British Empire.'

It was a curious arrangement that the Kirk Session had its authority bestowed on it through the Presbytery of Edinburgh while, on the other hand, it was also responsible to the Committee in Edinburgh for its ministry and its day-to-day management and work. This often created misunderstandings and confusion, especially in the early days and relations were not always harmonious. On the 28th January, 1935, concern was raised regarding the relationship of the Kirk Session and the Committee on a matter of authority. The minute notes that 'It is very important that the Home Committee should realise that a very competent Kirk Session exists in Jerusalem, and that they are fully capable of dealing with their own affairs, and it would be very stupid not to take their advice on every possible occasion. They realise they need the support of the Home Committee, and do not for one minute desire to break off from it. It is felt strongly that official communication should be conducted through the Kirk Session and not through the Minister.'

At the same meeting the relationship between the Kirk Session and their responsibility for the Hospice was discussed. From the outset, the Committee's intention was to separate the "management" of the Church from that of the Hospice. That was made clear when the respective responsibilities for the Chaplain and the Lady Warden were set out. As time went on and with the establishment of the Kirk Session this separation became a matter of uncertainty and concern. The Committee noted that 'The Kirk Session should be permanently represented on the advisory committee of the Hospice in order to create some liaison, but that the Hospice should remain responsible to the Home Committee for its conduct and management. The Minister should continue to have no official position in the Hospice but would be able to make such position as his personality warranted.'

At its meeting in August 1935, the Committee was read a letter from Hill who, at the time, was acting as Chaplain in St Andrew's. Hill complained that, 'on more than one occasion Mrs MacRae had permitted and encouraged dancing to take place in the Hospice.' He considered that 'at St Andrew's Hospice, such a thing was wholly out of place.' The Rev. William Ross confirmed 'that during his term of office nothing of this sort had taken place of which he disapproved. He said that on St Andrew's Eve and New Year's Eve and one or two other occasions, the dancing of reels and country dances had taken place, and he had felt that such entertainment was only right and proper. He considered the place should not be permitted to become in any sense a dancing saloon, but he thought there was not the slightest danger of that.'

The Committee agreed and resolved the matter noting that 'The question was raised in a communication from a Member of the Committee as to the nature of the evening entertainment at St Andrew's Hospice. The Committee recommended that the nature of the entertainments should in all cases be subject to the sanction of the Chaplain.'

There were two occasions when the status of the Chaplain was a matter of concern to the Kirk Session and the Committee. In February 1935, the Committee, 'felt strongly that the Minister's salary should be increased. It is only fair to him if he was to stand on the same basis as the Bishop and others, that he should be able to put himself in a stronger position.' Then, later in the year, the Kirk Session asked for assistance in ascertaining, 'the proper place in the order of precedence of the Chaplain of St Andrew's Church.' The Committee Convener confirmed 'that he had consulted Sir Francis Grant, the Lord Lyon, who gave it as his opinion that, there being two National Churches in the United Kingdom and both being represented in Jerusalem, the Chaplain of St Andrew's Church being the representative of the Church of Scotland, should rank immediately after the Anglican Bishop in Jerusalem, and that he had forwarded that recommendation to Jerusalem.'

Once the Kirk Session had been constituted it remained under the Presbytery of Edinburgh until the formation of the Presbytery of Jerusalem in 1941. At the time the Presbytery of Jerusalem had a wider membership than today with its two charges, St Andrew's Church in Tiberias and St Andrew's Church in Jerusalem. When formally constituted, the Presbytery oversaw not only congregations in Jerusalem, Jaffa, Haifa and Tiberias, but also in Alexandria and Cairo.

The first mention of a Presbytery within Palestine is recorded in the minute of the Edinburgh Committee meeting of the 12th January, 1940. It noted that Dr. Norman MacLean, while Chaplain at St Andrew's, Jerusalem 'had visited Haifa on the 25th October, 1940, and constituted the six ordained Ministers as an informal Presbytery for the purpose of inducting the Rev. John Gray to the Chaplaincy of the Scots' Congregation (in Haifa), and that these Ministers had resolved to petition the next General Assembly to institute a Presbytery of Jerusalem.'

On the 22nd April, 1940, the Committee heard the Petition from the Ministers and Elders in Palestine requesting the General Assembly to form a Presbytery of Jerusalem. 'The Committee discussed the matter very fully and after they had been assured that the formation of such a Presbytery would make no difference to the work of the Committee in any way, approved of the petition. They recommended that the proposed Presbytery should include the charges in Alexandria and Cairo as well as those of Jerusalem, Jaffa, Haifa and Tiberias.'

The "Presbytery of Jerusalem" was constituted on Saturday the 1st November, 1941. This event did not attract as much attention in the press as did that of the formation of the Kirk Session.   Soon after the event the Church's "Life and Work" noted:

'On the 15th November, 1941, there took place in St Andrew's Church, Jerusalem, an event which only the absorbing interests of the war have prevented from catching the imagination of the Church. On that date and in that place there was duly constituted the Presbytery of Jerusalem, as an Overseas Presbytery of the Church of Scotland. Visiting clergymen from many churches and a large number of prominent laymen were present at the opening ceremony. The black of Geneva gowns was relieved by the khaki and Air-Force blue uniforms of associated Army chaplains, and by the scarlet D.D. robes of the constituting Minister, the Rev. Dr. W.M. Christie. The Rev. S.H. Semple was appointed the first Moderator and the Rev. A. Scott Morrison, Presbytery Clerk. A correspondent tells of the thrill that passed through the Congregation as they sang from the 122nd Psalm, "Jerusalem, within thy gates our feet shall standing be." The ceremony was felt by all to be a fitting and worthy consummation of the hundred years of work, since the days of Dr. McCheyne, Keith and Black, among the Jews and Arabs of Palestine, refugees from Europe, Scots kinsfolk in business and administrative work, and thousands of soldiers in the Forces.'

The Scotsman of the 6th November also carried a small article on the event. Unfortunately both the "Life and Work" and the paper recorded the inauguration date as the 15th and the 3rd November respectively.

Constitution of the Presbytery of Jerusalem, 1st Nov. 1941

The Committee in Edinburgh had no direct involvement in the institution of the Presbytery. The Committee's principal concern was to ensure that the Presbytery did not conflict or interfere with its responsibility for overseeing the day to day management of the Church and Hospice. However there were practical matters which had to be dealt with as a result of the creation of the Presbytery. For example, all ministers now enrolled within the Presbytery of Jerusalem would have their names removed from the appropriate "home" Presbytery, and the Kirk Session of St Andrew's, Jerusalem, until now under the jurisdiction of Edinburgh Presbytery, would now come within the fold of the Presbytery of Jerusalem. A significant outcome of the first meeting of Presbytery was the decision 'to inform the Government of Palestine of the constitution of the Presbytery of Jerusalem, and to request that all official communications affecting the Church be addressed to the Presbytery Clerk, C/O St Andrew's Church, Jerusalem.' By and large this is a relationship which remains to this day with the State of Israel.

From the time MacLean and Hill travelled to Palestine in 1923 to take up an informal Chaplaincy to the Scots community in Jerusalem, securing the services of Chaplains/Ministers to the charge in St Andrew's has not always been an easy task. There are many reasons for this, for example, the level of remuneration, the length of appointment, the security risks, and often, today, the difficulty for Ministers relocating with Spouses wishing to pursuing their own career.

To some extent this difficulty was overcome by Church Committees, already working in Palestine, coming together to share the Ministry. During the Mandate the Church's Huts and Canteens Committee had appointed the Rev. Roderick Murchison as Chaplain to their work in Palestine. Following discussion between the two Committees Mr Murchison received a Joint Appointment on the 1st June, 1945, serving both the Congregation at St Andrew's and the Huts and Canteens Committee, with the costs being shared. Following 1948, a similar appointment was entered into by the Memorial Committee and the Jewish Mission Committee of the Church with its staff in Jaffa. However, this arrangement raised the issue of the nature of the relationship of St Andrew's with the State of Israel and the Jewish Community at large. It was and always has been a sensitive one and was called into question on a number of occasions.

At its meeting on the 12th June, 1951, the Committee noted that at the General Assembly a few weeks earlier a Minister present at the Assembly had expressed concern, 'lest St Andrew's Church might be compromised in the eyes of the Israeli Government by activities more characteristic of a Jewish Mission than of a National Memorial and simple Church of Scotland Congregation.' The minute noted that Dr. McQueen, as Convener, had given an assurance on behalf of the Committee 'that there was no intention of converting St Andrew's Church into a branch of the Jewish Mission. The Committee approved and instructed the Secretary to advise the Minister of St Andrew's to be careful in this respect.'

That advice to the Minister, the Rev. Scott Morrison, resulted in a letter from the Church's Jewish Mission Committee referring to the Bible class held by Mr Morrison in the Hospice and 'stating the difficulties which the Jewish Mission Committee had in finding other accommodation for this class.' After consideration 'The Committee resolved to raise no objection to holding the Bible class in St Andrew's Church and Hospice, but instructed the Secretary to suggest to Mr Morrison that it would more conveniently be held in the Manse than in the Hospice.'

Later, on the 20th June, 1961, the Committee agreed to the Joint Appointment with the Jewish Mission Committee of the Rev. Tom Gibson. His responsibility in respect of St Andrew's, Jerusalem would be 'to conduct the services there according to the forms of the Church of Scotland; that he shepherd the Protestants who adhere to St Andrew's Church and that in all ways act as a Minister of the Church of Scotland in Israel. In reference to work at Jaffa, Mr Gibson would teach scripture in Tabeetha School as arranged with the Head of the School, and keep in touch with former pupils and especially those who had moved to Jerusalem and were studying at the University there.'

One year later while on leave in Scotland and attending a meeting of the Committee on the 24th August, 1962, Mr Gibson 'described the congregation of St Andrew's as fluctuating with a nucleus of about forty people drawn from many nationalities. Although thus variously compounded, all there were very happy to be in St Andrew's and got on well together.' In answer to a question he added that 'It was in every way advantageous that the Church and Hospice of St Andrew's had never been associated with any "organised mission." It was, therefore, viewed by the Jews without any suspicion they cast on missions, and besides, the beauty of the Church and its surroundings attracted many Jews and others to visit it and ask questions about it and the Church of which it was part.'

A matter, not unrelated to the relationship of the Church to the State and the Jewish Community was and is the right of the Minister to baptise children and adults into the faith. The Baptismal Register records that from the first baptism on the 1st April, 1923, until the end of 2011, two-hundred and thirty-nine individuals were baptised, one-hundred and thirty-eight during the Mandate of which ten were before the Church was opened. The register provides a unique insight into the origins of those who made St Andrew's their spiritual home while in the city.

Unfortunately there are few records available relating to marriages conducted in St Andrew's. The one set found indicates twenty-four weddings taking place between June 1941 and August 1943, all of them between men and women serving in the Forces.

————————————————

Through time the ministry and witness of every congregation changes depending on a number of factors. One would be the skills, experience and personality succeeding Ministers might bring to the charge. Another might be changing circumstances within the parish. For St Andrew's Church with no geographical boundary defining its Parish, with its Ministers on contracts and changing frequently, and operating within an ever-changing, oft times hostile environment, it was a constant challenge to remain relevant with a ministry fine tuned to meet contemporary needs. The various reports sent by the Minister to the Committee in Edinburgh and the records included in the Annual Reports do, however, give an authentic insight into the life and witness of the Church.

At its meeting of the 12th January, 1937, the Committee received the following report from the Rev. William Ross while he was on leave from Jerusalem:

'My first appointment as Chaplain of St Andrew's Church, Jerusalem, dates from the beginning of April 1934 to the same date in 1935. The second appointment dated from the 1st September, 1935, to the same date in 1936, a period which was extended till the 18th October because of the difficulty that my successor found in leaving work in Scotland before that date.

'For ten months of my first period I acted as Officiating Chaplain to the 1ˢᵗ Seaforth Highlanders. They attended church at 9 am and 10 am on Sundays. The church was filled with military at 9 o'clock, and filled again with soldiers and civilians at 10 am. At 11 o'clock I had a Children's Church, small in numbers necessarily, but keenly interested. The children for the most part had been present at the 10 o'clock service. Their service accordingly was short, not more than twenty minutes. At 7.20 am on Sundays I conducted a service at Sarafend thirty miles distant, for companies of the Seaforths in garrison there. Once a month on Communion Sundays there was an evening service, – later every alternate month. Holy Communion is now celebrated six times every year, but also on Thursday evening of Holy Week and on Easter Sunday.

'During this period three memorials were unveiled, two in the Church and one in the Cemetery. One was a bronze tablet presented by the London Scottish Territorial Regiment in memory of comrades fallen in the Palestine Campaign. Colonel Ogilvy travelled from London to be present. The Seaforth Highlanders who also fought in the Palestine Campaign presented a Memorial in stone. The stone was placed in the north-west corner of the chancel, – the spot selected for it by the Officers. The third Memorial was a very handsome granite graveyard stone placed in the British Cemetery in memory of the late Dr. Ewing who died in service in Jerusalem. In each case the services of Dedication were attended largely by British people of all denominations, and the act of unveiling was done by His Excellency the High Commissioner. During these twelve months Palestine was peaceful and prosperous; service in it was a privilege and a joy.

'During the second period from December when the troops arrived I acted as Chaplain to the 2nd Battalion of the Queen's Own Cameron Highlanders. They also attended Church at 9 am and 10 am led by some twenty pipers and followed by the Band, – the first time in their history that they marched to the Church with bagpipes. I had no difficulty in giving the permission which the Colonel correctly and courteously asked. From the middle of April onwards, when the strike was declared, the services were conducted in the N.A.A.F.I. For seven months the troops were standing by and could not leave the barracks. On several occasions also, I conducted services for men of the United Board of English Regiments.

'Evening services at St Andrew's were not possible during the strike because of the curfew at 7 o'clock and latterly at 6.30 pm. Since early last summer a number of Palestinians, some of them Arab Protestants, others Greek Orthodox, and a few Moslems have worshipped with us in St

Andrew's. Your Chaplain was warmly supported and ably helped by the High Commissioner, by the Commanding Officers of the Battalions, by the members of the Kirk Session, and particularly by Dr Harkness, O.B.E., the Deputy Director of the Government Medical Department, who appreciates and encourages the spiritual side of Church work and makes an excellent Session Clerk. I should like to add how glad I am and grateful that this Committee asked me to do this work and that I was free to undertake it. The Chaplaincy presents a unique opportunity of service. In peace or in strife the work was congenial, sometimes alarming, but always interesting and richly rewarding.'

The Committee noted Mr Ross's additional observations that 'There were one or two aspects of the position in Palestine which had caused him disappointment. He felt that the measure of Christian liberality of St Andrew's Church could and should be increased. He regretted the lack of Sunday observance, and particularly remarked on the practice of holding yacht races, horse races, and hunting expeditions on Sunday. This compared unfavourably with the very strict observance of the Jewish Sabbath. He further commented on the sale of banned literature at bookstalls.'

Understandably, from 1939 to 1945, the work of the congregation had a different focus. The Rev. Duncan MacGillivray who was Chaplain at St Andrew's during the war years reports in a letter to the Committee in January 1941:

'Jerusalem has been very full of people and of course we are not without our quota of the uniform services. The result has been a very full Church the whole time. Sunday morning brings a Congregation of extraordinarily interesting people to Church, and I am really very happy to be among them. The visitors this year have been from rather nearer hand than before – mostly people who could not get home or north to Syria as their usual leave. We have also a surprising number of Scots soldiers who come, but there are no 'parade' services. The Church has also been a great goal of pilgrimage to successive groups of Australians.' After mentioning that the windows have been curtained for blackout purposes, he continues, 'I have been loath to alter the time of the evening services, as the Anglicans have done, as we have some forty to fifty attending, and are mostly men who have no other opportunities of worship. The Hospice remains quite full and with continual demands for accommodation that have to be refused.'

Church parade, 11ᵗʰ August, 1940

Later in the year, in the congregation's Annual Report, Mr MacGillivray wrote:

'My Dear People,

'I should like to say how happy my first nine months have been here among you. For this I owe a great deal to the members of the Kirk Session, to you for your own individual kindnesses, and, of course, to the Hospice.

'All this makes me appreciate more the value of what members of St Andrew's have done in their several ways to welcome and give hospitality to others who have come here owing to the requirements of the war. This of course, as all of you will acknowledge, cuts both ways, for our life as a Congregation and our worship have been greatly enriched by the many from the Churches at home who have joined us during the recent months.

'I should like also to acknowledge your forbearance in suffering my many absences from the work of this Chaplaincy and my divided attentions. I think, however, that all of us will be glad that this Chaplaincy has been the means which the Committee of the Church of Scotland on 'Huts and Canteen Work for H.M. Forces' has been able to use for initiating its valued war-time work in the Middle East. Within the past six months, six clubs or hostels have been opened in Palestine, and the splendid work started earlier in the war by the Scottish Churches in Cairo and

Alexandria has been multiplied in Egypt by the addition of three canteen cars, three huts, and a hostel.

'During the past summer we have had a surprising stream of visitors, not all of them in khaki. Many of them no doubt found Jerusalem the alternative to spending a longer leave at home. In addition there were the 'families' who came to Jerusalem for an all too short period of their changeful life.

'The opening of St Andrew's House in the autumn has kept many of you busy and has been an introduction for many men to the worship of our Church. Here let me offer a welcome to them, if they do not already count themselves among those addressed in this letter; and here let me say a word of appreciation of the services of the men's choir that has become in so short a time a valued part of the evening congregation.

'We cordially sympathise with Dr. and Mrs Maclean whose departure home has been so long delayed. (Because of transport difficulties due to the war) The delay, however, has been the means of enabling the Women's Guild to welcome Mrs Maclean as their President for whatever period they may still be with us. In spite of the numerous other engagements of Guild members there has been no slackening of their energies in the interests of the Church or towards their other commitments. All who were present at the "At Home" arranged on the eve of St Andrew's Day still agree that it was both socially and financially a well-planned alternative to the annual sale of work.

'All during the summer and throughout the winter the Hospice has been continuously full and the hospitality and attention of Mrs MacRae and her staff have been widely appreciated both by civilians and by members of the Forces. One is entitled to say that the tenth anniversary of the Scottish Church and Hospice, commemorated last St Andrew's Day, has been most fittingly marked by both the Church and Hospice being used to capacity.

'It is part of the nature of things that the British Community in Palestine should yearly lose yet another of its members. There will be many benevolent organisations, as well as St Andrew's Church and personal friends, who greatly miss the real altruism and sustained energy of Mr Griffiths, our Honorary Treasurer, who has recently intimated his imminent return home. To Mrs Griffiths and himself, who have both been such loyal friends and fellow workers, we express our deep appreciation, our best wishes and our desire for their safe journey.

'May God bless you all, and have in His keeping those who are away from us.'

The 1940 General Assembly recognised the need to provide both spiritual and physical welfare to soldiers and established the "Committee on Huts and Canteen Work for H.M. Forces." In addition to his commitment to St Andrew's Church the Rev. Duncan MacGillivray was also the first director of the "Huts and Canteen" work when it started in the Near East later that year in July. He managed its work from St Andrew's Church and from his annual report it is clear that the Congregation was also very much involved in St Andrew's House. An article in the Glasgow Herald of the 23rd December 1940, provides insight into both the level of need for this service for soldiers away from home and also the level of work requiring to be carried out by Mr MacGillivray and others in meeting the need:

'The Church of Scotland, it is announced, has established centres in the Near and Middle East. These are located at Jerusalem, Nazareth, Haifa and Jaffa, and in Egypt the canteen cars which serve as mobile units are performing a splendid service, and more are being arranged for.

'There will be an opportunity to hear of this work in the Empire broadcast at noon on Christmas Day, when a programme will be given from St Andrew's House, the Church of Scotland hostel and canteen in Jerusalem, which was opened by the High Commissioner for Palestine.

'Increased staff and equipment are needed immediately at Jerusalem and as other centres develop, and new ones are opened the needs will be greater. There is an urgent need for overnight accommodation for men on short leave, and suitable premises are now being sought in Tel Aviv and Haifa in addition to the club and canteen centres already opened there.'

Later in the war, the minute of the meeting of the Committee on the 3rd April, 1944, records that 'Mr MacGillivray paid warm tribute to the Women's Guild of the Scottish Community in Jerusalem. The numbers attending the church services were continually increasing. He went on to speak of the work of St Andrew's House – the first Hut work started in Jerusalem – and said that the Congregation of St Andrew's Church along with the Women's Guild were largely responsible for its inception. This House (a rented hotel) has since been extended and now sleeps two-hundred men. Mr MacGillivray also spoke of the work that was going to be done amongst the police in Palestine, and said that full-time Chaplains were going to be appointed to that work, but that meantime the Kirk Session had sent each man a letter as he arrived inviting him to the services, etc. He also spoke of the enormous increase in the cost of living in Palestine which was up more than 300%, and said that St Andrew's Hospice was the only hospice in Jerusalem charging less than the maximum charge allowed of £22 a month for accommodation.'

Mr MacGillivrey and CoS Huts and Canteen lorry

For many soldiers stationed in Palestine during the Mandate and the Second World War St Andrew's Church and Hospice was a familiar haven. In his memoires Captain Donald Erskine describes St Andrew's as 'A real place of worship and renewal,' and continues 'There is no doubt that there is one place I really loved and felt at home in, in Palestine, was that of St Andrew's Kirk in Jerusalem, which I visited as often as I could, even though we were about an hour away. There I felt I was at home in Scotland, with all the ambience and faith of our religious convictions surrounding us, as we worshipped in that beautiful church.'

Even before it was opened in 1930, there is no doubt that through the years St Andrew's Church has been blessed with the attention and service of Clergy of considerable stature and influence in their Ministry. Whether as Committee members in Edinburgh or serving in Jerusalem, or often in both, they have nurtured and developed the work of St Andrew's which, today, enjoys the respect of the Churches, the Communities and the Authorities in the region, and wider. In a short history of the Church such as this, it is extremely difficult to elaborate on the work of each and every one who has served as the Chaplain/Minister of St Andrew's. However, perhaps there is one whose story might exemplify the characteristics and the commitment of the many who have served at St Andrew's.

The Rev. William (Bill) Gardiner Scott was born in Bo'ness, by the Firth of Forth in Scotland, on the 23rd February, 1906. His father was an engine driver and his mother ran a restaurant in the town. After completing university studies Bill followed in her footsteps for a few years in the catering business. Tam Dalyell, a Labour politician and a good friend of Bill, writes that after four years of cooking and baking Bill 'received the call and entered Edinburgh's New College to study Theology. He was, as he put it later "all the better for having grown up in the real world and not having gone straight from university to the priesthood." In 1936 he won a prize which was to mark a turning point in his career – a travelling scholarship to Palestine. After the expiry of his grant he went as a ship's steward to America and to India, which strengthened a lifelong belief in Christian obligation to poor countries.

'Ordained as a minister of the Church of Scotland two months before the Second World War broke out, he became an army Chaplain in the Eighth Army in the Western Desert. He developed a community centre at the Gunners' Depot in Cairo, a welcome place for all us troops in Sir Claude Auchinleck's army.

'He was the driving force behind a weekly Scots newspaper, the "Clachan Crack," which lifted morale out of all proportion to the somewhat sketchy print it was. When General Montgomery relieved Auchinleck in 1942 Gardiner Scott founded Montgomery House in Alexandria as a community centre for all ranks and Allied troops. He won the greatest respect of Montgomery's Chief of Staff, General Sir Francis de Guingand, who whenever he came to the Parliamentary Labour Party defence group would ask after Gardiner Scott.

'At the end of the war he served as Church of Scotland Chaplain for Galilee and District during a time of enormous sensitivity. On returning home he became a senior Chaplain at Scottish Command in Edinburgh and then warden of the student movement house in London. However he felt the call of serving the church abroad and in 1950 accepted the position of Chaplain at Victoria University, Wellington, New Zealand, where he remained for four years.' It was while he was in Wellington that he met and married Darinka Glogovac. Tam notes that 'When I asked him why he didn't stay longer in Wellington he said he felt guilty about having too cushy a job.'

In 1955 Bill offered himself and was accepted as the Minister of St Andrew's in Jerusalem. For Bill and Darinka, this was no easy posting. Each had their own particular roles, Bill as Minister and Darinka as Lady Warden, with responsibility for the guests and the Hospice.

The first problem they encountered was the need to carry out extensive repairs to both the Church and the Hospice due to damage which, seven years following the "Israeli War of Independence" in 1948, had not been fully tackled. In his first letter to the Committee following their arrival, Bill noted that he was 'anxious to open the Hospice as a Christian home as soon as possible.' However to achieve this major repairs would be required and extra staff would need to be employed both of which would be expensive and the funds would need to come from the Committee as neither the Church nor the Hospice had any.

A few months later Bill's correspondence confirmed that three months experience had convinced them of the value of the Hospice and they were now in a position to assess the needs of the situation. It had taken a good deal of hard work to bring the Hospice into a state with which they could be reasonably satisfied, but even at that it was clear to both of them that much would have to be done before it would be in a fit condition to fulfil its purpose. Within the Committee there was a general agreement that it must do everything it could to support Bill and Darinka which meant that they must be enabled to put the buildings in respectable order. It was only reasonable to suppose that a good deal would have to be done to them. The Committee considered however that the state of its funds made it impossible for them to find £2000 [£48,000] immediately – the amount estimated it will cost to carry out the work. It would take some time to gather so much money. Further 'it was well known that the political situation in Palestine was passing through a critical phase. Present tensions might be peacefully resolved, but they might not. There was a general feeling among knowledgeable people that if no explosion took place by Easter the hopes entertained of maintaining peace would be strengthened.' At the end of the discussion it was unanimously resolved:

'1. That Mr and Mrs Scott should be assured of the Committee's firm support and that approval should be given in principle to the scheme of repairs in the Church and Hospice.

'2. That in order to enable the Committee to meet the cost of the repairs the scheme should be divided into several parts: only what was absolutely necessary to keep the buildings watertight should be done at once: after Easter £600 should be remitted to cover the first part of repairs; and four or five months later a further sum should be remitted to cover the second part, and so on, until the scheme was completed.'

The Convener then referred to Mr Scott's letter of the 3rd January, 1966, where mention was made of the Hospice staff. Mr Scott reported his satisfaction with the services of Mr Moshi Ben-Shmuel, a Hebrew-Christian, and stated that there was a real possibility that the services of his wife would be available also. They had both previously been employed by the Scots Hospital in Tiberias, and Mrs Ben-Shmuel was a Norwegian and a good cook. Mr Scott proposed that the couple should be employed to take over the domestic side of the Hospice and that they should live in. The Committee agreed.

There followed a prolonged struggle by Bill and Darinka to put the premises, particularly the Hospice, into good order to receive guests. Despite all, however, guests put up with the run down condition knowing that they would receive a warm Christian welcome.

While Darinka made every effort to provide the best possible experience for the guests of the Hospice, with the same vigour Bill was developing a ministry which, over time, achieved considerable influence and respect for himself and St Andrew's. This was evident not only within the Christian community at large but also within the different faith communities and authorities of the City and the State. Bill's "Annual Report" to the Committee for 1956, despite rising tensions within the City, provides a sense of solid ministry and hope. The Committee noted that 'this report showed that there were at the time of writing about thirty-five people attending services on Sunday mornings, a decrease in the number having taken place since the outbreak of hostilities. At that time a number of families were evacuated, no students came to the Swedish Theological Institute, and no tourists to the country in general. Mr Scott gave a list of those composing the hard-core of the congregation; among them were Americans, English, Dutch, Danish,

German, Jews, and sometimes both Arabs and Jews were occasional worshippers. The only Scottish family left was the Reids. Apart from the regular Sunday services Mr Scott held a short midweek service on Wednesday evenings, conducted prayers daily for visitors in the Hospice, celebrated communion every two months, and now intended to celebrate it monthly. Each year three of the services in St Andrew's were broadcast and much was made of other special services.

'It was customary for the members of the Congregation to meet for a cup of tea in the Hospice after Sunday services and once a month in the Hospice a Congregational social was held, and then, of course, special socials were a feature of St Andrew's Night and Burns Night. Every second Friday an enthusiastically supported class for Scottish country dancing was held. Mr Scott attended the fraternal of the Ministers in Jerusalem, which met once a month in the homes of the Ministers in turn. His chief extra-congregational activity was as Chairman of the "United Christian Council of Israel."'

The continuing tensions in the region did not appear to diminish the ministry of either the Minister or the Congregation. In his report to the Committee in July 1957, Bill noted that 'at Easter time the services in the Church had been well attended. A surprising number had stayed for the whole of the three-hour service held on Good Friday. On Easter morning a Dawn service was conducted on the terrace of the Hospice, and considering the early hour, 4.30 am, a goodly Congregation of over sixty was present. At the service on Easter Day, the Church was comfortably full. It had been beautifully decorated with lilies and carnations, the gift of the American Consul-General and his wife and of the British Consul and his wife. In the afternoon of Easter Day Mr and Mrs Scott had crossed into the Old City for forty hours. There they took leave of Bishop and Mrs Stewart, who were shortly returning to the United Kingdom. Bishop Stewart was to be succeeded by an Archbishop, the son of a former Bishop in Jerusalem, Bishop MacInnis. From these letters it was clear also that Mr Scott's relations with the representatives of other denominations in Jerusalem were exceedingly good. He had been appointed chairman of the United Christian Council in Israel and as such had been invited to attend an international conference held at Eastbourne from the 31st May to the 6th June. He had accepted the invitation and had attended the conferences, the expenses being fully paid by the Inter-Church Aid and the Service to Refugees Division of the World Council of Churches. While he was in the UK he had taken the opportunity to make a brief visit to Edinburgh and discuss the affairs of St Andrew's Church and Hospice with the Secretary. On his return he was able to report that there had been a good number of visitors at the Hospice, including a party of R.A.F. with their Scottish Chaplain from Cyprus. He also stated the cost of food was becoming more and more a problem. The most ordinary meat now cost fifty-six shillings [£64] per kilo. Still, they were trying to make ends meet and had raised the Hospice charges, for it was not only meat but everything else which had risen in price.

'Mr Scott stated that he and Mrs Scott had come to feel that during the past seven months the Ministry was developing in Jerusalem. Attendance at services, despite the rather abnormal times, had been encouraging. The Church and Hospice were obviously a much needed centre of social intercourse and Christian activity. They felt, therefore, that it would be a mistake to break the continuity of the Ministry at this juncture and therefore they offered to remain engaged for another tour of service in Jerusalem. They were, however, both tired and in need of the furlough which was due. They proposed to take this furlough, with the Committee's permission, in the USA where Mrs Scott's relatives live. Then, when they returned, they would resume their work in Jerusalem, having made provision for its continuance during their absence on furlough. The Committee resolved to put on record its pleasure at Mr Scott's willingness to re-engage for a further period of service and to offer no objection to his spending his three months furlough in the United States of America.'

During this time the work of St Andrew's Church and Hospice and the Gardiner Scotts was not without national recognition within Scotland. The November 1956 edition of the "Scottish Field" magazine produced an article "St Andrews Church in Jerusalem". Following a summary of the history of the Memorial, the writer of the piece, Shirley Cunningham, continues:

'On a clear cold Saturday afternoon, when a sharp "Scots" wind was blowing through the dark spruce and fir and the pale green olive trees that line the sharp curving drive to the church, I went up to the manse, which is part of the Hospice, and over a cup of tea and Scottish shortbread, Mr Scott and his wife told me of St Andrew's Church today.

'A congregation of between fifty and eighty attend the service held each Sunday morning. Few of them are Scots, for the days when the Scottish regiments were stationed there and three services had to be held each Sunday morning to accommodate them have long since passed. Today Finns, Swedes, Danes, Dutch, Americans, Germans, Poles, French, Yugoslavs and Irish are among those who make up the regular cosmopolitan assembly, for St Andrew's is regarded as a meeting ground for all the Protestants in Jerusalem. Many of the nations are there with their own missions and though, in Mr Scott's words, the services are 'out and out' Presbyterian they draw Anglicans, Congregationalist, Baptist, Lutherans, Armenians... The present elders of the Kirk are a New Zealander, an American and a Scotsman.

'To emphasise still further the international character of the Church, one of Mr Scott's first christenings there was an Anglo-Arab baby girl who received the exotic name of Scheherazade; on another occasion a Danish lady acted as interpreter when a German baby was christened. A Bulgarian lady, who wished to bring her friends to the service, asked Mr Scott to preach slowly so that she could translate for them. "I have to translate my Scots anecdotes into English anyway" said the Minister. "It's a critical audience and they know their Bible" he continued. "Bishops, professors and humble folk alike expect real preaching! We hope to have a choir soon."

'"This is a new country, and in a new country personal relationships, are often the first to suffer; people are lonely and that I think, is often why they come to church."

'On their Sabbath Jews, too, come to look at the church, and relationships are good with the new State of Israel. Last autumn there was a broadcast service from St Andrew's, a pleasing event in a non-Christian State.

'"Now we can't imagine ourselves anywhere else but Jerusalem" said Mrs Scott "Our friends keep writing to tell us to come home at once out of danger, but in fact it's the peace here we love. To read the Bible and the psalms with the well-known places all around us makes them seem so much more real and is a tremendous thrill. Who knows even what site this church is on – when the excavations were made what is probably a third century tomb and skeleton were unearthed. The dry stane dykes around here remind me of Scotland and I can even hear Yugoslav tongues in the city!" Mrs Scott, a lady of the manse in the best tradition, has the vital and energetic personality needed to help her husband to restore St Andrew's to its pre-eminent position. Since the War of Liberation appointments to the Church have been, until the arrival of the Scotts, temporary appointments, and Mrs Scott is the first Minister's wife to accompany her husband since then. After each service there is "open house" in the manse for the congregation. "Some of them are very shy at first but a count of the teacups shows that between thirty and fifty people take the opportunity each Sunday to meet the Minister and his wife at home." As they sometimes entertained forty students to tea in New Zealand such large numbers of guests hold no terrors.

'Mr and Mrs Scott, too, are the first people to combine the Ministry and the Hospice which is part of the manse building. Formerly there was a Lady Warden, a separate appointment, in charge of the Hospice, but now Mrs Scott has taken over the task, though she admits to disliking the formal title. The Hospice of St Andrew's was never actually closed, but because of the war and subsequent staff problems it could, over the past few years, only be run on makeshift lines. Now staff problems are easier and, in Mrs Scotts words, she is hoping to make it "a real Scottish home, with home cooking too, and not a professional boarding house, for Scots travellers to the Holy Land. We have room for twenty guests and the library here is one of the finest in the country. I just hate it that the guests have to pay at all," she added. "I like to think of the Hospice as just part of the manse."

'Both Mr Scott and his wife speak more than one tongue, which is almost a necessity amidst their cosmopolitan congregation. Mr Scott speaks some Arabic, Mrs Scott speaks French, Serbian, a little Spanish, and they are both studying Hebrew.

'From the tower of St Andrew's a wonderful view opens out, familiar names sound like chimes – the Mount of Olives, the black dome of the Church of the Holy Sepulchre on the traditional place of the Crucifixion, though these are inaccessible now from Israeli territory, and in the distance the thin blue line of the Dead Sea, the wilderness of Judaea by the Jordan Valley, the hills above Bethlehem. Close by are the massive yellow-white walls of the Old City on Mount Zion, and on Mount Zion too, in a tangled barbed wire enclosure of no man's land, the room of the Last Supper. Though divided, Jerusalem is still the Holy City, and there where mediaeval Crusaders fought and died, there could be no finer place for a Memorial for the sons of Scotland who also fell in the Holy Land.'

Bill and Darinka took their three-month leave from the 1st September, 1957, and used this opportunity to travel widely. When the Minister and Spouse each hold separate positions with separate responsibilities it is not easy to get away together on leave. Arrangements require to be made for maintaining the oversight of the congregation and, at the same time, the Hospice requires to be managed. With his well-connected fraternal relationships Bill was able to call on the services of a good number of colleagues, particularly those from within the

Y.W.C.A. and Y.M.C.A. to maintain the worship and pastoral care of the congregation.

Regarding the Hospice it is often the case that assistance comes from within the congregation. On occasions Mr and Mrs Cedric Conradi had deputised for short periods for Bill and Darinka and, again, willingly offered to take care of the Hospice while the Gardiner Scotts were on leave. Mrs Conradi was the organist in the Church and when the occasion arose had proved to exercise a skilful oversight of the Hospice. Their daughter, Kay, a young teenager at the time, remembers being in Jerusalem with great fondness. Her parents moved from their home in the Jewish district of Rehavia to rent the upper flat in the Hospice for a year. Kay describes it as a happy welcoming 'home from home which drew in a wonderful variety of interesting people.' She recalls that some of them were real "characters." There was "John the Baptist" who came to every Church service dressed appropriately, and Miss Bakewell, a shy retiring Nun who lived in the room/"cell" in the tower. Like young people through the ages who came to the Church, Kay had the responsibility each Sunday for tolling the bell in the tower. For Kay, at her age, while she was aware of the poverty and the general conflict in the area, she felt no threat to her security. She recalls her 'home' as a 'magical' place with a balcony providing a wonderful view over the Old City with its pink evening glow. Christmas with the Church filled to capacity was a special time for Kay, remembering the Carol Service when she, with a small choir, sang unannounced through the opening in the ceiling of the Church from the Cupola down to the congregation below – 'An angelic experience for many!' she says.

The Gardiner Scotts returned to Jerusalem in December 1957 and were, as reported at the Committee 'received with a great welcome home party held in the Hospice and the speeches made there were actually broadcast by Kol Israel. They were soon deeply engaged in the many activities of the long Christmas season. On Christmas Eve, after a united service in the Y.M.C.A., open house was kept at the Hospice, and many members came bringing Jewish friends with them. About ninety were served at a buffet supper. The evening ended with a short service at midnight in the Church. At a candlelit Carol Service the congregation was overflowing; there was also a very good congregation on Christmas Day, when the Sacrament of the Lord's Supper was celebrated. So also at New Year time, on Hogmanay, Mr and Mrs Scott again kept open house in the Hospice, and after supper the company listened to a recorded programme of Handel's "Messiah", the records having been sent as a gift by a former Lady Warden of the Hospice, Miss Mary Jackson. The evening concluded with the Watch Night Service.

The Hospice had been suffering from a dearth of visitors. Some guests had stayed there during the Christmas and New Year seasons, but tourists tended to avoid Jerusalem in the cold winter, much preferring the warmer climate of the plains of Sharon and the lakeside of Galilee.'

Bill resigned his Chaplaincy of St Andrew's in 1960 and took up a charge at Abernethy in the Highlands of Scotland. The Committee found it difficult to appoint a Minister in Bill's place and therefore his time at St Andrew's was followed by a number years of sporadic locumships and assistance from various sources within Israel, including from the Y.M.C.A.

An issue which had implications for St Andrew's and its work arose from the Committee's concern over the financial situation of the Hospice. That concern led to a "Commission of Enquiry" into the viability of the Hospice, an enquiry which also took the opportunity to review the Church situation. At its meeting in May 1963, the Committee, after taking the decision to close the Hospice (see Chapter 8) it also considered the future of the Church. 'Members who had visited Jerusalem in recent years all agreed that although there were very few Scots there, and with the exception of Mr Reid, none at present attending Church, there was a sufficient number of non-Roman Catholics in Israeli Jerusalem to justify the appointment of a suitable Minister to the charge of St Andrew's; for it was to St Andrew's that these people all looked as their spiritual home from home. Very few of such people, however, were posted to Jerusalem for long, so there was only a very small number that could form the more stable and enduring nucleus round which the temporary elements could gather. The Minister in St Andrew's was called not so much to visit his people as to be regularly visible to them in the city, so that they could make their approach to him easily, and at times visit him in St Andrew's at service on Sunday. The ideal Minister would be a man of great experience and riper years, who has something to say and could say it well on Sundays, and who would be out and about in the course of the week proving his genuine interest in the community and its members in any way that was open to him. Members felt it should be possible to find such a Minister from among the number who had reached an age when their existing charge had become too heavy a burden for them physically, and who would welcome a change to a place like Jerusalem where an opportunity was offered of useful service in the Ministry which made no more than a reasonable demand upon the Minister's bodily strength. It was noted that, with the best will in the world, the present Minister, the Rev. T. Gibson, just because he was a young man, could hardly be expected to fill the above role, and should, therefore, be informed of the Committee's policy so that he would be prepared to make a change once his present tour of duty was completed in about two years' time.'

Four months later, Mr Gibson, holding the posts of Minister in St Andrew's and teacher at Tabeetha School, resigned. With the Hospice closed and the Committee caught unawares and seeking to appoint a Minister of "riper years" sooner than anticipated it sought and received the assistance of the Rev. Herbert Minard, a United Church of Christ Minister and Director of the Y.M.C.A. Describing Mr Minard's's role as "caretaking" does not do justice to the work undertaken by him in both Church and Hospice. Using the resources of the Y.M.C.A, including staff and providing "up front" funding, he was, during this interregnum, able to completely renovate both properties and bring them up to a standard which had been not been achieved for some time.

Mr Minard continued to assist the Committee until the arrival of the Rev. William McIntyre, in May 1964, and the Committee 'unanimously and enthusiastically resolved to put on record its sense of indebtedness to Mr Minard and to the Y.M.C.A. behind him, and to thank him most gratefully for all he had done for St Andrew's Church and Hospice.' There is no doubt that the already existing relationship between the Memorial and the Y.M.C.A. was greatly strengthened during this period, a strong link which survives to this day.

Unfortunately due to his wife's illness, Mr McIntyre had to resign his position a year later. Once again the Committee called on the services of Mr Minard while it sought to replace Mr McIntyre. Following a period with more locum Ministers from Scotland the Committee recognised that this temporary arrangement could not continue. With no suitable applicants to fill the post, the Committee approached Bill Gardiner Scott and invited him to return to Jerusalem as Minister at St Andrew's again.

Bill's second ministry was very much a case of picking up where he had left off when he returned to Scotland in 1960. Old acquaintances were renewed and new ministries were developed. The Committee's report to the 1967 General Assembly celebrated Bill's return to Jerusalem noting that 'through his friendly contacts in Church and State the Rev. W. Gardiner Scott has made St Andrew's a centre of attraction for all who are interested in the Christian Faith. He has reopened the Hospice, and encouraged old and new friends. At the services in St Andrew's, on the great national occasions, the Government and City officials attend divine service. It is recognised that here is an embassy for Scotland, and that in this beautiful and simple Church there is a living Memorial to the common suffering of our people and to our mutual struggles for freedom and survival. What was originally a War Memorial has now become an active centre of outgoing goodwill, an open door to which people of all nations and creeds come and go and meet one another, giving friendship, aid, and comfort.'

Under Bill's leadership the Congregation's outreach and ecumenical foundation grew in strength through his continued involvement with the United Christian Council in Israel. The importance and relevance of this participation was recognised back in Edinburgh with the Church's "Special Group on Jewish Christian Relations." Following a visit to Israel in 1968, the Rev. J.M. Hamilton reported to the Group that 'the unity of Christian witness in Israel was evidenced by the activity of the United Christian Council in Israel. Church of Scotland Ministers and Missionaries took full share in the work of this Council, and the Hospice at Tiberias had been the venue for some of its major meetings.'

The development of the Hospice with Darinka's help was a continuing challenge. In 1968, following the Committee's review of the role of Minister and Spouse in the Hospice, Bill agreed to the Committee's decision to appoint Mr John Samson to the post of Manager of the Hospice. It was not a successful arrangement. Within four months of his arrival Mr Samson resigned and Bill and Darinka returned to running the Hospice.

On his retirement in 1973 Bill and Darinka remained in Jerusalem. When Bill died in 1998 the Rev. Hugh Kerr wrote of him on the 16th June in the Herald newspaper. "Jerusalem was, as in ancient maps, for him the centre of the universe, and it was there at St Andrew's, or later in the little manse on the grounds of St John's Hospital, or in their retirement flat, that Bill and Darinka were best known exercising the blessed ministry of hospitality, kindness, love, understanding, and concern. In an area where taking sides is all too easy, Bill had friends everywhere. His couthy, kindly manner endeared him to all who crossed his path. At home as much in an apron as in a cassock there was no one, Arab or Jew, old or young, rich or poor, with whom he was not in constant rapport. His leading of worship combined his simple Presbyterian background with liturgical and charismatic emphases. In the years leading to his retirement, his ministry was revitalised by the spiritual renewal of that time in Jerusalem. On retirement Bill and Darinka, though never abandoning their love of St Andrew's, found their spiritual strength in the services of St George's Anglican Cathedral. On Sunday, 8th October, 1939, William Gardner Scott was ordained to the Holy Ministry of the Church of Scotland by the Presbytery of Edinburgh in the Pleasance Church in that city. Countless others have cause to thank God for his gracious, gentle, and effective ministry throughout the years.'

Bill Gardiner Scott's unique and remarkable ministry is not untypical of that of the many Chaplains and Ministers who before and since have taken up the challenge of a ministry very different in many ways from that they will have experienced in Scotland. While in the view of the Memorial Committee arguably the ideal Minister for St Andrew's will be one of 'riper years' with much experience under their belt it is certainly not a charge which makes 'no more than a reasonable demand on the Minister's bodily strength.' In a ministry which has few boundaries and certainly no walls the records clearly indicate that the demands are numerous and varied – as are the rewards.

—— CHAPTER EIGHT ——
A Ministry Of Hospitality

WHEN OPENED in 1930, St Andrew's Hospice was one of many in Jerusalem. H.V. Morton in his book "In the Steps of the Master" [11] describes the concept of a hospice within the context of Jerusalem and details those available when St Andrew's Hospice was opened:

'If you arrive in Jerusalem and discover that all the hotels are full up with cruising parties from Haifa, someone is sure to suggest that you try to find a bed in a hospice.

'A sense of fear and panic assails the European traveller who, unaware of an earlier tradition, feels safe only in an hotel. The word "hospice" has for him a chilly and unfamiliar ring. It suggests possibly a St Bernard dog, or a bed on the floor. But how little he has to fear! He pulls a bell in a small postern gate, set in a high wall somewhere within the Old City, and his ring is answered by a monk, who stands aside automatically, for this sort of thing has been happening in Jerusalem for over a thousand years.

'The monk leads him to a frugal room with a bed in it, and a crucifix above the bed, a wash basin and a chest of drawers. And the traveller, glancing with approval round the little room, feels, if he has any sense in him, that he is seeing Jerusalem from the right angle.

'Since Charlemagne founded a hospice, with a library and a vineyard, sometime during the eighth century – it was swept away by the storms of Islam – Jerusalem has specialised in hospices. It was to the hospice of the Knights Hospitallers that pilgrims found their way during the Crusades: it was also a hospital in the modern sense of the word, for in those days many a Pilgrim arrived stripped, wounded, and robbed. Hospices maintained by the various churches, often under the most appalling difficulties and dangers, have ever since welcomed the Christian to the Holy City.

'At the present day there is the Casa Nuova, the hospice of the kindly and charming Franciscan Fathers, the Hospice of Notre-Dame de France, the Hospice of the Fathers of the Assumption, the German

Catholic Hospice, the Austrian Hospice, the Russian Hospice, and the Anglican hostel of St George's Cathedral. There are Maronite, Greek, and Armenian Hospices, the American Colony's house (which is really a hospice), and the huge, new and rather incredible American Y.M.C.A., the pious gift of a millionaire.

'The latest country to build a hospice in Jerusalem is Scotland. It is a beautiful white building that stands on a rise of ground facing the Old City walls and Mount Zion. The Scots Hospice contains also the only Scottish Kirk in Jerusalem, the Church of St Andrew.'

Morton goes on to describe his visit to the Hospice a few years after it was opened:

'One morning I walked down the dusty road from the Jaffa Gate to have a look at the Scots Hospice. Its site was chosen with real genius, for the white building shines from afar. There is nothing Scottish about its appearance, which is a tactful blend of Eastern and Western architecture.

'I rang the bell and found myself in a circular hall, very modern in design, yet very homely. I soon encountered a charming Highland voice and was told all about the Hospice. Since it was opened over one-thousand Scotsmen and Scotswomen have stayed there: tourists, students, and missionaries.

It is, in my opinion, one of the most charming and comfortable places in Jerusalem. The bedrooms have hot and cold running water in them and lights near the bed so that you can read yourself to sleep. There is a fine theological library for the use of students, a dining room (in which I am sure they give you bannocks at breakfast time) and a large drawing room, or lounge whose tall windows lead to a paved garden and a view straight ahead to the walls of the Old City

'One of the curiosities of the Scots Hospice is the dead man near the front door! While the place was being built the workmen blundered on the usual rock-hewn tomb, with an early Christian skeleton inside. He was photographed and reverently replaced under one of the ground floor windows.'

Morton's reference to the Hospice "containing" "the only Scottish Kirk in Jerusalem" resonated with the intention of the Committee in developing the concept of the Memorial. When it met in March 1925, the Committee confirmed 'the twofold character of the Memorial – the old-time idea of a Scots College or hostel with the Chapel attached.'

As the opening of the Hospice grew closer, the Committee made considerable effort in contacting Universities in Scotland advising them of the opportunities for students to spend time in Jerusalem with the Hospice as their centre. Publicity was spread amongst the student body bringing to their attention the list of nineteen scholarships available to them for the purpose. In February 1931, while still in Jerusalem following the opening of the Memorial, Hill sent a circular around the Divinity Faculties in the Universities:

'Rev and dear Sir,

'I have pleasure in informing you that the St Andrew's Hospice is now open for the reception of visitors.

'The Committee will be obliged if you would kindly draw the attention of your students to the advantages to be derived from a visit to the Holy Land. The Hospice contains a library of about 500 volumes from the collections of Prof. W.B. Stevenson, Prof. Dalman, the late Prof. James Robertson and other sources.

'The Newman School of Missions announces a Summer School of languages for Hebrew and Arabic from the 17th July to the 21st August. Classes are held in the mornings, leaving the afternoons free for excursions. The fee for the course of six weeks is £6. For further particulars apply to the Rev. E.F.F. Bishop, M.A., Thabor, Jerusalem.

'The American School of Oriental Research also announces a Summer School to meet at Beirut on the 21st July and continuing at Jerusalem for a fortnight from the 25th July. Lectures will be given, and visits paid to the more important sites excavated between Galilee and Jerusalem; fee for tuition £2. Autumn and Winter Terms extend from the 5th October to the 13th March; fee £5 per term. There is also a Spring Field trip from the 6th to the 25th April. For further information apply to the Director – Prof. C.C. McCown, American School of Oriental Research, Jerusalem.

'The Ecole Biblique et Archeologique, St Stephen's (Dominican) Convent provides, in French, courses of study including various Semitic languages. The Session begins in November and closes in July. Afternoon archaeological visits are made once a week and whole day excursions once a month. No fees are charged.

'In the Hebrew University the language used is Hebrew.

'Divinity students will be received in the Hospice at the reduced charge of eight shillings [£33] per day. It is hoped to reduce the charge still further when the debt on the buildings is discharged. Students should be provided by the Professor with an introduction and apply for accommodation to the Lady Warden of the Hospice.

'Attention is drawn to the P&O Branch Line service carrying one class only, the fare being £28.12.10 [£1,585] London to Port Said, 2nd Class rail to Jerusalem and return to London. Reduced summer fares begin about the 1st April.

'I am,

'Yours very truly,

'Ninian Hill, Chaplain.'

This had limited response. The first formal visit was a small group of students from Edinburgh Faculty of Divinity and New College, which travelled out in 1933 for an Easter "Vacation Tour." It was a start but much more publicity was required. A further effort was made by the Committee to publicise the "Institute" in 1934, this time giving all the practical information the student might need in making travel plans:

'Rev and Dear Sir,

'A party of nine Divinity students from Edinburgh University visited Palestine last April and stayed for about a month in St Andrew's Hospice. During that period they had opportunities of studying the topography and antiquities of the Holy Land, and of becoming acquainted at first hand with the historic Churches of Christendom and also with Judaism and Islam. It was for such a purpose that the General Assembly resolved to erect the Hospice building so that it might become an Institute for Biblical Studies.

'In the Committee's Report to the General Assembly for 1933 will be found a list of the educational facilities available for study in Jerusalem. The Chaplain is always ready to make arrangements for students to visit sacred scenes and to render all possible assistance. In the Hospice Library there are over 700 volumes relating to Palestinian subjects from the collections of Professors W.B. Stevenson and G. Dalman; Dr. W.M. Christie; the late Professor James Robertson and D.M. Kay, and other sources.

'The Committee is very desirous that the advantages of a period of study in Palestine should be enjoyed by as many students as possible in all our Divinity Halls and Colleges. We therefore beg that you will kindly bring the matter under the notice of your students.

'Application for accommodation should be made as early as possible to – the Lady Warden, St Andrew's Hospice, Jerusalem. Reduced terms for students are eight shillings per day. For other visitors the charge is from twelve shillings.

'As regards routes and fares, Messrs Mackay Brothers and Co, advise as follows: –

'1.University Students Special Rates

'The Blue Funnel Line from Liverpool and P&O Line from London issue special return tickets in ships carrying one class only to Port Said for bona fide University students under the age of 35 years at the current single fare for the return journey. The periods of availability are:

'Easter – between the 15th March and the 15th April outwards; return journey to commence before the 30th April.

'Summer - between the 1st July and the 31st August outwards; return journey to commence before the 15th October.

'Christmas – between the 15th December and the 5th January 1935; return journey to commence before the 31st January, 1935.

'The special summer single fare to Port Said of £22 will be quoted outwards between the 1st April and the 31st August and this will be the rate charged to University students for that period. Outside that period the rate will be £32.'

The circular continued to include travel details for a further five shipping lines together with train travel details from Port Said to Jerusalem. As a result a number of small groups of students did make use of the facilities, including student groups from various parts of the world, but certainly not in numbers which justified, as was hoped for, the appointment of appropriately qualified and experienced staff for the "Institute."

At the time the Hospice was first considered, it was to be a centre for theological students rather than a Guest House. With this in mind an effort was made from a very early stage to acquire appropriate books. An important collection was obtained by the Rev. W.M. Christie of Tiberias 'at a cost of £100 without charge to the funds of the Committee' and comprised the many Hebrew books and documents collected by Prof. Dalman, Director of the German Evangelical Archaeological Institute.

Over the years the use of the "Dalman-Christie" Collection as it became known, and their safe keeping, proved much more of a problem than their acquisition, and featured in the minutes of many meetings. Reluctantly, following much discussion, the decision was taken to explore if it might be of interest to another library or institution. In 1945, at its meeting on the 12th September, the Committee 'agreed that a list of the Hebrew books in the Hospice should be made and submitted to the Committee before disposing of any of them.'

Initially the National Library of Scotland confirmed an interest in the Collection but having been made aware of its condition, many of the one-hundred and eighty volumes requiring to be rebound, it doubted whether it was wise to transport it as it was. Approaches were made to a number of other institutions and individuals, including the Hebrew University in Jerusalem and the Chief Rabbi in London, with no success.

In 1947 the Committee agreed that the Collection would best be preserved and accessible for study if kept 'in a Church Library such as the Library at New College' in Edinburgh. The Collection was packed and sent to Scotland and, today, is held in New College as one of its "Special" collections. (See online catalogue http://catalogue.lib.ed.ac.uk/, shelfmark Dal-Chr)

In parallel with the concerns regarding the future of the "Dalman-Christie" Collection the role of the Hospice was also being reviewed. It gradually became apparent that the difficulty that students found in taking sufficient time away from their colleges, and the cost of such a period in the Holy Land meant that the concept of the Hospice being a theological college gradually had to give way to the reality that there was not a demand for such a service and this was eventually appreciated. Discussions between the Memorial Committee and the Committee on Education for the Ministry culminated in a conference with representatives of both Committees in January 1947. In acknowledging the issues they agreed 'to report to the next General Assembly that the Conference was not in favour of the establishment of a Theological College in Palestine. It thought such a College neither desirable nor practicable. The Conference was, however, of the opinion that facilities should be increased for sending students out to Palestine for the study of archaeology, historical geography and allied subjects. The Scots Memorial, Jerusalem, Committee to get in touch with the four Divinity

Hall Senates regarding the provision of facilities for students travelling to Palestine.'

Three months later the General Assembly noted the report and acknowledged the "sympathetic and promising responses" from the four Divinity Halls. To date, however, the situation regarding organised and structured student visits to the Holy Land using the facilities of the Hospice remains, essentially, as at 1947. Many attempts to encourage such visits were sporadic, as was the response. Today the only successful programme of student visits is the Scholarship Scheme under the auspices of the "Society of Friends of St Andrew's, Jerusalem." The Society also supports a Bursary programme for Ministers of the Church of Scotland wishing to use the Hospice as their base for study.

———•◦•◦•———

While the Committee struggled over a number of years to bring the "Institute of Biblical Studies" into existence, the task for the Lady Warden on her arrival in Jerusalem, with the Hospice still a building site, was one which required much more immediate attention. Three years after her appointment as "Organising Secretary" of the Committee and her management of the highly successful fundraising Bazaar, Mrs Isobel MacRae was appointed the first Lady Warden of the Hospice in February 1930, and travelled to Jerusalem in April to take up her duties. With six months to go before the Church and Hospice were due to be opened her presence there at this time must have been a considerable boon to the design team in finalising the many construction and fitting-out details. However even after the opening in November, 1930, the work was not complete and it took another two months before the Hospice could open its doors for guests.

Once opened, the task was not only to compete with the many other hospices and hostels in the area and make St Andrew's Hospice financially viable, Mrs MacRae had the additional burden of creating a profit from the business in order to pay off the £1,743 debt (plus interest) due to the Contractor who had built the Memorial, and at the same time make a financial contribution to the upkeep of the Church. There is very little detail of how the Hospice fared in the day-to-day records of the early years. However in July 1935, Mrs MacRae presented to the Committee a comprehensive report providing an excellent overview of the achievements and the issues she faced over the first four and half years:

'Report of the Lady Warden for the years
'1931, 1932, 1933, 1934 up to 30 June, 1935

'Scope of Hospice

'It will be remembered that the Hospice contains twenty rooms apart from kitchen and servants quarters; five rooms on the ground floor and fifteen bedrooms upstairs. Three of the upstairs rooms are occupied by staff, the Warden's bedroom, and the Chaplain's bedroom and sitting room, leaving twelve for visitors. As five of these are double rooms, seventeen visitors can be accommodated. During the very busy season, which may last from November until May, use can be made of a room in the Church Tower and of offices near the vestry. There is no water laid on in the Church section of the building, and access to these rooms can only be gained through the Common Room or by the front door of the Church, so that it will be seen that this arrangement is only an emergency one; inconvenient and involving considerable extra work. It has, however, worked well on the whole, enabling the Hospice to accommodate as many visitors as the Dining Room will hold comfortably, i.e., about thirty.

'On the land adjoining there stands a small house, known as the manse, which is rented by us along with the piece of land extending to the station road. This house has four rooms and a bathroom, and has been utilised by us in many ways. For one year it was occupied by the Chaplain and his family. It can be used, however, most profitably by letting it to Jerusalem residents who will gladly pay about £38 per month for two people with meals in the Hospice.

'Therefore the Hospice can find room for twenty-nine or thirty people; three staff, seventeen visitors in the main building, two to three in the manse or annex, and from four to six in the Tower rooms.

'On one occasion beds were found for over forty, but this is only possible for a few nights during an emergency.

'Domestic staff

'To carry on the work at least six servants are employed, seven for the greater part of the year, including a boy who gives part of his time to the garden. All the women servants are Christian, the two boys are Muslim, one having had some Christian training. Three of the servants have been here for five years, having been engaged to help in the preparation of the Hospice, and others have been with the Hospice for four, three and two years.

'Statistics

'It has not been possible to keep a daily book of statistics but from the visitors book and from the list of accounts paid the following figures have been compiled with a fair degree of accuracy:

	1931	1932	1933	1934	1935	Total
Missionaries	47	87	117	69	31	351
Ministers & Wives	35	57	53	82	35	262
Students	12	4	13	28	25	82
Other Visitors	137	248	379	384	185	1333
	231	396	562	563	276	2028

'With the half-year figures for 1935 it will be seen that the Hospice has steadily gained in usefulness, and that about five-hundred appears to be the maximum number of visitors per annum if overcrowding is to be avoided. Remembering the limited accommodation it cannot be doubted but that the Hospice is now being fully used and is filling a real need.

'In addition to the groups of students from Edinburgh who have come during the past three years, students have come independently from Scotland and Ireland, from Oxford and Cambridge, from New Zealand, Australia and America, as well as missionaries from the field for a period of language study. An increasing number of these described as "other visitors" are Church members from home.

'Scale of charges

'The charges vary from eight shillings per day to twelve shillings per day, the average charge being ten shillings. These rates include meals and a shower bath.

'Service to the Church

'Of course the Hospice exists to serve the Church; but it has been able to give special help from time to time. On two occasions, for instance, at the request of the Foreign Mission Committee, two Chinese workers, returning to China after a period of training at home, have had a visit to Palestine arranged for by us, from Port Said to Jerusalem; to Galilee and back again to Egypt.

'Financially, the Hospice has contributed directly towards the reduction of the debt the sum of:

1931	£ 200
1932	£ 620
1933	£ 500

1934   <u>£ 500</u>
Total   <u>£ 1,820</u>

'It also cares for the upkeep of the building, and is almost entirely responsible for the cleaning, lighting and heating of the Church. On several occasions it has contributed to the maintenance of the Chaplain.

'As regards the congregational life in Jerusalem the Hospice has tried to foster this as far as is possible. Every Sunday, since the opening day, tea has been provided for all those who care to wait to meet their Minister after Church. During the busy months this may involve from fifty to seventy teas every Sunday, but it has been found to be well worth doing. During the first years regular work in the entertaining of Scottish policemen was undertaken, but with increasing numbers in the Hospice such work could not be continued. The Church work party for the Christmas Gift Service meets in the Hospice, and the children of the congregation are entertained.

'Service to the Community

'As regards the community the Hospice has organised four annual dinners for women on St Andrew's Night, the men having had another tradition for many years. To these dinners women have come from all parts of Palestine, and His Excellency and other Scotsmen have been present during the evening. On the arrival of each new Chaplain and on other occasions, receptions have been given to all communities, and in other ways the Hospice has taken a share in the public life of Jerusalem. From time to time as the numbers in the Hospice permit, the work parties for the Social Service Committee and for the Order of St John meet in the Hospice Common Room.

'Policy

'The task set before the Lady Warden seems to be two-fold. The first, to run a Hospice which shall be in every way a worthy adjunct to St Andrew's Church in Jerusalem, and to the church at home; secondly, to run it so that it will not only pay its way, but will, as far as possible, make a surplus available for reduction of debt, purchase of land, or for an endowment fund.

'From the figures given regarding the different types of visitors it will be seen that the large majority do not necessarily have any interest or share in the work of the Church. There has to be a nice adjustment between the claims of these visitors who have made a purely business arrangement, and the claims of the Church upon the Hospice. This has not always been easy, but it has been done with some measure of success.

There has been established during its four years a Scottish Hospice tradition, and it attracts, to a large extent, only those who are in sympathy with that tradition.

'In any measure of success achieved the Lady Warden would like to acknowledge with gratitude the help given to her by each successive Chaplain, by the members of her Advisory Committee, by the Honorary Treasurer, Mr Turnbull, and lastly by her loyal staff of servants.

'Finally, it may be of interest to record the during these four and half years, the Memorial has been one of the special sights of the city, and has attracted to it many eminent visitors among whom may be mentioned the Princess Royal, the Earl of Athlone, the Archbishop of Canterbury, and last spring Mr H.V. Morton who has done so much to make the Memorial known through his book "In the Steps of the Master."

'Names Recorded in the Church Visitors' Book

1930	17
1931	294
1932	218
1933	287
1934	266
1935 (6 mths)	363

1445

'The marked increase in 1935 is doubtless due to the publicity given by Mr H.V Morton.

'The Lady Warden would like to take this opportunity of thanking the committee for their trust in her. She hopes that this report will satisfy a continuance of that trust.'

In her report Mrs MacRae raised the issue of the charges for accommodating the Chaplain within the Hospice:

'Hitherto no instructions have been received by the Lady Warden from the Committee on this matter, and arrangements have been made with each Chaplain on arrival.

'It would be a great advantage if now, after four years experience, a definite rate for the Chaplain were fixed and made known to him by the Committee at home.

'After consultation the Honorary Treasurer and the Lady Warden propose the following for your consideration:

'1. That if there is a rate, common to other Chaplaincies of the Church of Scotland on the Continent that would be applicable to Jerusalem, that rate should be adopted here.

'2. Failing that, it is proposed for consideration that the Chaplain should be received at the student rate, eight shillings per day, for board and lodging and bedroom only, a charge from £1-£3 per month being made for a sitting room, according to the size of the room. There should be no other charge made by the Hospice beyond that of starched laundry, which cannot be done on the premises, and private entertainment of guests.

'3. The family of the Chaplain should receive the most advantageous terms possible according to the accommodation required.

'4. The Lady Warden would welcome an arrangement by which it would be possible for the Committee to remit to her the payment of the Chaplain's charges, leaving only the incidental charges to be dealt with on the spot.'

Hospice staff between 1940 and 1946

In his report to the Committee in January 1941, Dr. Stuart, Session Clerk, reports, 'Of the part played by the Lady Warden in creating an atmosphere reminiscent of Scotland at its best it is unnecessary for me to write. Let it suffice if I say that she bravely carries on that tradition of Scottish hospitality which has ever been associated with St Andrew's

Hospice. Further, although doubtless often footsore and weary from too much serving, she seems to go from strength to strength, becoming more and more indispensable to the Memorial's ordered existence.'

After eighteen years service in various capacities to the Committee in Edinburgh and the Hospice in Jerusalem Mrs MacRae retired in 1944. There is no doubt that the success of the Hospice in these early critical years was very much due to her belief and commitment to the wider work of the Memorial. The Chaplain at the time, the Rev. Duncan MacGillivray, paid warm tribute to Mrs MacRae noting that her name is widely known in the region for her kindness and thoughtfulness for everyone she came in contact with. On her return to Scotland Mrs MacRae continued to support the Memorial by participating in the work of the Committee in Edinburgh.

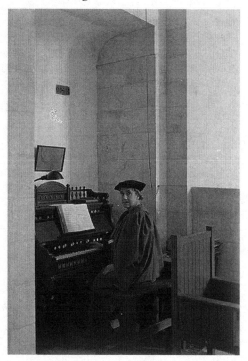

Mrs MacRae at the Church organ

Mrs MacRae died on the 1st November, 1960, and at its meeting on the 4th January, 1961, the Convener acknowledged the tribute paid to her by Dr. John McQueen of St Andrew's congregation:

'Mrs Isobel MacRae died suddenly at Ovingham House, Northumberland, on the 1st November. She was the grand-daughter of Thomas Legerwood Hately, composer of the well-known Psalm tune -

Leuchars. She went to Palestine first in 1923, where she met Dr. Norman MacLean and Dr. Ninian Hill and joined forces with them in the effort which eventually produced the Scots Memorial, Jerusalem, St Andrew's Church and Hospice. When it was opened in 1930 she became the first Lady Warden, which post she held until 1944, when she retired. She was loved and respected by a wide circle, not only in the congregation but among people of various races and creeds who dwelt in Jerusalem. Those who had the good fortune to be her guest in the Hospice will never forget the kindly Scottish home she made for them, always greatly appreciated, but never more than in the war years.'

———————————————————— ··•·· ————————————————————

Throughout World War II and the Mandate, with the presence of troops and personnel from the Palestine Police Force the popularity of the Hospice was assured. In the four years from Mrs MacRae's retirement until 1948 two Lady Wardens from Scotland were appointed. Their responsibilities were made increasingly difficult due to the escalation in the violence and unrest in the region especially during the lead up to the departure of the British Troops in May/June 1948. At the same time they had to cope with an economy destabilising under the strain. In April 1944, the Committee noted 'the enormous increase in the cost of living in Palestine which was up more than 300% and that the St Andrew's Hospice was the only Hospice in Jerusalem charging less than the maximum charge of £22 per month.' And in May 1946 'The cost of living had risen in Jerusalem by 250% while the Hospice charges could not be raised beyond 30%,' a condition of the license to operate as a Hospice laid down by the Jerusalem Municipality.

Each Lady Warden dealt with this situation in her own way. For many years the Hospice was treated as a permanent residence for individuals and families, mostly with a government or military background, with the accommodation arranged to suit particular circumstances. In April 1944 it is recorded that there were fifteen permanent residents living in the Hospice. While this provided some guarantee of income it was a departure from the original intention of the Hospice meeting the short term needs of students and travellers. Because of this arrangement many potential guests were turned away and complaints were being received by the Committee. In May 1946, with the arrival of Miss Margaret Brownlee as Lady Warden, Dr. McQueen, a member of the Kirk Session and himself a resident of the Hospice suggested 'that priority should be given to Ministers, Missionaries and Church of Scotland people generally, who wished to be guests in the

Hospice.' This 'suggestion' was later enshrined in a revision to the policy by the Committee stating that 'the Hospice was in the first place meant for pilgrims and students, though it has never been possible to reserve all its accommodation for them. At the present time they are likely to be few in number, and the rooms should, therefore, be available for others. These others, when admitted, should always be given clearly to understand that they are not being taken as permanent residents in the Hospice. Any accommodation given them is given them temporarily.'

Miss Brownlee's term as Lady Warden was cut short in May 1948 when she was recalled by the Committee in Edinburgh at the time the British troops and the Palestine Police Force withdrew from Jerusalem to Haifa and Jaffa for departure from the country at the end of the Mandate sparking the Israeli "War of Independence". This left the Minister, the Rev. Clark Kerr, on his own in the Church and in charge of the Hospice, not that there were any guests willing to run the risk of been shot at while seeking a bed in the Hospice situated as it was in an exposed position in "no man's land" between the warring factions. With the departure of Miss Brownlee, to be followed six months later, in November, by the Rev Clark Kerr's return to Scotland, the Committee gratefully accepted the offer of caretaker of the Church and Hospice from Mr John Reid, Elder and Session Clerk/Honorary Treasurer, and described by Clark Kerr as the only Scot in the Congregation.

From May 1948 until during the first half of 1949 when the intensity of the fighting eased off the Hospice remained closed. With the arrival of Clark Kerr's replacement, the Rev. Scott Morrison, the Committee began to consider preparing the Hospice for reopening. Miss Brownlee was invited to return to Jerusalem as Lady Warden but was unable to take up the offer due to failing health. On the suggestion of Mr Morrison who, by this time, had developed a strong relationship with the Reids, Mrs Mary Reid was invited to take up the post of Lady Warden in October 1949 on a temporary basis for one year until the Committee could appoint a Lady Warden from Scotland. This "temporary" appointment lasted six years until the arrival of Bill and Darinka Gardiner Scott in 1955.

Mrs Mary Reid

With her appointment as Lady Warden Mary, John and their three children, Melville, Mary and Katherine, took up residence in the Hospice leaving their home in the Jewish district of Upper Bakaa. Being "on-site" made preparing the Hospice for re-opening a more convenient arrangement. However with the position of the Church and Hospice and sporadic gunfire coming from the battlements of the Old City wall it remained an exposed and dangerous location.

The first task was to carry out repairs to the buildings. The damage was extensive both externally and internally and securing reliable labour to undertake the work under the prevailing conditions was difficult. Employing permanent staff for the Hospice was also extremely difficult and if found, was expensive. When the Hospice managed to open its doors again the local staffing situation had not been fully resolved. The result was that Mrs Reid found herself not only managing the Hospice, taking reservations and relating to guests, but also being involved in the hands on day to day activities in the kitchen and guest accommodation.

The situation was such that even the Reid children helped out with a variety of chores around the Hospice and the Church. Mary notes that

'As children living in the Hospice, we were aware of the dangers so to speak and learned to be very careful. We helped our parents where we could with the ironing on wash days, the breakfasts for the guests on weekends and holidays, dusting the pews of the Church every Sunday and we took it all in our stride.' On Sundays Melville rang the Church bell and Mary and Katherine took up the collection. Such chores, however, were not without their danger. Mary recalls on one occasion with sniping still going on, Melville had a close shave 'when he went up on to the top of the tower to raise the Saltire and was shot at. Minutes later, after he had fled, the wooden flagpole was shot down!'

There is no doubt from the records that for the Reids there was a total family commitment to the life and work of the Church and Hospice. This was a loyalty which, despite the many difficulties and dangers, saw Mrs Reid willing to twice extend her contract as Lady Warden. A mark of her dedication and drive made evident by the fact that throughout her six-year period of employment she took no annual leave.

While Mrs Reid and the family continued to manage the Hospice and fill it with the few visitors who were around, in the background the Committee, under the circumstances - its lack of funds and seeing no end to the conflict in the region - struggled to define the Hospice's long term purpose and direction. At its meeting in January 1950, the Committee considered a proposal from the Rev. Clark Kerr, now a member of the Committee. He noted 'Now that the seat of the Israeli Government had been removed to Jerusalem it would be necessary for Legations to follow, and it was likely that the British Legation were now looking for quarters in Jerusalem. Since these would be very difficult to find, Mr Clark Kerr's suggestion was that the Legation should be offered a long lease of the Hospice. After the conversation with Mr Kerr the Secretary had written to Mr Scott Morrison in Jerusalem advising him that this project was being entertained; and Mr Clark Kerr had written to a friend of his in the Foreign Office to find out if the project was feasible. Mr Clark Kerr reported to the Committee that he had received a letter from the Foreign Office stating that they were interested in the idea, and will give it serious consideration, but they asserted that the lease would have to be at least for two years before they could accept any proposal to rent the Hospice.

'Discussion followed when it was pointed out that owing to the disturbed state of Palestine it was unlikely that the kind of guest for whom the Hospice was designed would be found in any number for a long time yet. In these circumstances the advantage of housing the Legation was considerable, and outweighed the one disadvantage which was mentioned by Mr Murchison, i.e. – the risk of housing Government officials in a Church building. It was resolved to offer a two year lease of the Hospice to the Foreign Office for the purpose of housing the British Legation in terms that would be acceptable to both parties.' In response the Foreign Office did not take up the offer.

In July 1950, under the Minute heading "Hospice: Future" the Committee considered 'letters dated, Jerusalem the 10th June, from the Rev. A. Scott Morrison; the 10th July from Mrs Reid; and from Ramleh, Egypt, dated the 18th June from Mrs Isa M. Bury, all dealing with the Hospice, its use and organisation. The Rev. Scott Morrison, being present, dealt with the situation in Jerusalem, and showed how far the possibilities of using the Hospice were limited by circumstances.

'The position generally in Jerusalem was conditioned by the fact that there was no final settlement of the future status of the city as yet agreed-upon. The truce, therefore, was still an uneasy one and the Old City was still cut off from the New. It was only now that the barbed wire which surrounded the Church and Hospice was being removed. In consequence pilgrims and visitors to Jerusalem were still comparatively few and not disposed to seek accommodation in a building that looked like an outpost in the firing line. That apart there were other serious difficulties in preparing the Hospice to receive visitors; at present rates payable in Israel the wages bill for a full staff would be about £300 per month. It would also be exceedingly difficult and very expensive to get adequate supplies of food. There were two alternatives immediately open to the Committee in respect of the Hospice. On the one hand a Jewish staff could be engaged and the Hospice run on commercial lines, charging prices for accommodation which would be far above what could be afforded by Missionaries, Ministers, and the ordinary type of Pilgrim. On the other hand Mr Morrison could continue conversations he had already started with the Y.M.C.A., with a view to letting some of the rooms in the Hospice to the Y.M.C.A. for accommodating some of their senior staff. In any case Mrs Reid's contract as Warden expired at the end of September, and if she were to be continued in her present capacity it would be necessary to increase her salary. But if the use of the Hospice was developed along either of the lines above mentioned she would need a colleague, and it might be a senior colleague. Mrs Bury, who wrote from Egypt, was a lady with much experience in Hostel work, was interested in the Warden's post, and was known to members of the Committee as one whose qualifications merited the most favourable consideration. The Committee resolved that the only possible development in the use of the Hospice at the present time was along the line of an agreement with the Y.M.C.A. and that Mrs Reid should be asked to continue as at present, but that from the 1st October, her salary be increased by £50 per annum; and that the Committee should meet sometime in November with Mrs Bury present, and reconsider the whole position of the Hospice and its organisation.'

The Y.M.C.A. took up the offer of occasionally renting rooms in the Hospice which helped considerably with its income. Mrs Bury turned down the offer of the appointment of Lady Warden.

Mrs Reid wrote to the Committee in April 1951, and it noted 'conditions were very unsettled, there were practically no visitors, and so far she had been unable to get suitable staff. In order to get supplies for the Hospice a licence was necessary, and she had taken up this matter with the authorities and hoped to get the licence in about six months time. Five guests were at present permanently resident and the Hospice had been fairly busy during last summer and autumn accommodating visitors for a night or two.' Mrs Reid wrote 'I have been trying to draw a fine distinction between "no hotel," obligations to the Y.M.C.A. and "make a bit of money" and have, I think, reasonably met all three.' Finances were reasonably good, and IL400 had been banked from income. The considerable question of repairs and replacements had still to be faced, but Mrs Reid did not consider the present a suitable time to start work. Occasional bullets still struck the building, and the previous week a coloured pane had been smashed in one of the Church windows. She envisaged important replacements in the plumbing system.

For the next ten years with Mrs Reid and then the Gardiner Scotts putting every effort into trying to keep the Hospice going as a financially viable concern, the Committee rarely gave consideration to developing a long-term strategy. Its problem was that whatever was proposed required investment of capital funds, which it did not have. In addition it was vital to have the support of a good reliable local staff team of which there was no guarantee.

A "delegation" of Committee members was sent to review the situation in 1954. Its report recognised the extremely difficult circumstances the Lady Warden, Mrs Reid, was working under but offered no better long-term strategy for the Committee's consideration. Despite that, there was no shortage of ideas coming forward from time to time:

– 'Turn the Hospice into a modest first class hotel, run by a professional hotelier who would be given a free hand to make it a paying concern.'

- 'Treat it as an extra large manse where the Minister and his wife would take a paying guest from time to time.'

- 'Co-operate with other Churches or ecumenical bodies, like the World Presbyterian Alliance, to provide facilities for pilgrims from other lands.'

The objection to this last proposal was the perceived difficulty of getting other Churches or the World Presbyterian Alliance to co-operate or, on the other hand, of persuading 'our own' Church that this would be desirable solution to the problem.

With the imminent departure of the Gardiner Scotts in 1960, once again a Committee delegation was sent to determine a viable strategy for the long-term future of the Hospice. When the Committee met in May that year, the delegation report noted that 'with the establishment of the armistice line in 1948, and the generally unsettled state of affairs in the Middle East, pilgrims and tourists have been few in number, and as the majority of the holy sites are in Jordan the average visitor is not interested in spending much time in Israel – or at least not in Israeli Jerusalem. This year it would appear that the situation as regards tourists is slightly improving, and this improvement is likely to be continuous if conditions remain stable. But apart from the two main religious festivals of the year, the Scotts have found that the clientele of the Hospice has been mainly missionaries on short leave, an occasional student, and parties of varying sizes from different countries. For some time now they have not been able to give full board, receiving guests only on a bed-and-breakfast basis. The reasons for this are completely understandable. Firstly the fantastic cost of living in this country, with its compulsory high rate of wages, has made the procuring of paid assistants a most difficult matter (for example, a house maid gets £36-£40 per month, a cook £50-£52) and even when such help is obtained, it has often proved most unsatisfactory. But the main difficulty has been that in expecting Mr and Mrs Scott to manage both Church and Hospice. The Committee have been expecting the humanly impossible. Here it should be said that the "impossible" has in fact nearly been achieved; for however exacting the demands upon their time, and no matter how hard they have been pressed by their innumerable duties, Mr and Mrs Scott have nevertheless maintained in the Hospice the atmosphere of a Christian home. We have had abundant testimony to this fact, and wish to make it quite clear that if the Hospice has not been functioning as fully as it might, the fault is in no way theirs; we cannot think of any couple who could have done it better.

'Some points regarding the potential future of the Hospice:

'1. Tourism is likely to increase in this country if peace is preserved.

'2. The Archbishop, Dr. Kosmala, and others, encouraged us in the idea of attracting students here whether under – or post–graduate. The Archbishop is hoping to develop St George's, on the Jordan side, along this line, and would gladly co-operate in all possible ways. This would be more feasible if we had, say, a Hebrew scholar here in residence, and could give full board to students. The Swedish Institute would also willingly co-operate, and there are possibilities as yet untapped in the young and vigorous Hebrew University.

'3. Should Jerusalem come to be recognised by the UN countries as the capital of Israel, the embassies would move up here from Tel Aviv; this would have a vitalising effect upon both the Church and Hospice; but of course this is a problematic event.

'It is clear to us, therefore, that not only must the Church and Hospice both be retained (we have never for a moment doubted this,) but both must be developed much more fully than they have ever been in the past. There is one main pre-requisite to this end. There must be a Minister whose duty will be purely and simply that of a Minister (with all the unusual ministerial duties which this unique charge demands); preferably he should be a Hebrew scholar, or at least willing to learn modern Hebrew, the language of the country in which he works. And, in addition, there should be a man and wife sent out from Scotland to be Warden and Hostess–Housekeeper of the Hospice. We can envisage the possibility of these duties being undertaken by, say, two women, but the ideal would be a man and wife – a similar set-up to the management of the homes run by our Social Service Committee in Scotland. With the somewhat spasmodic local help obtainable, this should be sufficient to lift the Hospice back on to a full board-and-lodging basis. Nothing less will suffice. (It should be added that the Presbytery of Jerusalem are in full agreement with the policy outlined above.)

'We are aware of the financial demands that such a policy will make upon the Committee and upon the Church, especially during the first year or so, until the new facilities become well known. But we are confident that, while it may never completely "pay its way" (taking into account the salaries that would have to be paid) the Church would be making a grave mistake if it did not seek to improve the Hospice amenities, either in the way we have suggested, or in some other way. We have the most wonderful assets here in Jerusalem, and if we do not use them to the full, when other organisations are able to take full advantage of much more meagre premises, the inevitable question is asked, "What is wrong with the Church of Scotland?'

With the exception of confirming that in future the Minister and the Warden of the Hospice should not be a team of Minister and wife, the Committee took no other decision in respect of the report. Instead it "recorded" its existence and proceeded to find a Minister to succeed Mr Gardiner Scott and also someone to manage the Hospice.

In this respect and despite their best efforts it was the locum Ministers appointed to fill a gap in the Ministry of the Church, Dr. John Gray from Aberdeen University and Dr. Bathgate from the Edinburgh Medical Mission Society Hospital at Nazareth (E.M.M.S.), who ended up managing the Hospice. They did get assistance eventually from Miss Penelope Brough who commuted a few days a week from the hospital in Tiberias until she was confirmed the full-time Lady Warden living in Jerusalem. In 1961 the Rev. Tom Gibson was appointed as Minister and arrived just in time for Miss Brough to resign as Lady Warden due to ill health. To replace Miss Brough, and in contradiction to the Committee's previous decision Mr Gibson's wife was appointed to the post of Lady Warden. To assist Mrs Gibson, the Committee later appointed Miss Elizabeth Tennant, a school meals manager from East Lothian County Council as Hospice Cook.

However, for many reasons these were not happy times. There were personality issues compounded by the stress of ongoing conflict in the area and the constant pressure on the Committee not being able to find a long term workable strategy for the Hospice. In May 1963, Committee members 'addressed themselves to the question of the viability of the Hospice in present or immediately foreseeable circumstances. Reference was made to the disappointing record of the Hospice for a long time back, and not merely recently. It was noted that the maximum number of beds for letting was only sixteen in eleven rooms, and apparently one could count on letting even that number for a comparatively short period of the year; for the rest sometimes very few would be let at all. Members were reluctantly driven to the conclusion that to maintain the Hospice on the standard demanded if it was to do credit to the Church of Scotland, would necessarily cost a good deal both in capital outlay and in maintenance charges. The annual loss would, therefore, be serious, and on the other hand the compensating gain to the Church was not very obvious. It was generally agreed that the Hospice had become a financial drain on the Committee's resources, which the Committee, on its own responsibility, could not allow to continue. The Convener stated that he had already indicated to Mr Gibson that the closure of the Hospice was a real possibility and they had actually discussed it together.

'It was resolved to suspend operations in the Hospice at the earliest possible date compatible with the faithful discharge of existing commitments, which date, according to the Rev. Gibson, would be the end of August. A thorough survey should be made of what the Hospice has been costing the Church, also of urgent repairs and renovations required, and a thorough assessment made of the whole situation, before resumption of the Hospice on its present scale could be contemplated.'

With the closure of the Hospice, the Church would continue under the leadership of Mr Gibson, local staff would be paid off and Mrs Gibson, 'would revert to her original position as the wife of the Minister.' The cook, Miss Tennant, was asked to take up the "post" of Church Beadle and take care of both Church and Hospice. Included in her new role was providing refreshments after Sunday Services in the Hospice which was to be opened for the occasion. Miss Tennant did not accept the offer of these new responsibilities and resigned. She later sued the Committee for Breach of Contract and received compensation.

Miss Tennant was not the only one unhappy at the decision to close the Hospice. The Presbytery, which had no input into the decision complained as did the staff of the E.M.M.S. Hospital in Nazareth. The staff of the Hospital, many of whom were Scots, considered the Hospice as a "home from home" when visiting Jerusalem. The Foreign Office sent a letter to the Committee advising that 'It was the opinion of the Consul General in Jerusalem, Mr Alastair Maitland (an Elder in the Kirk Session), that the closure of the Hospice would represent a considerable loss to this Community where British Christianity was no longer widely represented.'

One of the guests requested to vacate his accommodation in the Hospice when it closed was the Rev. John Sawyer, in Jerusalem on extended study leave. Mr Sawyer had been able to assist with Sunday worship in the absence of Mr Gibson, which service was greatly appreciated and recorded as such in a Minute of the Committee in Edinburgh. However the closure of the Hospice was a considerable concern for Mr Sawyer, so much so that he wrote an article on the matter which appeared in the Scotsman newspaper on the 18th November, 1963:

'Close-it-Down Church

'Dismay Over Scots Hospice Move

'The St Andrew's (Scots Memorial) Church and Hospice in Jerusalem has been 'Closed for Repairs and a Review of the Future', causing widespread dismay. There is evidence of a new interest among the people of Scotland in Israel but that country sees little proof of this. In this article the Rev. John F.A. Sawyer points out that the Church of Scotland has a long history of endeavour in the Holy Land and stresses the need for it to be continued.

'"Is this the tomb of King David?" A face peered through the French windows. "Oh, excuse me!" The voice faded away, when several Scots faces looked up from their coffee.

'The mistake is easily made, because besides Jerusalem's old railway station, where crowded trains end their steep climb up the 'corridor' from the coast, there are two hills: on one, traditionally Mount Zion, stands the tomb of King David; on the other, St Andrew's (Scots Memorial) Church and Hospice. Pilgrims coming up to Jerusalem for the first time to join in the Lamentations on the Ninth of Ab or the rejoicing during Passover week soon find out which is which.

'But now there is another reason for confusing the Scots Hospice with the tomb – since the end of August St Andrew's Hospice has died, 'Closed for Repairs and a Review of the Future.' There are now no more Scots faces to look up from their coffee, and the popular nickname of the 'Close–it–Down' Church seems justified once more.

'This year Tabeetha School in Jaffa celebrated its hundredth anniversary and Dr. Wardi, the adviser to the Minister of Religion, suggested that this would be a good time to print an article entitled "One-Hundred years of Scottish endeavour in the Holy Land." "You have so much to be proud of," he said, "and there is so much ignorance about what you have achieved here." Then he was horrified to hear that the Scots Hospice was closed. Just at this time, too, when the many friends of Tabeetha have been offering their support and proving their appreciation, both at the centenary celebrations and after the recent attacks on the school by Orthodox students, there are rumours that it too is to close before long.

'Needed in Israel

'From all over the world missionaries, teachers, journalists, UN personnel, tourists and pilgrims write as usual to St Andrew's for accommodation for themselves or their friends, and they are told the place is closed. Another old friend, Dr. Hans Kosmala, Director of the Swedish Theological Institute in Jerusalem, makes no secret of his disappointment. "We need the Church of Scotland to work with us in Israel," he says. "My students have long and happy connections with St Andrew's." Professor Brevard S. Childs, of Yale Divinity School, has also expressed his dismay at recent events here.

'This year the first Church of Scotland youth group to visit the State of Israel looked proudly on their Church's prized possessions in the Holy Land, and put forward their enthusiastic suggestions. Then they were told that things were closing down. The United Christian Council, which is composed of all Protestant Churches in Israel, expects more from the Scots than dying hospices, resigning ministers and closing schools. Some months ago the Edinburgh Rabbi, Dr. Weinberg, on a visit to Israel, made a point of visiting the Scottish Church in Jerusalem, and was very impressed by what he saw. "It seems, however," he said, "that I know more about the Church of Scotland in Israel than the Scots themselves!" But more recently, thanks to his efforts (hundreds of Scots Church folk know him and learned of Israel and the Jewish people from him) and thanks to the increasing number of returning pilgrims from the Holy Land, there seems to be a new interest in Israel arising among the people of Scotland.

'Unfortunately, Israel – and that means not only the Jews but also the United Christian Council and all our friends there – sees no evidence of this new interest. What Israel sees is our "Close-it-Down" Church. Is the famous old school in Jaffa going to be next? If Israel sees all that, how can the life and interest and enthusiasm and hope of Scots survive?

'A Take-Over?

'Of course, if Scotland cannot continue in Israel – and there are problems – then our friends from the United States have always shown a keen interest in our Church; and perhaps the World Council of Churches would take over the Scottish Hospice in Jerusalem and make it once more into a students' study centre – the purpose for which the building was originally intended by the Scots who built it – and Tiberias Hot Springs, Ltd., might be only too happy to buy up the thriving Scottish Hospice in Tiberias.

'But the Israeli Jesuit, Joshua Bloom, who is on the interdenominational panel for the translation of Christian terms into Hebrew, expects some special contribution from the traditions of the Scottish Church. "What has happened to your Church these days?" he asks. The United Christian Council has just met for its annual conference in the Scottish Hospice at Tiberias, and have a special respect for the Church of Scotland. The Scots at the E.M.M.S. Hospital at Nazareth, and another in Kafr Yassif, look down from the north of the country, and can hardly believe their eyes when they see Scotland giving up and closing down. One of them, Dr. Doris Wilson, a graduate of Edinburgh University, believes that we have a special duty to provide, along with the hospices and churches, a good Christian school, quite apart from the special contribution of such a school to Israel in general.

'The Church has a duty to itself, too. Israel today judges according to the highest standards of vitality, creativity, progress and success. If there are signs of this new life in other parts of the world – in the participation for the first time of the Pentecostalist Churches at New Delhi, in the new spirit alive in the Ecumenical Council at Rome and in the Anglican Congress at Toronto and in that of the Orthodox Churches in Rhodes, in the lively, creative controversy over "Honest to God", in the success of new experiments in our Church's youth work, in all the ideas for the Church in Israel that have been going about for so many years (such as starting a Scottish Theological Institute in St Andrew's Hospice, Jerusalem) – if all these signs of life are real, then Israel, which associates Scotland with the life and colour of the Scottish regiments, are being misled by our "Close-it-Down" Church. The theology, liturgy, culture and spirit of Scotland are known here already, respected and sought after, the years of Scottish endeavour must not end either with a bang or with a whimper.

'There was once a patient in the E.M.M.S. Hospital in Nazareth for whom there seemed to be no hope. Then Dr. Bathgate, a man still known and loved by thousands, took out his bagpipes and began to march up and down the balcony, playing them outside the patient's room. So amazed and excited was the patient that he leapt out of bed and ran to the window to see what was happening: life returned to his dying body and from that moment he never looked back!'

Four months after the decision was taken to close the Hospice the Rev. Tom Gibson unexpectedly resigned as Minister of St Andrew's throwing the Committee into disarray. As noted in the previous chapter, it was at this point that the Rev. Herbert Minard of the Y.M.C.A. stepped forward to assist. Using the resources of the Y.M.C.A., during its closure, he was able to undertake a thorough investigation and completely renovate the Hospice and bring it to a standard which had not been achieved for some time.

At its meeting on the 21st April, 1964, the Committee noted the accounts for the Church and Hospice submitted by Mr Minard. 'These showed that as at the 1st January there were credit balances on both accounts amounting to IL3,756 in the Church account and in the Hospice account IL6,350, in addition to a small cash balance. The income from collections have been well sustained during the three months, with the result that Mr Minard had been able to meet a very large bill for repairs and replacements and also offered to pay for ordinary running costs, without calling for a remittance from the Committee, although, in the Secretary's opinion, some remittance would soon be necessary. Nevertheless, the Secretary had been surprised to note how much had been accomplished with the money on hand in Jerusalem, which spoke volumes for Mr Minard's efficiency. It also underlined his generosity in making available workers regularly employed by the Y.M.C.A. whose services in large part represented a very considerable contribution from the Y.M.C.A. to the Church and Hospice.'

In his covering letter Mr Minard stated that the hot water boiler, which was leaking, would have to be replaced, in addition to work already accounted for, and in a previous letter he had estimated this to cost about IL600. In that same letter, dated the 18th March, he gave an account of the work that had to be done to restore the hot water and central heating systems to efficiency. Since no plumbing plans were available, and since much of the piping had perished through disuse, the workmen had encountered many difficulties, but in the end these were all surmounted and the whole system put in working order. Furthermore a cursory examination of the foundations of the ground floor, which in part was built over the water cistern, had revealed no apparent weakness; Mr Minard intimated that a thorough examination would be made soon, before the present phase of repairs was ended.

The Convener referred members to the correspondence with Mr Minard, and stated that 'it was abundantly clear that the Committee and St Andrew's Church and Hospice owed a great debt to Mr Minard for the signal service he had rendered in so many respects, especially since the departure of Mr and Mrs Gibson. No one could have done more than he to keep the congregation in good heart. The amount of care and concern he had shown in the practical affairs of the Hospice compelled the Committee's gratitude. Reports received indicated how much had to be done by way of renovation and repairs to the buildings, and also how competently and economically it had been done on Mr Minard's initiative and under his supervision. The Committee, therefore, unanimously and enthusiastically resolved to put on record its sense of indebtedness to Mr Minard and to the Y.M.C.A. behind him, and to thank him most gratefully for all he has done for St Andrew's Church and Hospice, Jerusalem.'

In May 1964 the Rev and Mrs William McIntyre arrived in Jerusalem as Minister and Warden to take over from Mr Minard, complete the repairs to the Hospice and prepare it for opening which it did a few months later. However during the period of the closure of the Hospice the records give no indication of the Committee using this time to address the issues it raised in May 1963 when it took the decision to close it – to undertake 'a thorough survey of what the Hospice has been costing the Church' and 'a thorough assessment to be made of the whole situation.' With no work having been undertaken on either and with no strategy in place the Hospice opened in a climate of continuing tension in the area and with very few tourists around.

Mr and Mrs McIntyre had to return to Scotland prematurely in August 1965 due to Mrs McIntyre's ill health. Once again Mr Minard from the Y.M.C.A. stepped in to arrange Sunday worship and safeguard the Hospice which, by this time, had very few guests. It took some time to find a replacement for Mr McIntyre but in May 1966 Bill and Darinka Gardiner Scott, with their daughter Tanya, were warmly welcomed back to St Andrew's to begin their second tour of duty as Minister and Warden. With their vigour and enthusiasm the Scotts soon managed to breath new life into the Hospice which began to fill with guests.

One year later a major opportunity for the development of the Ministry of the Church and Hospice arose out of the Arab-Israeli War of June 1967. The "Six-Day War" was short, sharp and brutal. It changed the geopolitical scene in the region including making for easier access into the Old City and today's "East Jerusalem." The travel agents were quick to recognise the new opportunities. Soon after the war "Fodor" printed a supplement to its "Guide to Israel" entitled "After the Cease Fire" and describes "A New Look for Tourism":

'The new state of affairs in the Middle East promises a glowing future for tourism in the Holy Land. Though some 30,000 tourists were lost to Israel due to the crisis and the war, this figure should be more than made up by the new influx of visitors that will be coming for pilgrimages and vacations or just to see the nature of the modern-day David that confounded Goliath. Israel's Director General for Tourism,

Meir de Shalit, predicts that 1967 would bring a record 350,000 visitors to Israel despite the brief setback. As in 1966 when Christian visitors outnumbered Jewish for the first time since independence, the majority will be non-Jewish. In 1968, Israel's 20th anniversary year, as many as half a million tourists are expected as special celebrations, congresses and commemorations will be held throughout the year. Visitors coming on pilgrimage will particularly benefit (for obvious reasons if they are Jewish), while Christians will now be able to follow in the footsteps of Christ without having to flash passports in the midst of their journey.'

At its meeting in October 1967, the Committee agreed that 'the time had come to consider the implications of the unification of the City of Jerusalem. It was pointed out that the barriers were down between the Old City and the former Israeli sector. This meant that the Church and Hospice of St Andrew's had now more opportunity to serve pilgrims in the Old City. It was desirable to consider the full use of the Hospice in Jerusalem and that such use could more amply fulfil the original vision of the part which this Hospice could play in the life of our church.'

A major scheme for the development of the Hospice which would add more bedrooms was drawn up by Dan Ben Dor, the Church's local architect who had been an assistant to Clifford Holliday, the architect of the Memorial designed and constructed forty years previously. The enthusiasm for this extensive project stumbled when the Committee considered that the cost was prohibitive. It was another twenty-five years before the work as envisaged was undertaken. In the meantime it was decided that even if the larger proposal for development could not proceed that, at least, work could be done to refresh and refurnish the bedrooms. To raise funds for this Bill Gardiner Scott contacted congregations and individuals in Scotland and invited them to send a contribution of £150 [£2,400] which would allow them the opportunity to "name" a room and have it furnished. Through Bill's persistence and hard work this turned out to be very popular. It was not long before locally produced ceramic tiles with the names, Warrender, Murchison, MacGillivray, Templeton, Elsie Rankin, Morrison, Bathgate and Sym were being fixed to bedroom doors.

The early story of the Hospice is one of struggle – a lack of funds for investment, difficulties with securing staff and the volatile and fluctuating situation in the region, all of which limited greatly the Committee's ability to carry forward any of their many ideas and plans.

However what was happening in Committee meetings behind "closed doors" was not a concern for the many thousands of Hospice guests and visitors over these years. As the Committee struggled with its business, the Hospice was doing what it was meant to – meeting the needs of travellers seeking very much appreciated rest and recreation. A further forty years on and while the room names have long since disappeared St Andrew's Guesthouse strives to live up to its heritage and continue to provide that sought after traditional Scottish rooted ministry of hospitality.

—— CHAPTER NINE ——
An Islet in a Savage Scene

CONCEIVED as a result of a World War and born into a region of strife, the Scots Memorial in Jerusalem has experienced and survived conflict in its many forms throughout its eighty plus years of existence. Today the building still carries its "war wounds" and the scars are noticeable in a number of places on its outer walls. Not a "monument", the Memorial with Church and Hospice together has people at its heart, providing life and meaning and driving it forward in its work and outreach within the communities in which it exists. These are the same people who through the years have maintained its presence and, on occasions, its very existence. There have been times when they have continued their work under extremely difficult conditions and suffered the consequences from the stress and anxiety in doing so.

There were obvious and notable occasions when outright conflict found property and people literally in the firing line and in mortal danger, as in 1948 and 1967. However for most of the time, for Ministers, Staff and members of the Church community, it was the distress of witnessing communities pushing each other apart and at the same time, in the midst of it all, being open to provide a reconciling word, a sanctuary and a voice of hope – a ministry which continues to this day.

With increasing Jewish immigration into Palestine during the Mandate tensions in the region grew. Inter- communal violence was commonplace with many killed and injured. British troops and the Palestine Police Force found themselves in a difficult situation maintaining law and order.

Into this volatile situation, in June 1946, the Rev. William Clark Kerr arrived as Chaplain to St Andrew's, Jerusalem. A man of considerable experience of the Middle East, Clark Kerr was first inducted to the charge in Stamboul, Turkey, in 1929. In 1941 he was appointed by the Church's Colonial and Continental Committee to its charge in Haifa and in addition to that responsibility was appointed as the Middle East Director to the Church's Huts and Canteen Committee in April 1946.

Induction of the Rev Clerk Kerr to St Andrew's

In November that year Clark Kerr wrote to the Committee describing the level of disorder in Jerusalem and the strain on everyone living there. He noted that the situation was having a serious effect on the work in general, but more specifically, described the damage caused to the windows in the Church, Hospice and the Manse. This was as a result of the bombing on the 30th October, 1946, of the railway station only two-hundred yards from the Memorial when an Arab policeman and a British bomb disposal officer were killed and the station was very badly damaged.

In February 1947 Clark Kerr sent a further letter to the Committee 'describing the measures taken by the Palestine Authorities in connection with terrorist attacks and how these affected Church organisations. Amongst other things he stated that the Hospice had been almost emptied of its former guests, whose places had been taken by Government officials. The Memorial buildings were to be brought within the perimeter of the defended area. Mr Clark Kerr foresaw great difficulties in maintaining Church Services under the new security conditions, but both Miss Brownlee (Lady Warden) and himself had been exempted from the evacuation measures.'

At the same meeting of the Committee 'The Secretary reported having received the following cablegram from Mr Clark Kerr "Strongly advise immediate representations to Colonial Office against rumoured military requisition of Hospice. Brownlee and self remaining." The Secretary further stated that he had consulted with the Convener and written to the Secretary for the Colonies protesting against any attempt that might be made by the Military to convert any part of the Memorial buildings into a military establishment, which would be exposed to attack by Jewish terrorists. At the same time letters had also been written to the Earl of Selkirk, the Lord Advocate, General Sir Arthur Wauchope, and Mr Walter Elliot, asking for their assistance in this matter. Favourable replies had up-to-date been received from the Earl of Selkirk and the Lord Advocate.'

The closing months of the Mandate were characterised by increasing problems concerning the security of anyone linked to the administration. An additional problem was the polarisation between Jew and Arab, which left Hebrew Christians the victims of both sides. The excellent report from the Rev Andrew Scott Morrison, appointed as evangelist and teacher in Jaffa by the Church's Jewish Mission Committee, paints such a clear picture of the descent into chaos that it is recorded in full [12]. There is no record of this period in the annals of St Andrew's but the problems facing the Minister, the Lady Warden and the Congregation were very similar. First hand accounts from St Andrew's covering the period after the end of the Mandate pick up the story later in this chapter:

'Without the least shadow of a doubt the past twelve months have been the most disturbed single year in the whole history of the mission. It might be described as a year of "alarums and excursions." Nor have all the noises been "offstage," somewhat remote from the actual work, and forming a "political background" to the even tenor of the institutional work of an ordinary mission. The political struggle has even invaded the precincts of the mission compounds, so that converts and even some of the missionaries find themselves torn by conflicting loyalties over the intense political issue which touches the life of every soul in this troubled Holy Land. It speaks highly of the calibre of missionary personnel that in spite of these differences of opinion they are still able to maintain "the unity of the spirit in the bond of peace." Perhaps just there lies a witness to our non-Christian neighbours of how an acceptance of the Christian faith could help to heal the wounds in the body politic.

'All our institutions were working smoothly when the first blow fell on the 1st February, 1947. All British personnel in the town were summoned to an urgent meeting in the Jaffa Club to hear the District Administrative and Police Authorities outline the difficult political situation which had developed through the threat of Jewish extremist organisations to kidnap and hang British nationals, as a form of reprisal for the execution of Jewish youths found guilty of being in possession and making use of arms contrary to the Emergency Security Regulations. We were informed that all non-essential personnel would be evacuated, and should be ready in three days' time to leave the country.

'At first it appeared that all missionaries, without exception, were included in this category of non-essential persons. Through the Presbytery, for Scottish institutions, and through the Anglican Bishop of Jerusalem, for English religious bodies, cabled representations were made direct to the Colonial Office, as a result of which heads of institutions, and an essential skeleton staff, were allowed to remain, provided they agreed that the Government took no further responsibility for them, and would consent to live within Security Zones approved by the Authorities.

'Through this evacuation scheme, known as "Operation Polly," we lost from our mission only the housekeeper and one teacher from Tabeetha Girls' School, who later obtained permission to remain in Egypt and help with the work of St Andrew's School for Girls in Alexandria. Two British teachers and the Minister were allowed to remain and the other members of staff, being of other nationalities, were not affected by the scheme.

'The Authorities also suggested that all mission schools – three in number in Jaffa – should unite for joint instruction within the Security Zone. After lengthy negotiations the impracticability of this arrangement as far as our school was concerned was demonstrated to the Department of Education, and it was further conceded by the Administration that clergymen and nursing sisters need not live in Security Zones. Thus it was possible for all the work to continue, though under restrictions and difficulties in respect of staff; the British staff lived in the Security Zone and came out daily for work, sometimes with a police escort.

'The next blow fell at the beginning of March, when, for a fortnight, Tel Aviv was placed under Statutory Martial Law, forcing our clinic to close down for lack of patients, and making it impossible for students to come to our evening class school on the boundary line between the two towns. During this period the Sherwood Foresters occupied the big hall and the clinic as off-duty sleeping quarters and one night fought an epic rifle duel with the Palestine Police, each party unfortunately mistaking the other for a band of the Irgun Zwei Leumi, or the Stern Gang. Fortunately no casualties resulted, and "a good laugh was had by all" in the morning, when the mistake was discovered! From this period until the end of June we gave sanctuary to three families of Hebrew

Christians, evacuated from their own homes, to make room for a Security Zone which had been established nearby.

'By the end of June the state of security made it possible for Government to relax Security Zone Regulations. The two members of our staff residing there were allowed to return to Tabeetha School, and permits were secured for the return of the two evacuated to Alexandria.

'During July, August and September the situation again deteriorated to such an extent that it became impossible for Church Services to be maintained or the clinic to function, and schools of course were closed for the long vacation in any case. This deterioration was due to the series of events which culminated in the hanging of two British Army sergeants, and the curfew regulations imposed by the military by way of preventing further disorders.

'By October it was possible to resume services, evening classes, clinic and day school, but the atmosphere was supercharged with the intensity of feeling with which all shades of opinion followed the broadcast deliberations of the United Nations' Special Committee on Palestine. With the publication of its decision to partition Palestine (November 30th), the fourth heavy blow fell upon us and our work. This time the cause was not Jewish terrorism, but Arab indignation, backed by armed force, at the proposed partition of the land between Jews and Arabs.

'So far, at the time of writing, three months after the publication of the U.N. decision, the position is still "fluid", as the journalists say, and it is both impossible and unwise to attempt to assess the full extent of this blow to the ordered work of our own and other missions. After three months of bitter racial disturbances, in the course of which, in the whole country, one-thousand, three-hundred and seventy-eight persons of all communities have been killed, and over three-thousand seriously injured, we cannot yet see how more serious clashes can be avoided on the withdrawal of the British Administration and police on the 15th May of this year 1948.

'Since November 1947, this boundary area between Jaffa and Tel Aviv has been under continual dusk to dawn curfew; consequently evening classes, as well as evening services on Sundays, are impossible. The entire population has left the boundary districts, so that the clinic has no patients by day. All our work, save that of Tabeetha School, situated well in the centre of Jaffa, and so spared the worst noise of shooting and bombing, is well-nigh at a standstill. Even there the attendances are only about two thirds of the former strength, and several Palestinian teachers have left the country. Instead of having all our congregation to worship together there is a morning service at 10 a.m. in the Security Zone for the British members, a 3 o'clock service at the Mission for Hebrew Christian members, and an early evening service at 5 p.m. for Arab Christians.

'Despite the continual sniping from rooftops, sound of near and distant firing, the explosion of bombs, and the blowing up of houses left tenantless and suspected by the military of being snipers' nests, our building has so far sustained only broken tiles from rifle fire resulting in a flooding of the kitchen and study when it rains heavily. The whole staff are at their posts again, after some preliminary disorganisation and inability to get passes through restricted zones at first; they are exercising mainly a ministry of visitation among the scattered members of the congregation, evening classes and club work. The doctor and nurses go to their patients instead of having them come to the clinic.

'What will be the future of our work when the proposed non-Christian States are set up in Palestine? Is the Christian Faith for ever destined to be a minority faith in the land of its birth? Or is God about to open some new door of opportunity in the Holy Land, through which his Kingdom will come in?'

The Journal printed this article at the end of June 1948 and included a post script from Scott Morrison:

'This article was written in March. Thereafter the political situation deteriorated even more rapidly. Rumours spread in Jaffa of the penetration of the Jewish Haganah forces beyond the boundary line between the two towns. Wealthier Arab families began moving away to Egypt and the Lebanon, and some to the South American states where they had relatives. The Jewish Mission Committee had put the responsibility of deciding the time of evacuation upon the people on the spot. In mid-April we decided that it was time for the ladies to be evacuated. At the Barbanel Street premises on the boundary line mortar shelling became more and more intense until one night a bomb cut off the water supply by cutting the main pipe about fifty yards up the street. This made it imperative to evacuate the staff to Tabeetha and the refugee Hebrew Christians to a specially rented building inside the British Security Zone, provided by the kindness of the District Commissioner. They could not be taken to Tabeetha School on account of being regarded as Jews by the neighbouring Arabs. The Hebrew Christian members of the staff were next evacuated by air, after receiving permits from the Hagenah authorities to leave the country. By the beginning of May all the work at Barbanel Street was at a complete standstill, and with the aid of the Palestine Police Force, who were most helpful, five three ton lorry loads of furniture and equipment were removed to storage in Tabeetha School and the Church Missionary Society's School in the Ajami quarter of Jaffa, for greater safety. Also early in May the last pupils of Tabeetha School were safely evacuated by their parents to the Lebanon or Transjordan.

'The fall of Haifa to the Jews utterly demoralised the Arab defenders of Jaffa, and the British Forces had to take a hand in the fighting to secure their own supply lines to the Jaffa Security Zone. At this point the District Commissioner sent an armoured car to the Mission to bring Miss Rosie and myself to the Zone, where we were hospitably entertained in the Police Officer's Mess for seven days before being escorted to Haifa for evacuation on the troopship "Georgic". We arrived in Liverpool on the 15th May, the date set for the termination of the Mandate.

'Shortly after, Jaffa was occupied by the Haganah forces and letters from members of the congregation indicate that the Barbanel Street premises have received a direct mortar bomb hit which penetrated through the roof in the region of the bathroom. So far as can be ascertained Tabeetha School is intact and in the care of the International Red Cross.

'Some twenty-five persons, Hebrew Christians, who were in danger of their lives, because of being regarded as traitors by the Jews, and as Jews by the Arabs, were brought home to Scotland for safety by arrangement with the Home and Colonial Offices. The Church has undertaken the responsibility of providing accommodation and work and the eventual resettlement of these persons in Palestine or elsewhere.'

In Jerusalem various attempts were made to reduce the violence and even bring about peace in the City and the surrounding area. Richard M. Graves, the brother of Robert, the poet and writer and of Philip and Charles, both noted journalists and writers, was the Mayor of Jerusalem and Chairman of the Municipal Commission from 1947 to 1948. In his diary "Experiment in Anarchy" [13] he writes on the 26th February, 1948:

'I have had it in my mind for some time past to make proposals to the combatants for a ceasefire in Jerusalem as a preliminary to a general peace, though without much hope of success, and when I read the leader in the "Post" I sat down and wrote a Project for Peace in Jerusalem, which I shall hand to the political leaders on both sides, after ascertaining that my proposals do not conflict with the views of the High Commissioner in respect of ways and means. In principle Sir Alan

Cunningham is as anxious for peace as anyone in the country. My "project" which is written in everyday language and has none of the style of the major or minor prophets, contains a number of concrete proposals, which would certainly establish peaceful conditions if followed.

'This afternoon I handed a copy of it to Roger Pawle for the High Commissioner, who is giving an address to the unofficial British community at the British Council's house. There I had a few words with Sir Alan, who said he would be glad to read my paper, but reminded me that projects for peace were being constantly discussed "at the highest level". I am sick of this phrase. It gives a mysterious weight and importance to the conversations of ill-informed politicians occupying high places, which are never reported to the public and which are too often full of high-flown sentiments and banalities and seldom get down to the heart of the subject. This judgement would not apply to H.E's conversations with community leaders in Jerusalem so much as to the discussions at Lake Success, and probably in London. What I want to emphasise is that at the highest level (20,000 feet or so) the persons who live on it can only faintly discern the movements and needs of the earthbound peoples who make up the world.

The advantages of my project are: (a) that it calls for detailed action and (b) that when it is published – as it should be – it will help to form public opinion. We are supposed to be living in a democratic age, but in fact partly owing to the secretiveness, sometimes justified, of Ministers, and partly owing to the shortage of newsprint, the public seems to be taken less into the confidence of the Government than at any time in the past sixty or seventy years. This is especially applicable to Palestine which has no democratic institutions, no British Press – only strongly partisan local newspapers – and no government propaganda worthy of the name. Anyhow, the public in Jerusalem have not an inkling regarding the peace overtures in this country or for this country, which have been made by the Palestine or British Government.'

Graves' "Peace Project for Jerusalem" was published and distributed by the District Commissioner on the 28th February, 1948:

'Peace Project for Jerusalem

'During the past three months hundreds of people have been killed or injured in Jerusalem in a species of warfare devoid of rules and humanity. Many more have lost property or their livelihood. Nobody has gained anything and no good can possibly come to either side from the continuance of strife and bloodshed to the City.

'The vast majority of the inhabitants desire to live in peace and to be freed from the increasing dangers of communal disorders. They recognise that while there must be political disagreements these can never be solved by violence, and that if the life of the City is to survive *modus vivendi* must be found to enable the two Communities to live together until their political relationship can be permanently settled. For this purpose I ask that both Communities should henceforth conscientiously observe a truce of God and the following rules of conduct:

'(a) Each Community should for the time being restrict the movement of its members to its own areas which will be policed by its own members of the Municipal Police Force.

'(b) Each Community should solemnly undertake not to attack the other by sending armed men into that Community's area or by firing from one area into another.

'(c) Each Community should bind itself to exercise the utmost self restraint and control of violent elements in its midst.

'(d) Each Community should refrain from retaliation and reprisals which can only make it more difficult for the leaders of either Community to prevent further attacks and counter-reprisals. This recommendation is the most difficult of fulfilment, but it is the most important of all.

'(e) Each Community should fully respect all vehicles carrying the Red Cross, Red Crescent or Red Shield, and should undertake that any such vehicle would not be used for any purpose not authorised by these signs.

'(f) Passage by members of one Community through the territory of the other would be permitted in the case of funeral parties or revictualling parties under a flag of truce. A minimum number of omnibuses should be permitted to operate.

'(g) No armed men should be permitted to live within any area reserved for the other Community.

'(h) All armed men should leave the portion of the Old City occupied by Orthodox Jews, whose safety would be guaranteed by the Arabs if this were done, and the Old Montefiore quarter should be similarly evacuated by all armed men and placed under the protection of British forces and the Municipality.

'This appeal has the support and goodwill of all the people of Jerusalem except those who are determined to submerge this entire City in chaos and bloodshed for political ends.

'If these rules of conduct are observed peace, if not at first goodwill, will be restored, and the life of this City, so often destroyed in the past, will be able to continue.

'March, 1948

'District Commissioner,

'Jerusalem District, Jerusalem.'

To push forward with the Project Graves met with Dr Khalidi and David Ben Gurion, the recognised leaders of the two Communities, and reported on the 9th March of his meetings to the Chief Secretary of the Government:

'1. I have the honour to inform you that I have handed copies of my Peace Project for Jerusalem as amended by you, and with a few minor additions, to Dr Khalidi and Mr Ben Gurion.

'2. Dr khalidi was very polite and thanked me for my initiative, promising to submit the Project to his Executive. He has now sent me a letter, of which I enclose a copy, stating that he and the Higher Executive consider that the arrangements contemplated are premature at the present stage.

'3. I saw Mr Ben Gurion yesterday and discussed the Project which had been in his hands for a few days.

'4. He disagreed with the number and the variety of the clauses, and would not accept the proposal that the Jews of the old City should be guaranteed by the Arabs after the withdrawal of the Haganah which he said was insulting to Jewry, and considered that the proposed restriction of Jews to Jewish areas and Arabs to Arab areas was undesirable and offensive to both Communities.

'5. However, he said that he and the Yishuv were very anxious for the peace of Jerusalem and were prepared to undertake that not a shot would be fired by any Jew in the City for a specified agreed period – a week, a month or a year – if the Arabs would make and observe a similar undertaking. When I mentioned that he might have some difficulty in making Jewish dissidents comply with such an undertaking, he said that he would be able to do so.

'6. I promised to convey his views to the Arab Higher Executive.

'I have the honour to be, Sir,

'Your obedient servant,

'R. M. Graves, Chairman, Municipal Commission.'

It is often in these situations that people perceive the Church to be a help in troubled times, just as in such times the Church can be the recipient of much needed support. On the 26th March Richard Graves wrote in his diary, 'It seems to me that at this stage of the world's regress into barbarism it wouldn't be a bad thing to seek for peace in the bosom of religion. The thought reminds me that this morning, being Good Friday, Clarissa and I went to Church at St Andrew's by the Scottish Hospice. We had a very distinguished panel of Ministers, the leader of whom was the Chief Moderator of the General Assembly of the Scottish Church. He read an excellent sermon which he had composed for the occasion and I wouldn't have had him alter a single word of it. St Andrew's is a beautiful building, and large enough to hold a good size congregation, which we had.

'It gives me some satisfaction to think that the Christian Churches, and in particular our Churches, Anglican and Scottish, will carry on in Jerusalem however much the nations furiously rage together, and will form islets of civilisation in a savage scene.'

Describing the continuing Sunday worship at St Andrew's in the Committees' Report to the 1948 General Assembly, the Chaplain, Clark Kerr, in the midst of the conflict notes 'the large numbers not only of civilians but also of military and police in attendance, of the thrill and challenge of ministering to an almost all-male congregation in circumstances of great tension and danger. Often the noise of shooting and explosions has been so great as to make it impossible to hear any word spoken in the service. Worshippers have had to hide behind walls to shelter from flying bullets on the way to Church. Many have had to secure special passes to enable them to come into the Zone at all, and some have run the continual risk of assassination in order to attend Church. His Excellency the High Commissioner, Sir Alan Cunningham, and the General Officer Commanding, General MacMillan, have given a great lead to the Community by their loyal attendance at Church worship and their friendly interest in all the affairs of the Church.'

At its meeting of the 1st April, 1948, the Committee considered the safety of both Clark Kerr and the Lady Warden, Miss Brownlee. The Committee decided that for Clark Kerr the matter of his own safety, security and evacuation was for him to decide. However he was instructed to make arrangements for Miss Brownlee to return to Scotland.

The issue of the Church's property was also of concern at this meeting noting that a month earlier, in March, the Commission of the General Assembly agreed 'to the appointment of a Committee to watch over the interests of the Church in view of the partition of Palestine in conjunction with the Committees concerned and the Presbytery of Jerusalem, the Committee to consist of two representatives from each of the following: – viz., General Administration, Jewish Mission, Colonial and Continental, Scots Memorial, Jerusalem, Huts and Canteens, Education for the Ministry Committees, and the Church of Scotland Trust, the Procurator, Convener.

'The Commission further resolve that if and when an approach is made to the Civil Authorities the Committee shall be the medium through which the negotiations shall be carried on.' (This "Special Committee on Church Property in Palestine" reported to the May 1949 General Assembly the contents of which are included in Appendix [5])

At the same meeting the Committee confirmed its support for a "call to prayer" for the Christian Community in Palestine. The call was initiated by the Church's Colonial and Continental Committee following its receipt of a letter from Clark Kerr 'in which complaint was made of the apparent indifference of the Christian world generally to the difficulties and dangers which confronted the Christians of Palestine.'

Following Miss Brownlee's departure from Jerusalem there was a flurry of communication from Clark Kerr to the Committee. The Committee was concerned, as was Clark Kerr's mother that their correspondence was not getting through to him. At its meeting in June 1948, the Committee considered 'correspondence from Mr Clark Kerr and read in full a letter from him dated Jerusalem, 12th May, in which he stated his resolve to stay in Jerusalem with three Arab servants, so that he might protect the Church and Hospice from looters. The question of his means was raised and Miss Brownlee stated that she had left him with £58 in cash. In addition there were £71 in the Treasurer's Account and £24 in the Lady Warden's Account. In the above letter also Mr Clark Kerr stated that he had over £700 of the Church's money. Moreover according to Miss Brownlee he had a good store of food. It was reported that he had been deprived of the three Arab servants when the Jews took possession of the area in which the Hospice stands, two having been arrested. The last word received from Mr Clark Kerr was a cablegram dated Haifa ex Jerusalem, 5th June, which read as follows: "Quite alone but all well at Hospice." After discussion the Secretary was instructed to send a letter of appreciation and sympathy to Mr Clark Kerr's mother and to make an effort through the Foreign Office to get in touch with Mr Clark Kerr himself.'

The Committee, on being advised that the records of St Andrew's Church were kept in an iron box in the vestry 'the Secretary was instructed to request Mr Clark Kerr, as soon as communication with him was opened up, to have these records put in a safe place, if possible under British Government protection.'

Meeting in October 1948, the Committee considered 'letters dated Jerusalem 7th July, 6th August and 14th September, all from the Rev. Clark Kerr. Also read was a letter dated Bedford 23rd September from the Rev. P.E. Adeney (of St George's Cathedral, Jerusalem). Mr Adeney's letter described, from personal knowledge, the difficult position of Mr Clark Kerr, and strongly urged his relief at the earliest possible date. Mr Clark Kerr's own letters described the situation of the Church and Hospice in detail and stressed the danger of looting which threatened them. He also stated that he himself was feeling the effects of the long strain, and petitioned the Committee for immediate relief. His efforts to find someone who might take his place as guardian of Church and Hospice had so far been unsuccessful, and he asked the Committee to seek a Minister at home who would be willing to succeed him.

'The Vice-Convener expressed on behalf of the Committee the highest appreciation of the courage and devotion to duty shown by Mr Clark Kerr under the prolonged and severe strain to which he had been subjected in Jerusalem, and the conviction that the continued safety of the Church and Hospice was largely due to the fact that he had remained at his post. It was agreed that in view of all the circumstances all possible measures should be taken to relieve Mr Clark Kerr.

'The whole question was discussed at length and finally the following resolutions were adopted unanimously:

'(1) That the Rev. Clark Kerr should be encouraged to continue his efforts to solve the problem by enlisting local help in Jerusalem;

'(2) That a notice should be published asking for a Minister to volunteer to go to Mr Clark Kerr's relief;

'(3) That any candidate should be interviewed by the office-bearers, who should be given powers to make an appointment on terms they should decide;

'(4) That a letter should be written to the International Red Cross, to discover if they could take over temporarily the Church and Hospice, and so protect them;

'(5) That a letter should be written to the Stated Clerk of the Presbyterian Church in the USA describing the situation and invoking their help to interest the State Department in the matter;

'(6) That a letter should be written to the Foreign Office requesting them to make representations to the Israeli authorities, concerning the safety of the Memorial;

'(7) That a letter should be written to Mr J.M. Reid, informing him of the Committee's desire that he should take Mr Clark Kerr's place in the hospice.'

During his time as Chaplain in St Andrew's Clark Kerr kept a hand written daily diary of events which he faithfully maintained until his departure from the country on the 8th November, 1948. The diary not only describes in vivid detail the events of each day it also provides a frank self-assessment of his spiritual and mental well-being as the stress of living on his own in a "war zone" took its toll. He was not totally isolated, however. The Church was still open for those who wished to worship on Sundays and he continued to provide pastoral support when necessary and when safe to do so. Furthermore throughout this time he developed and nurtured the close relationship with John and Mary Reid and family all of whom would go on to play a significant role in the story of the Memorial.

The following brief excerpts from the diary provide a forceful illustration of Clark Kerr's day-to-day life and innermost thoughts over this period:

'*Wednesday, 8th September* – Today I enter the 23rd week of my solitary confinement at the Hospice. It is difficult to assess its effect upon me. I feel a great mental fatigue and spiritual deadness and am weighed down by an awful feeling that the morale and spiritual emptiness and powerlessness of the Christian church and world is being more clearly revealed from week to week. The thing that saddens me is that I do not feel challenged by such a thought but rather enervated and weakened.

Friday, 10ᵗʰ September – Mr Reid tells me that the Arab League have declared their intention of fighting it out to the last man. So we may have full-scale war very soon again. Luckily our building here has been missed by the heavy stuff flying about though more bullets have come in through the Church windows and brought the plaster down.

Monday, 13ᵗʰ September – My desire to get away is always very strong on a day like this and I began to wonder what I shall do if I cannot get the assurances from the Jews of Mr Reid's demand for a guard. Tonight I feel I would just like to turn the key and go.

Wednesday, 15ᵗʰ September – I got back to the Hospice without incident to find Mr Reid waiting and after tea came the news that the guard had been refused by the Military Governor which seems to make my arrangement with Mr Reid impossible so we have come to a dead end there. I must wait now for a final reply from the Home Committee.

Thursday, 16ᵗʰ September – The building here was hit many times with the shooting during the night.

Friday, 17ᵗʰ September – We had another great battle last night during which the whole city rocked, this house shook, Bonnie (Clark Kerr's dog) ran from place to place and I played the loudest gramophone records I possessed.

Saturday, 18ᵗʰ September – These ought to be days of deep thought and great creation but I seem incapable of either. Nothing seems real.

Monday, 20ᵗʰ September – I have decided to make this a scrapbook as well as a diary and to put in such cuttings of pictures and illustrate it and so make the record as complete as possible. As a story of inner development however it does not get very far. One feels so morally and spiritually dead and negative reactions of dislike and distaste seem to come more easily than love and interest and helpfulness and yet I so much want to gather up all the powers of my soul to help others and give them courage and affection.

Tuesday, 21ˢᵗ September – U.N.O. has put Palestine in the forefront of its programme and seem anxious

to come to a quick solution, so that is encouraging. Meanwhile the Jews are pressing on with their own programme for Jerusalem, clearing Christians from whole areas and filling up the houses with their own people. There has been a shooting match in Talbeih and Mount Zion has been noisy.

Wednesday, 22nd September – Last night after I got to bed there was a series of violent explosions and glass began to fall and furniture to topple over. I did not get up as I thought that bombs were bursting nearby but soon I began to see the glare of flames and thought the Hospice was on fire. When I looked out however I saw that a whole area near the Jaffa Gate was burning and the Old City was weirdly illuminated by the fires. I think an ammunition dump must have gone up.

Thursday, 23rd September – Shelling and shooting continues here as I write. I heard today that the big explosion last night was at poor old "St Andrew's House (Fast hotel)".★ It has been looted twice, burned twice and now blown up and is the second St Andrew's House in Jerusalem to go down into rubble.

★ (Ex "Huts and Canteens'" Soldiers' Hostel)

Tuesday, 28th September – We had one of the narrowest escapes of the war this evening. Mrs Reid came as usual to sit in while I went to pay some visits. I got back at dusk as usual and she left. I had just got back into the house when there was a loud explosion that shook the building. I soon realised that a mortar must have fallen in the direction that Mrs Reid had gone. I rushed out to see where she was and met her coming back looking very quite shaken. Sure enough a mortar had exploded only a few yards from her and she had small cuts on her wrist and knee. It looked as if a fragment of shrapnel had gone into her wrist but she was all right otherwise. I quickly put plaster over the cuts and realised she must get home to get attention and to keep the family from worrying so we set off together through the dusk. The bombardment started up while we were on the way and three shells exploded quite near and we were forced to crouch behind trucks on the railway line. I took her beyond the power station and watched her on the way to her own house then turned back towards the shelling expecting any moment to be blown to pieces. However after much dodging I got back safely. There have been very many explosions and I sit here worrying as to how Mrs Reid is. I'm afraid we cannot risk her coming alone any more along that way.

I am wondering if there will be definite instructions from the Home Committee this week for I really would like to be on my way.

Wednesday, 29th September – We had another fiendish night with shelling, sirens wailing three times and the house shaking from explosions. I hurried through the cleaning and called on the Reids shortly after 9.30. Mrs Reid looked very white and shaken and the splinters have not been removed though the doctor had given her an anti-tetanus injection.

Thursday, 30th September – Mrs Reid got her shrapnel splinters removed today for which I am very glad indeed. Psalms are chosen and the sermon is ready for Sunday but I am afraid that the congregation will be small for the mortars have increased considerably in the last few days making the journey more dangerous.

Sunday, 3rd October – A new development today was that congregations have now to be "escorted" to Church. I suppose that this is because of Arab infiltration in the area or the danger from increased mortaring. The escort today was a young giant of a Jew from Egypt who had attended the English Mission College in Cairo and who was a member of Scripture Union so he asked if he might come to the Service for which of course I was very pleased.

A high-ranking Haganah group went through the garden at dusk and I was afraid they might start up a burst of shooting but so far this has been one of the quietest nights for months.

Wednesday, 6th October – I have had another slight fit of exhaustion, not so serious as some of the previous ones but making me feel fairly tired. The worst of this present way of living is that it encourages one to think of one's own feelings and emotions all the time. The day has been unusually calm and still though now at dusk shooting is starting in every direction. I have tried to work off my lazy feelings, sweeping out the upper floors of the house, nailing back the three ply fanlight on the front door (which had been blown in again) and finishing the mangling. I was glad to see that there was practically no more interior damage in the building since the last time I was around though there are very many more scars on the outside walls.

Thursday, 7th October – No letters, no papers, no visitors, no surprises today! But perhaps I ought not to think of the things I have not had but to think of the things I have had. I was up very early and got all the household chores over quickly. I got the Manse cleaned up. Every time a bomb goes off nearby plaster falls from the roof and from the bullet holes in the walls all over everything but now it is habitable and usable again.

Monday, 11th October – There is a test blackout on tonight and a wild cold storm blowing. The city is still as death with no shooting at all. I have been round pulling blinds and shutters. I'm feeling very lost and depressed.

Tuesday, 12th October – I collected four letters from Mrs Reid, one from Miss Robinson at Haifa, one from Ireland, one from Mother still bewailing my silence and the most important from the Home Committee at last. Evidently Mr Adeney had been in touch with them. They want me to leave without delay – to make some arrangement if I can but anyhow to get out at once – no successor to be appointed. Suddenly everything has become full of meaning again. Bonnie looks at me sadly, questioningly as if she knows I was planning desertion and the thought of leaving Church and people at this point hurts terribly. But I feel I must comply for all this is beginning to affect me mentally and spiritually. How strange is the way that God has led me!

Friday, 15th October - Another tired and depressing day. I did a few hours work on the expository Times in the morning with a Sermon subject in view but I did not get anywhere. I feel the need of thunderous Sermons on great themes but have to content myself with simple talks because more than half my present congregation don't know English and the rest are too strained, tired and depressed to cope with theological abstractions. But I must get away from the "Don't worry, have Faith in God" theme.

Saturday, 16th October – There has been severe fighting all day today on Mount Zion. I have been watching bombs and shells exploding and buildings crumbling and as I write the whole hill seems to be in flames. So are the "Holy Places" cared for and respected today in Jerusalem. I made rough notes for a Sermon on "Fiery Trials" though if the present shooting continues I'm afraid there will be no congregation tomorrow.

Sunday, 17th October - The day has been full and reasonably satisfying. I was glad to be able to start it at all for the fighting was furious all night, the house shuddered with shell blasts and doors and windows flew open. The (three ply) fanlight over the front door blew out for the fourth time and all sleep was impossible. The congregation was quite good and I was delighted to see two seats of U.N.O. men there. I preached on "Fiery Ordeal" – not very original or profound but reasonably apposite and interesting.

Tuesday, 19th October – Still the noisy battle rages around. When coming back from "visitation" a shell burst over my head and I had to duck. Mrs Reid was hurrying away in panic as I got near the Manse and we both had to shelter for some time before a quiet spell came along and she was able to go on. A shell has just struck the house as I have been writing but I dare not go and see how great the damage is as another may come any moment. The situation gets worse and worse from hour to hour.

The strain of the fighting is telling on the people. Everyone looks tired and weary and longing for some real peace. When and how will this all end? There seems to be no light and no solution. Try as one will one cannot help being saddened, weakened and depressed by events. Oh Lord, how long, how long?

Wednesday, 20th October – Today came the news that the Military Governor had worked out an arrangement for the security of the Hospice that would allow me to get away. They are to recruit a civil guard to stay here with Mr Reid and are ready to go ahead at once. So now that my going seems to be a real possibility I am back at the main struggle with my own conscience. I hate the idea of leaving when the people of the Community need me more than ever and when the U.N.O. men are beginning to show an interest in the Church.

Thursday, 21st October – Mr Adeney arrived for tea. I saw the letter written by Alex King to him re myself the gist being that I had disregarded repeated orders to come home and in general I am being rather difficult and over conscientious.

Saturday, 23rd October – It is strange to think that tomorrow may be my last or second last Sermon here.

The day has been hot and unusually quiet but shelling began again at Sundown and I was driven in from the garden by a tremendous salvo of shells that fell all around.

Wednesday, 27th October – Life has been rather a toilsome business today for in addition to all the ordinary chores I seem to have been poking into all the plumbing. The system is in a shocking state, taps and washers and baths are rusted so with the water coming on there are leaks everywhere so that I have had to wipe flooded floors and try to stop leaks. I was shot at twice when I went to inspect the bathrooms on the top floor. I stood for half an hour making some pancakes for tea but when carrying the tea things through I dropped the tray in the passage and was left with nothing but a heap of broken crockery, mixed up with jam, milk, tea and crushed pancakes – a real tragedy.

Thursday, 28th October - I got the news today that the guard has now been appointed to begin duty next Monday. Now, at last it looks as if I can leave after all after the service on Sunday. I feel stunned now that going is a real possibility and how I shall get everything ready tomorrow and Saturday. I cannot think and yet I shall be glad once I am on my way for I feel that I cannot cope with this existence very much longer. A battle is going on now and this never ceasing shooting and bombing becomes unbearable

Friday, 29th October – Met with Mr Reid and we went over the stores, etc., in the Hospice and discussed arrangements for the "transfer of authority". I went off down the Colony to see the "guard" who is to come here and also pay my respects to the Military Governor.

It is strange to look back on these last years in Jerusalem. The Huts side of things have given me much worry and pain and a great sense of inadequacy. I cannot think of anyone among the British staff who tried to show sympathy and understanding. The Church was cold at first but slowly thawed and filled and the young folks especially showed me friendship. I realise however that I do not now attract and make friendships easily indeed I seem to shy off from them and thus repel advances. And yet I hate this emotional isolationism and long for affection, understanding and friendship. Soon I shall have to begin a new chapter. Will it be a good, successful and happy one or has the period of decline really begun? Just now I feel flat and empty, as if there was no more achievement in me but I know that that is a temporary feeling which I shall surely get over.

I feel that I am going leaving nothing but debris and chaos; that all my work has resulted in nothing and that even my going has hurt and disillusioned those who have looked to me in the present crisis. It is all very humbling.

Saturday, 30th October – I have not been able to keep the tears back today as I have gone about doing many of my duties for the last time and I stood for a long time looking over the city as the sun went down. It wrenches my heart to go just now though, of course, I ought to be glad to go. These poor people so depressed and sad, the whole future so obscure it is terrible to leave but it seems I must go.

Sunday, 31st October – It is impossible to put into words the tears and heartbreaks of today's parting. I was up very early after a noisy night and quickly and very sadly went over the household routine again that I have so often hated. I gathered the few remaining belongings I was taking and realised with horror that I finally had seven pieces of baggage but it was now too late for jettisoning. Mr Reid arrived and I handed over keys, etc., and soon the congregation were arriving. The service was a failure from start to finish. I had begun with "Come let us to the Lord our God" at Mr Reid's request but few know "Kilmarnock" and it went badly. We also sung "Aberystwyth" which went worse still. The sermon was spoiled because I was disconcerted by a group of giggling flappers ogling American soldiers. I had a hard struggle to control myself at my farewell talk and afterwards everybody seemed to be in tears. It was not what I did for them personally, that was all too little, but I was a symbol of the world church and a link with a saner, kinder world and so, as some of them said, they felt they had lost their last friends.'

At this point Clark Kerr moved out of the Hospice to take up residence in the Y.M.C.A. for what he thought would be a few days while he got his passport renewed and the permit to leave the country. On Monday the 1st November he wrote in his diary 'I could not sleep all night thinking of Mr Reid alone at the Hospice. It was a terrible night of shooting and bombardment and I thought of Bonnie not having me to run to in her fear. I never imagined that I should feel so badly about all this.'

Finally with all his papers in order and ready to travel to Haifa in preparation for sailing to Cyprus he records his last view of the Memorial on the 6th November 'Loud explosions shaking Abu Tor as usual and I looked sadly at St Andrew's standing proud and alone on her devastated battlefield.'

Following his departure from Palestine Clark Kerr returned to Scotland via Cyprus and attended the Committee's meeting on the 26th November, 1948. 'The Convener referred to the letter dated Famagusta, Cyprus, 12th November, from the Rev. Clark Kerr, in which he stated that he had been able to make an arrangement whereby Mr J.M. Reid had relieved him of the charge of the buildings in Jerusalem and had taken up his residence in the Hospice on the 31st October. The Jewish Military Authorities had consented to allow him the use of a civilian guard to assist in the protection of the property. Mr Kerr had agreed that Mr Reid and the guard should each be remunerated at the rate of £30 per month plus food from the store in the Hospice. Mr Kerr had then left Jerusalem and after visits to inspect Church of Scotland property in Haifa and Galilee he had left Palestine for Cyprus. From there he had returned to Great Britain, and the Convener now welcomed him in the name of the Committee, and expressed to him its gratitude for the invaluable services he had rendered, especially during the last troubled months after the withdrawal of the British Authorities from Jerusalem. The Committee had felt proud of him for the courage and enterprise he had shown in remaining at his post, in spite of hardship and danger, and congratulated him on the success of his efforts to protect St Andrew's Church and Hospice. Mr Clark Kerr then spoke. He recapitulated shortly his experiences in Jerusalem after the departure of the British as stated more fully in his correspondence. He explained that one of his difficulties was caused by the failure of letters and cablegrams to reach him so that he was largely ignorant of what the Committee planned to do. In the end he had been obliged to leave, much against his will, by the discovery that five months of living for the most part in complete isolation, combined with the tension of his position between the firing lines of Jews and Arabs, had begun to affect his mental health. He paid tribute to members of the Christian remnant in Jerusalem, and especially to Mr and Mrs Reid, whose devotion to the Church and Hospice had been beyond praise. He referred in particular to the wounds sustained by Mrs Reid on the last occasion when she had visited the Hospice to take his place for a few hours in which he was enabled to visit the Christians in the city. Speaking of the arrangement made for the continued protection of the building he stated that the emoluments agreed upon were reasonable in view of the high cost of everything in Jerusalem. Amplifying the statement in his letter he explained that the emoluments to Mr Reid and the guard could be paid out of balances held in Jerusalem. Mr Reid was also to draw his food supply from the stores in the hospice gratis, but the guard was to be charged eight shillings a day for the same privilege. Mr Clark Kerr's view was that the present arrangement would secure the Hospice for the next three months, but that, since the Reid family planned to leave Palestine, the Committee should consider what was to be done after Mr Reid had left. Mr Kerr himself strongly urged the appointment of a Minister, not only to secure the building, but also to take pastoral care of the mixed community of Christians, numbering about five-hundred, who still remained in that part of Jerusalem, and had no Minister of the church to care for them.'

The man described formally in the diary and elsewhere as Mr Reid is John Reid from Forfarshire in Scotland. In 1921 he travelled to Jerusalem to join the Palestine Police Force. There he married Mary Georgian in 1937 in St Andrew's Church. Their three children, Melville, Mary and Katherine were each baptised in St Andrew's.

Given the risk of the property being commandeered John Reid decided that the only effective way to undertake the role of caretaker was to move into the premises leaving Mary and the children at home in their house in Upper Bakaa, some distance from the Hospice. A decision he took despite the fact that his health was deteriorating with the onset of Muscular Dystrophy. With the Church and Hospice situated in "no man's land" and a prominent target all too clearly visible to the Jordanian troops positioned behind the parapets of the Old City wall around

Mount Zion the dangers were all too obvious. Mr Reid writes to the Committee on the 3rd December, 1948, noting that he is being protected by a young armed guard 'provided by the Jews at a cost of £30 per month, which is expensive but impossible to get the service for less.' Without explanation by the Authorities this protection was terminated four months later. With its strategic position the land surrounding the Church and Hospice was also an ideal vantage point for the Haganah to mount attacks on the Jordanian forces in the Old City. The key to protecting the buildings was to ensure that there was no military presence in the area and John Reid, an ex-Chief Superintendant of the Palestine Police Force, with his long experience of dealing with delicate situations was well able to achieve this. His daughter, Mary, notes his use of 'diplomatic forcefulness when he met anyone on the premises and informed them that they were trespassing on private Church property!'

There is no doubt that with his twenty-five years of experience in the Police Force John Reid would not have been unaware of the real dangers he faced when he made his lonely rounds of the Church and Hospice grounds. This was made very clear to him when he heard of the fate of a former colleague, an ex- Police Inspector, who had taken on a similar job in St John's Ophthalmic Hospital not more than one-hundred yards from St Andrew's who was murdered and his body dumped in the Hospital well.

But these dangers were not just confined to Mr Reid. Living in the Hospice was far from comfortable with the windows shot out and no heating. The resupply of food and fuel had its own challenges and dangers. To overcome this problem Mrs Reid began to take supplies from home to the Hospice, a journey she knew very well having undertaken the same for Clark Kerr until she was injured. To avoid snipers these trips were made at night along the narrow back roads and through the railway station. On many occasions, to relieve their mother, these journeys were undertaken by the Reid children.

For four months the Reids maintained their dangerous vigil of the property until the arrival of the Rev. Scott Morrison in February 1949. In June that year Scott Morrison reported to the Committee that 'St Andrew's Church and Hospice has been well preserved through the care given to it by the Rev. Clark Kerr until November 1948 and by Mr John Reid, Treasurer of the Kirk Session, since that time. The glass and stone work of the Church have been damaged and birds have been coming into the building and liming hymn books and furnishings. Just recently I have arranged for a glazier to put in plain glass where the holes are large enough for birds to enter. Damp is showing along the three arches, suggesting that the rocking of the building during the bombardment has caused cracks on the roof. One corner of the mason work at the north-eastern gable is in a precarious condition, and must be repaired as soon as labour is available. One north balcony of the Hospice has been severely damaged.'

It took some time but three years later in acknowledging John Reid's commitment to ensuring the security of the property, despite the many dangers to himself and Mary Reid, in December 1951 the Committee approved wholeheartedly the Convener's wish 'to have the devoted services of Mr and Mrs Reid reported to the British Authorities in Palestine with the purpose of having them recognised by the King.' The result of this initiative was the awarding in 1953 of the M.B.E. to Mr Reid for 'remaining alone in the hour of danger and crisis and arranging for worship to be held in the Church every Sunday.'

John and Mary Reid and family

On the 25th September, 1955, the Congregation paid tribute to the Reid family on the completion of Mary Reid's appointment as Lady Warden:

'In demitting her office as Lady Warden it is only right and proper to lay on record the faithful and zealous manner in which Mrs Reid has served the Scots Memorial. This is all the more praiseworthy when one bears in mind the fact that her years of service have been marked by acute economical labour, political and civil problems, and difficulties of the first magnitude. The fabric of the Memorial suffered much damage and it is mainly due to her initiative and ingenuity that the building's exterior and interior are in such a good, serviceable condition today.

'Also, I am in honour bound to say that, humanly speaking, the Church of Scotland is in possession of the Memorial and its contents today thanks to the Rev. Clark Kerr and Mr Reid who, after the Chaplain withdrew, remained alone in the hour of danger and crisis and every Sunday arranged for worship to be held in the Church. For this he was awarded by the late King George the M.B.E., but he would be the very first to acknowledge how much he is indebted to his wife for this decoration as she, at the risk of her life, nobly attended to his physical needs.

'Nor must we forget Melville, Mary and Katherine – now, I am glad to say, full communicant members of the Congregation – for the innumerable ways in which they have served Church and Hospice.

'To Mr and Mrs Reid we all owe this debt of gratitude for all that they have done for the Lord and his church. Their presence will always be welcome in St Andrew's which is so dear and sacred to them and us.'

The establishment of the April 1949 Israel Jordan Armistice Demarcation Line did not halt the conflict. The situation remained tense and from time to time erupted in gunfire and sniping across the Hinnom Valley towards the Church and Hospice and elsewhere in "West" Jerusalem.

This uneasy truce continued for eighteen years until the 5th June, 1967, after a period of increasing tension in the region, the "Six-Day War" broke out. Early in the morning of that date Jerusalem experienced an increasing exchange of machine gun fire which quickly escalated to the Jordanian use of mortar and heavy artillery. Bill Gardiner Scott, the Minister in St Andrew's at the time, reported that the Church and the Hospice had been damaged by shellfire but that 'all were in good heart in Jerusalem.' The Committee recorded the situation in its Minutes in these few words. However the 1968 Report to the General Assembly provides a fuller version of events:

'The Rev. W. Gardiner Scott and his family were in personal danger during the bombardment of Jerusalem. Situated on the hill facing Mount Zion, and within easy range of the Jordanian batteries, St Andrew's Church and Hospice could hardly escape. One direct hit by shellfire on the south wall of the Church, and much shrapnel and damage from bullets scarred the buildings. Fortunately, none of our people were injured. Jerusalem itself suffered gravely and many died. Yet the Minister reports that he is now able to go freely into the Old City to visit the members whom he could only visit by special permit twice a year before the war. He also reports that his Congregation has been giving generously to the relief of the poor in distress, especially those who have been separated from their families by the new frontier.

'St Andrew's, Jerusalem, is recognised by Government circles in Israel and by the Mayor of Jerusalem as a centre of Christian leadership and co-operation. When the Lord Provost of Edinburgh was the guest of the Mayor of Jerusalem last year the Mayor visited him at St Andrew's Church.

'A restoration fund for St Andrew's Jerusalem was instituted shortly after the war and the friends of the Church and Hospice have given generously for its renovation, not only to repair war damage, but to cure the wear and tear of years. Mr Scott answers the question, "What in the World?" by saying that the whole world comes to Jerusalem where the people pray for the peace of Jerusalem and for the peace of all mankind for the promised day when the beam which shines from Zion's Hill shall lighten every land.'

Bill and Darinka's daughter, Tanya, provides a dramatic account of her experience as an eight-year-old living in the Hospice at the outbreak of the "Six-Day-War" [14]:

'"Where were you in 1967?" you asked me. My parents and I lived in West Jerusalem, at St Andrew's Hospice, where my father was the Church of Scotland minister and ran the thirty bed hostel for guests. It overlooked the Old City and Mount Zion, with only the Hinnom Valley separating us from what was then mostly Jordanian territory. So when the firing began on June 5, we were right on the front line. In fact, the Israelis had asked my father if they could use the Church as a lookout post, but he had refused, reminding them that it was a holy place.

'"What was it like for you? You must have been scared," you said. I started to answer – and suddenly, to my horror, I was back in Jerusalem in my eight-year old body, hearing that funny click and then the air raid sirens, running to the room with no windows to which my father had told me to go, clutching the first aid box with its cold metal edges as if it were my mother's hand.

'There were others at the Hospice, but my father was at the supermarket, my mother at language school, and I was alone inside, determined not to show my fear and clutching that damned box for dear life.

'I hope nobody will be hurt – I don't know what I'll do if there is blood. I wonder how we'll all fit in here. What will we eat?

'And then reloading – suddenly – where's the noise? The silence yawned like a bottomless pit. The minutes were eternity.

'This noise HURTS! It doesn't matter that I couldn't see – I could hear. The bullets whining, shells bursting, the tinkle and sudden crash of broken glass falling one hundred feet and the shudder of the building as a mortar penetrated half of its outer wall. The older girl cried a bit – she was fine – her mother, our housekeeper was with her. We had been at school together that morning, and my father had brought us home and then gone shopping for food, just in case.

'Suddenly my father came bursting in, shopping bags, unbelievably, still in hand, with a story about forcing the manager to let him leave the supermarket, driving as far as he could before the Israeli Army stopped him, and then using his training in the Black Watch (an elite Scottish Regiment) to dash from door-to-door on his way through the bullets. He says he was in one door way and decided that if a clergyman died with beer bottles in his bags it wouldn't look good... He left his beer. Hoping *somebody* had a free drink!

'"Any word of your mother?" He asked. My guts clenched with icy passion. Mother – I need you – and I bulldoze that thought as it started to erect itself in my heart.

'All right, father – and we went into the small room with no windows next door, while the others stayed in the room he'd secured with mattresses over the windows and a protective cliff outside.

'We were crouching by the phone and calling the number of the language school. When there was an answer my father started to shout, and I wished I could shut up the shooting so he could hear. The noise was deafening. I'll just sit here and maybe – "HERE, honey, say hello to your mother."

'"I love you." BANG. CRASH... RAT TAT TAT – faster than the words of love could blot out, my mother's voice drowned by the cacophony outside. My father, trying not to cry, me trying not to cry, knowing that she was under a table talking to us while the phone line held. BANG. CRASH. "That was your end this time. I love you. See you soon." And the line went dead. Shot down.

'My father opened the door to the next room and said "I'm going to feed you all now." Then he ducked and dodged to the kitchen and boiled a chicken he bought so we had fresh food between the now ten of us in there. Oh, we had things to do. We had a fiddle, and a recorder and, most important of all, a radio. Blankets. Candles – candles that I'd made him buy even when he didn't think we'd have a war. And I STILL can't keep down sardines and tomato sauce to this day.

'BANG. CRASH. Twenty minutes later by someone's watch. BANG. CRASH. Time had stopped and the only sounds were silence and the barrage. How long? Well, we still had water and food, and we sat there grimly trying to talk and sing and listen to the radio. Mustn't let the side down. Must support my father. Mustn't think of mother. Sleep. And then suddenly I sat bolt upright on the mattress the other girl and I were sharing – the glass was crashing. The old Armenian caretaker was shaking my father saying, "Make it stop! Make it STOP! MAKE IT STOP!"

'Well, yes, I can talk about it. I'm here, two decades and more later, a college professor continents away. Not the ghosts my mother's family in Serbia thought we were when we showed up four years later unannounced. Solid. Flesh and unspilt blood.

'So why, when you asked me so gently if I was scared, did I run to my room clutching the congealed fear like a metal box, close the door and go into MY windowless room and not be able to stop crying? The medicines I had used then were useless now; the wounds were open, bleeding, the tears unsobbed back then, and I rocked and cried, wept and cried, screamed and cried. CRIED. CRIED.CRIED, and finally slept.'

Clark Kerr and John and Mary Reid showed astonishing selfless devotion at a critical time of great danger, and the Gardiner Scott family continued this wonderful tradition in the later war. Without them it is questionable whether the Memorial buildings would have survived as they are today. In the years which followed the region suffered from continuing conflict both local and international; the inter-communal violence of two Intifadas and the continuing strife in Gaza; the 1973 "Yom Kippur" War; two "Gulf Wars" and the sporadic hostility between Lebanon and Israel, particularly the 2006 "Lebanon War." While the properties were not under direct threat as in 1948 and 1967, the Church and Hospice, with others, continued to "form islets" of faith and hope in the midst of "a savage scene."

──── CHAPTER TEN ────
Epilogue

THE OUTCOME of the Six Day War in 1967 dramatically changed the geopolitical situation in the region. Israel conquered the Palestinian Territories of Gaza and the West Bank, previously occupied by Egypt and Jordan respectively, and has maintained control of them since. The boundaries are generally regarded by the international community as being defined by the Green Line, the 1949 armistice lines established between Israel and its Arab neighbours in the aftermath of the 1948 Israeli War of Independence. The Green Line effectively divides Jerusalem in half with the Israel–Jordan border running through the middle of the city with the Old City on the Jordanian side of the Line, "East" Jerusalem, and the Scots Memorial on the other, within "West" Jerusalem.

The opportunity to travel more freely came as a result of Israel's occupation of the Palestinian Territories and created new opportunities for the ministry of St Andrew's Church and Hospice. In time the occupation also raised new concerns in respect of the effect of the occupation on the Palestinian communities. Whereas in the past it was difficult to travel between the two areas of the divided city, with the occupation and the removal of the physical partition such problems were eradicated and Ministers and Staff of the Church and Hospice could engage more freely with the communities, predominantly Christian and Muslim, not just in Jerusalem but in the Territories at large. Through the 70's and 80's and the work of Bill Gardiner Scott and the Ministers who followed him advances were made in cementing ties and developing relationships with indigenous Churches and organisations involved with the welfare of the people of Palestine.

Through time and as Israel began to exert its control and occupation of the Territories inevitable tensions arose resulting increasingly in open conflict in the streets. To enforce its position even more, Israel began its process of building settlements within the Occupied Territories having first removed people off their land. The rising tensions came to a head in December 1987 following incidents at Jabaliya Refugee Camp in northern Gaza which sparked the First Intifada (Uprising) which spread throughout the West Bank and continued until 1993. Strict controls on the movement of people within the West Bank and Gaza and between these areas and Israel were put in place.

St Andrew's Church and Hospice was not immune from the deteriorating situation within the West Bank. The establishment of the checkpoints and the need for passes to travel from Bethlehem to Jerusalem meant that it was not always possible for the Arab Christian members of the Congregation to attend Sunday services or the staff from Bethlehem to get to work in the Hospice. While that remains the situation for the Church members unfortunately the need to ensure an adequate daily level of staffing meant that the Hospice could no longer depend on staff from Bethlehem and they were released from their employment. Seeing no end to the developing situation many Palestinians, particularly those from the Christian communities, began to emigrate. The indigenous Churches came under growing pressure in trying to deal with the matter, exploring peaceful means to stop the violence and seeking justice for those displaced and endangered by the occupation.

When the Rev. Colin Morton arrived in July 1988 to take up his post as Minister at St Andrew's the First Intifada was well underway. At an early stage in his ministry it was very clear to Colin that to understand more fully and address the difficulties Palestinians were facing required the Church of Scotland to have much closer ties with the indigenous churches and the many local community organisations working in the areas. One outcome of that proposal was the establishment of a formal written partnership between the Church of Scotland and the "Episcopal Church in Jerusalem and the Middle East". Later, during the ministry of the Rev. George Shand, a similar partnership was entered in to in 1910 with the "Evangelical Lutheran Church in Jordan and the Holy Land." – the same Church which hosted the Church of Scotland's first ministry in the Holy Land in March 1923 with Norman Maclean and Ninian Hill.

These partnership arrangements were a significant development for the ministry of the Church of Scotland in the Holy Land. By working alongside its Partners the Church achieved a deeper insight into the issues facing the local Churches and their associated organisations. This was and is a practical, working arrangement including opportunities for sharing ministry and resources. With a greater understanding of the issues facing the people of Palestine and Israel the witness of the Church of Scotland was not only enhanced locally, it also provided a firmer footing in Scotland in advocating a just peace for all people in the region.

During Colin's ministry links with many groups and organisations working in issues of human rights and the promotion of peace and justice were developed and strengthened and continue to this day, for example, with:

- Dar Al Kalima College of the Evangelical Lutheran Church; an ecumenical institution serving the Palestinian community in Bethlehem with an emphasis on children, youth and women.

- Israel Committee Against House Demolitions (ICHAD).

- Sindyanna of Galilee; a women led Arab-Jewish cooperative supporting and financially empowering Arab communities in northern Israel.

- Al-Shurooq School for Blind Children in Bethlehem.

- Rabbis for Human Rights; working in partnership to provide support for the Bedouin communities in the Negev and the Jordan Valley.

- Wi'am, Palestinian Conflict Resolution and Transformation Centre; based in Bethlehem, providing a service for women and children and seeking to educate the local community on human equality and basic rights.

During this period a major project was initiated by Carol Morton, Colin's wife, drawing on her Fair Trade experience in Scotland. While travelling around the West Bank, including visits to Gaza, Carol and Colin were very much made aware of the plight of marginalised groups of women and disabled people and families attempting to survive financially often with their menfolk killed, in prison or incapacitated in one way or another. It was noted that due to their circumstances a number of women's groups had developed, their object being to create crafts and other products which could be sold with the profits shared as a means of family income. Modelled on Traidcraft in the UK Carol established "Craftaid" initially operating out of a small room in the Hospice. It was an outlet for crafts and goods from these self-help groups which have difficulty in finding other markets. Importantly, the project was also educational, raising awareness of guests and customers to the realities of life in the Occupied Territories. Prior to returning to Scotland Carol created "Sunbula" the successor to "Craftaid" which remains to date operating from the Guesthouse. On their return to Scotland in 1997 Carol continued her support for the self-help groups through the establishment of "Palcrafts" in Edinburgh as a Scottish charitable body, with "Hadeel" as the retail outlet for the goods from Palestine.

After a long period of illness, Colin died in June 2011. At his Thanksgiving Service in Edinburgh the Rev. Clarence Musgrave said of Colin's ministry, 'It was his absolute conviction that God's love was not limited to one person, one group, one tribe, one nation, or adherents of one religion. God's love embraced all, and because of that, we also had to embrace all. So, throughout his ministry in Jerusalem, two words were like guiding beacons – Justice, from which flowed a recognition of the Humanity of everyone. Justice and Humanity – to love God was to love all his creatures – be they Christian, Jewish or Muslim.'

Colin was instrumental in developing the strong link between the Church of Scotland and the Sabeel Liberation Theology Centre established in East Jerusalem by the Rev. Canon Na'im Ateek of the Episcopal Church. There is no doubt that Colin did much to shape the current direction of the Church of Scotland's ministry in the Middle East. This was acknowledged by Na'im Ateek who, at Colin's Memorial Service in Jerusalem, noted that he had, 'shaped and educated the understanding of the Church of Scotland of the issues here, the problems local people and the Christian community are facing, and where the Church should stand in terms of its care for everyone.'

This ministry of the Church's 'care for everyone' has been reflected through the years with the General Assembly's consistent support of efforts for a just and peaceful end to the Israeli occupation of the Occupied Territories, as well as recognising the rights of both Israelis and Palestinians to a secure and peaceful future.

The Rev. Clarence Musgrave arrived in 2000 to continue the ministry at St Andrew's now well established in its partnerships with the local Churches and their related community organisations. Clarence established the Congregation's relationship with the Muslim village of Jayyous in the north of the West Bank supporting income generating projects for women, which included the development of a crèche thereby enabling women to go out to work to provide an income for their families. He also considered it vital that whatever work was being undertaken in Israel and Palestine in its name, the Church of Scotland and its members had to "own" it and be part of it. To Clarence it was fundamental that if the ministry from St Andrew's Church was to have maximum effect it must include the involvement of Church members in Scotland. Together with his wife, Joan, Clarence set about organising and guiding pilgrim groups from Scotland on a regular basis. The purpose was not just to visit the familiar sites associated with the Bible but also to meet and spend time with the communities which live in the Holy Land. In providing group participants the opportunity of first hand engagement with the people of the land the intention was that the experience and new understanding gained would be shared more widely on their return to Scotland. Even after Clarence retired and left Jerusalem in 2006 he continued, with Joan, in this ministry of taking groups from Scotland to the Holy Land until his death in 2014 following a short period of ill health.

Involvement was integral to Clarence's ministry and he worked hard to encourage the wider Church's participation in Israel and the Occupied Territories through the financial support and Volunteer involvement in the "Ecumenical Accompaniment Programme in Palestine and Israel" (EAPPI), an organisation of the World Council of Churches. The Volunteer ecumenical accompaniers provide protective presence to vulnerable communities by monitoring and reporting human rights abuses and support Palestinians and Israelis working together for peace.

From 1967 the Hospice, now called St Andrew's Guesthouse, continued in its ministry of hospitality within the overarching ministry of the St Andrew's Minister and Congregation. Through the years, with constant use and the need to keep in tune with the latest regulations and safety standards this resource of the Church found itself constantly requiring funding for maintenance and upgrading. In the mid-1990's additional bedrooms were added to cope with the growing numbers wishing accommodation while in Jerusalem. The Church continues its policy of ensuring no discrimination in the staffing of the Hospice. Staff, be they Christian, Muslim or Jew, are today drawn locally from within Jerusalem, East or West. One significant difference today is that the Warden, now the Manager, is no longer recruited from Scotland to oversee the work of the Guesthouse. This post is now appointed locally, the first being Mr Rimon Toubassi from East Jerusalem.

This staffing arrangement within the Hospice goes some way in resolving an issue which has been a problem for the Church and Hospice from their beginning. With Committee members, Ministers and Staff from Scotland being replaced every three to five years, sometimes even less, often with little handover, how is it possible to maintain a level of continuity in the work so that established policies effectively continue and wheels are not re-invented? Today this concern for ensuring a high degree of continuity within St Andrew's Church and Hospice, and indeed, in Tabeetha School in Jaffa and the Scots Hotel in Tiberias, has been addressed by the decision to locate the Church's Middle East Secretary in Israel.

Prior to this and since the 1950's St Andrew's Church and Hospice was greatly blessed by the presence in the Congregation of Rizek Abusharr and his wife, Alice, and were an invaluable support to all who came from Scotland to take up their responsibilities in the Church and Hospice. Their service was enhanced by Rizek's appointment as Session Clerk in 1976 and Presbytery Clerk in 1977, positions held until 2006. From their years of experience Rizek and Alice were very much aware of how important it was to ensure that the new Minister was properly introduced not only to the Charge but also the local Church Leadership. Similarly for new Hospice Staff, Rizek ensured that they had the necessary "local knowledge" to enable them to fulfil the ministry of the Hospice. Rizek was appointed the local Director of the Jerusalem International Y.M.C.A. in 1975 and continued in that position until he retired as the Director General in 2001 after having served the Y.M.C.A. for fifty years. Through this connection the Church and Hospice were able to maintain and develop its long standing relationship with the Y.M.C.A.

The Church of Scotland in Jerusalem and Tiberias is in the unique position of being the only UK-based Church in Israel and Palestine of the reformed tradition which has buildings and a history predating the State of Israel. As a consequence as well as reaching out beyond the walls of the Church to the communities at large the ministry has a pastoral role for Christians of this tradition visiting the region for longer or shorter periods. From its opening in 1930 the international make up of the Congregation has been a mark of the service and witness of St Andrew's in Jerusalem, with some visitors attracting a little more attention than others. On Sunday the 11th March, 1979, the Rev. Tom Houston led the service of worship with the U.S. President Jimmy Carter and the First Lady in the congregation. Rizek recalls that he had the opportunity of greeting them and showing them to their seats. 'President Carter said he did not want to sit in the front row, so I led them to a row behind. As I handed him the Bible I noticed that by chance I had chosen for him the seat which had on it the name "Cairo." As it happened the purpose of his visit to the Middle East was to explore the options for peace in the region and as part of that process he was travelling to Cairo the next day.' (The Jerusalem Post's report on President Carter's visit to St Andrew's can be read in Appendix [6]).

———————————————————————

The need for maintaining a level of continuity does not mean that there is a responsibility to doggedly stick to the *status quo*. One notable change was made in the early 21st Century. "Hospice" has recently become associated with places where dedicated staff care for terminally ill patients, rather than the earlier meaning of a lodging for travellers. It was therefore decided that the name should be changed to St Andrew's Church and Guesthouse. The Rev George Shand, Minister at St Andrew's Church from 2009 to 2014, provides two further examples of how the Congregation must endeavour to seek new ways of expressing its ministry in the region:

'The building speaks eloquently of the past. Its role as a 'Memorial' Church is written into every wall of the building through memorial plaques for the First and Second World Wars, and for the Palestinian Police. But there is nothing that suggests a forward looking and engaged congregation worships there.

'I decided there was an opportunity to introduce a piece of artwork in the Apse area, which would speak to today's work and world. We commissioned a Palestinian artist from the Lutheran College in Bethlehem – Faten Nastas – to come forward with a design which reflected our priorities today, and also was based on 'the burning bush' – the symbol in the Church of Scotland logo. Faten's design was brought to life by a Bethlehem project working with people with learning disabilities, part of the international L'Arche community. This project works with felted sheep wool, and created the hanging now in the Apse - a 'burning bush' on the rear wall, and hanging over the Communion Table further representations of the flames of the bush in the shape of the Cross.

'The design is particularly powerful because of its contrast with its surroundings. Within a solid, stone building, the installation is suspended on wire, and moves gentle in any breeze. It gives a sense of being alive, and also speaks of vulnerability. This reflects the work of today's church in its support for vulnerable humanity here in this region of much conflict – the vulnerability of people of all backgrounds, and particularly of those who seek to build community and peace in the midst of conflict.

'The flames which make up the Cross can also represent God's spirit at work here.'

In the same vein, George and the Congregation were concerned with how the space surrounding the Memorial buildings can be used to declare its ministry within Jerusalem, an international city and the spiritual home for people of many different faiths:

'Jerusalem is a city which bears the imprint of many different cultures and faiths, yet today there are still groups which make exclusive claims. The result is that different faith groups find it very difficult to live and work together in harmony.

'The hill on which St. Andrew's is built has been in use for millennia. In front of our church building there are important Jewish graves which date back to the 7th Century, BC; at the entrance gate of the property are the foundations of a Byzantine period church; and close to the Guesthouse garden is a Watchtower dating back to the Ottoman period. Jewish, Christian and Muslim influences on the same site – a microcosm of Jerusalem.

'We aim to treasure that diversity, which is why we built the Peace Garden behind the church. The plants in the garden reflect the seven species, important in Jewish scriptures (and therefore Christian) and in Islamic tradition – the wheat, barley, grape vine, fig, pomegranate, olive, and date. Alongside this we planted a number of local herbs with medicinal value – 'God's pharmacy'. The design and installation of the Peace Garden was the work of a young Muslim garden designer, Jessica Yasmin Barhum.

'There are further plans to develop a walkway down to the lower garden, with stopping off points for reflection, so that the whole of this back area can be, amidst the hustle and the bustle and the division, a place of pilgrimage for those who value diversity and peace.'

The Church of Scotland has, through time, evolved a ministry in the Middle East, particularly in Israel and Palestine, which is unique for a UK-based church. The diverse nature of that ministry is important for the Church's work both in the Holy Land and in Scotland and the key roles played by Tabeetha School in Jaffa and the Scots hotel in Tiberias are integral.

Over the last forty years particularly, the development of the Church's ministry, reaching out to communities and developing and creating working partnerships with churches and organisations in the region, to a considerable extent exists today as a result of the foundations laid down by successive Ministers and Staff based in the Memorial buildings of St Andrew's Church and Hospice. To appreciate the Church's ministry today is to acknowledge a vital part the Memorial has played in its development. It is also important to recognise its pivotal role as the ministry continues to evolve.

A key question is what would the Church of Scotland's role or position in the Middle East be today if there was no Memorial for it to work out of? Would the Church have the same ministry or impact it has today, with an authentic and legitimate voice in the affairs of the region, without the physical presence of St Andrew's Scots Memorial? For over eighty years the Church and Guesthouse have been the centre from which a long line of Ministers and Staff have witnessed their faith and developed a unique ministry for the Holy Land. There can be no denying that today's Church of Scotland has inherited a remarkable asset through which it has been able to expand its work and voice in the region. It is a resource made possible through the dedicated service and commitment of many – the vision and skill of Clifford Holliday, the Architect of its distinct and acclaimed design; the huge contribution made by Mrs Isobel MacRae both in managing the wide ranging funding appeal and in setting the Hospice on to a profit-making basis soon after its opening; De Farro, the Contractor in generously accepting delayed payment for his work thereby saving the organising Committee's enormous embarrassment; the many Chaplains and Ministers who set out to engage with the challenges of this new and unique Charge, to Clark Kerr and John and Mary Reid who through their actions saved the property for the Church; and the Committees, in Edinburgh and Jerusalem, which, through the most trying of situations, saw the task through to a successful completion. The list could continue.

However it is to one man that the Church must owe the greatest debt of gratitude. From that motion on the 12th December, 1917, without Ninian Hill's stubborn determination and persistence in pressing forward when the target kept receding from his grasp, and his injection of considerable personal funds, his dream would never have been achieved. At the outset he could not have imagined that through his perseverance he was making provision for a practical and invaluable resource for the work and witness of his beloved Church of Scotland in a Middle East totally different from that in his lifetime. To quote Ninian Hill's obituary by his friend Dr. Norman Maclean printed in the Scotsman, 'all this has flowed from Ninian's motion, though he dreamed not of it – which shows that the ordering of life is in other Hands than ours.'

―――― CHAPTER ELEVEN ――――

The Society of Friends of St Andrew's, Jerusalem

THE MEMORIAL Committee met in Edinburgh on the 8th December, 1955, during which it considered 'ways and means of arousing interest in the Memorial and securing support for it. Mention was made of the possibilities amongst Scots' communities abroad, Scottish Regiments and other units of the Armed Forces, Rotary Clubs, of a "Friends of St Andrew's Jerusalem Society."'

The proposal was pursued and the Committee finally approved the Society's Constitution in October 1956 with its inaugural meeting taking place in the Martin Hall of New College, Edinburgh, on the 29th May, 1957. The Objects of the Society as set out in its Constitution are described:

'1. To co-operate with the Committee on the Scots Memorial, Jerusalem, in exercising a constant care for St Andrew's Church and Hospice, Jerusalem, a National Memorial to Scots who gave their lives in the Holy Land and in the Middle East generally in the two World Wars and during the Mandate. This involves helping to maintain the Church as a centre of Protestant worship and religious life in Jerusalem, and the Hospice as a centre for visitors and pilgrims; and also studying means whereby both can be used to their fullest value.

'2. To maintain the interest of those Scots at home who have at one time or another visited Jerusalem, and to arouse the interest of others by informing them of the work, purpose and potentialities of the Church and Hospice. To suggest and operate means of publicity to this end; and to keep constant touch with the Minister and Warden in Jerusalem, and encourage them in their work.

'3. To pray for the peace of Jerusalem.'

Membership was 'open to all who profess an interest in the objects of the Society. Associate membership shall be open to Congregations,

Congregational organisations and other groups.' Subscriptions were set at '5/- for ordinary members; 2/6d for husband, wife or child of ordinary members; 2/6d for junior members under 15 years of age and £1 for each group of associate members; ordinary life membership fee £5 [£110].

The Constitution of the time also noted that "All money received by the Society shall be handed over to the Treasurer who, after meeting the Society's expenses, shall make an annual contribution to the Committee on the Scots Memorial, Jerusalem, to be applied for the Committee's work in Jerusalem.'

Membership of the Society grew quickly from one-hundred and ninety members in 1957 to over nine-hundred in 1961. Even with this number the Committee at the time was concerned that new members were not joining and launched a membership campaign. From that period membership has fluctuated around six-hundred.

Since its inauguration the Society has raised and supported the work of St Andrew's Church and Hospice in raising funds for a variety of purposes, for example: £1,800 [£29,000] for carrying out repairs to the property arising from damage inflicted during the Six Day War in 1967; £25,000 [£68,000] for the purchase of the church organ in 1986; £150,000 [£240,000] towards the overall cost of over £400,000 for the Hospice Bedroom Extension project in the 1990's. In addition the Society has been able to assist on an annual basis with the provision of grants to enable the staff to undertake ongoing refurbishment of the fabric and amenities of the Church and Hospice, including providing various items of equipment.

The Society also provides financial support for the work of the Minister and Congregation in their outreach to local groups and organisations which they relate to in their ministry in the wider community. Very often these projects appear quite basic yet are vital to the beneficiary. These might range from helping a struggling new childcare project with no resources except voluntary input by buying a fridge for the group so that children's lunches could be kept fresh, to assisting an embroidery project in a local community centre, assisting summer school activities in villages in the West Bank, or in a Bedouin school, or helping a project working with people with learning disabilities to run their annual Christmas party, or helping a family who have fallen on very hard times by paying their electric or water bills.

A major programme of the Society is the provision of annual scholarships to Students and bursaries for Church of Scotland Ministers to enable study in the Holy Land using the Church and Guesthouse as their base. In doing so the Society goes some way towards meeting the unfulfilled vision for the Memorial - the establishment of a "Scots College", a recognised place of study in the Holy Land for divinity students from Scotland.

The Society reminds its Members and their guests of its historic link with the Memorial through its annual St Andrew's Day service of worship marking the day in 1930 when the Memorial was consecrated. Traditionally, the service takes place in St Cuthbert's Parish Church in Edinburgh where Ninian Hill and Dr. Norman Maclean were Ministers. The Society also provides financial support to the Memorial for its own celebration of St Andrew's Day in Jerusalem.

Working today alongside the Church of Scotland's World Mission Council, the body responsible for the Memorial and its ministry, the Society operates with a Constitution updated to ensure that its objectives and organisation are relevant. In this way it maintains an effective support of the Church and Hospice in their continuing work and ministry.

A key task of the Society today is 'to maintain the interest of those who have visited the Church and Guesthouse, and, in cooperation with the World Mission Council, to actively encourage the interest of others by informing them of the purpose, work and potential of the Church and Guesthouse.'

It may be that having read this story of the early years of the Memorial and of its life and work today, as an individual or as a member of a congregation or associated organisation you may be inspired to know more about the Society or you may wish to become a member. For more information please contact:

The Membership Secretary,
c/o The World Mission Council,
The Church of Scotland,
121 George Street,
Edinburgh EH2 4YN

email: partnership.world@cofscotland.org.uk

—— APPENDICES ——

—— APPENDIX ONE ——

Mrs Alice Todd Osborne

MRS ALICE Todd Osborne, a formidable lady from Glasgow had taken upon herself a passionate interest in the welfare of ordinary servicemen and women. Her story is best summed up in the obituary printed in the Glasgow Herald on the 20th April, 1926:

'Soldiers' Friend
Glasgow Lady's Work for the Garrisons

A notable Glasgow lady with a splendid record to the men of the fighting forces over a long period has passed away in the person of Mrs Alice Todd Osborne, founder and honorary superintendent of the Mission to the Mediterranean Garrisons. She died at Cairo yesterday and was buried with semi-military colours. Mrs Osborne, who had reached her eighty-fourth year, was proud to be known as "The soldiers' Friend". It was a title worthily earned. No one has done more in the interests of the welfare of the British soldier in various parts of the world than the venerable lady whose death has now taken place. For over half a century she has laboured incessantly to better the lot of the soldier, and the best monument to her work is to be found in the various institutions devoted to military uses. One agency will always be devoted to her name – the Mission to Mediterranean Garrisons, of which she was the founder. Mrs Todd Osborne belonged to a military family and it was her early environment that caused her to devote her life to the care of the soldier. She had felt what Kipling had put into heart–searching verse – that Tommy was a hero when the guns began to speak but that he was apt to be neglected when there was no fighting to be done. Her work had its genesis in a visit paid to the Gallowgate Barracks, Glasgow, in 1870. A soldier had remarked that if there was a Soldiers' Home he would never visit the canteen. 'I walked home from the barracks that night' Mrs Todd Osborne was wont to say 'and I prayed God to give me a Soldiers' Home.' Her prayer was answered, and through the kindness of a generous-hearted donor a Home was opened in July, 1876. Then she turned her attention to Maryhill Barracks (in Glasgow) and the second Home was opened there in December of the same year.

'Then came a call from Gibraltar she could not resist. When the Cameron Highlanders were transferred there in 1879, a cordial invitation came there from the Rock Garrison to Mrs Todd Osborne to pay a visit. When she went out in 1882, that gallant soldier, Lord Napier of Magdala, took a keen personal interest in her work, and gave her every help and encouragement. As a result of that visit a Soldiers' and Sailors' Home was established, and to meet the growing needs, it was subsequently extended. With a larger vision ever before her, and confident that the way would be opened up, Mrs Todd Osborne began a new venture in South Spain, a work that has been fruitful of much good. Then followed the old Macedonian call from the Eastern Mediterranean, 'come over and help us.' Ever charitable in her outlook, Mrs Todd Osborne declared as late as 1909 that Cairo was just what it was, unspeakably evil. Writing in 1897 a soldier said – 'I have read in the Bible of Sodom, but I think that Cairo is worse'. The challenge was quickly accepted. A home was opened there in the following year, but the accommodation was inadequate. A notorious gambling-house which had been suppressed by the Egyptian Government came into the market, and through Mrs Todd Osborne's eloquent and touching appeal at the Keswick Convention the money for its purchase was forthcoming. The Home was opened as the Russel Soldiers' Home in 1900, and there followed King George's Home in Abassia and Lord Kitchener's Home in Alexandria. But home interests were not neglected while the work was proceeding abroad. In 1896 the Cameron and Seaforth Highlanders' Home was opened in Inverness and the Wauchope and Black Watch Home at Perth in 1903.

'A home in Jerusalem.

'During the war Mrs Todd Osborne undertook ten journeys through the Mediterranean prosecuting her devoted labours. When Palestine was freed from the bondage of the Turks, her dearest wish was to establish a Home in the heart of Christianity, in memory of those who died and as an institution for the men who volunteered to take their places. A site was granted on the road to Bethlehem, near the Barracks, and the Jerusalem Home is now an accomplished fact. Mrs Todd Osborne, who was mentioned by General Allenby in his dispatches for devotion to duty, kept in constant personal touch with the stations that owe their existence to her. She was tireless in her devotion to what constituted her life's work, and vigourous in body, she made numerous voyages to help and inspire her workers. She had a gracious personality that endeared her to all with whom she came in contact, and work for her became a pleasure. Of Mrs Todd Osborne it may be said she lived to render service to others, and that her Christian labours were blessed even beyond her asking. The soldier will mourn the passing of one who was in the fullest sense of the word a friend.'

—— APPENDIX TWO ——
Ketef Hinnom

GABRIEL Barkay is one of Israel's most prominent archaeologists and describes the beginning of the exploration:

'I've lived in Jerusalem for more than 59 years. I sometimes feel I can put myself in the shoes (or minds) of ancient Jerusalem-ites. I think I can tell better than most where these ancient Jerusalem-ites would have located different facilities.

'I came to Ketef Hinnom in the early 1970's looking for evidence of these ancients, such as quarries, farms, orchards, military encampments, burials, roads, forts – even cultic activity that took place outside the city.

'Ketef Hinnom is located just opposite the Old City – to the south-west, across the Hinnom Valley from Mount Zion. When I began collecting potsherds and looking for terrain features, I found evidence of human activity over thousands of years. In each period, the inhabitants had cleared away the remains and looted the treasures of their predecessors.' [15]

At one time the area was part of the Upper City of ancient Jerusalem. A simplified timeline provides an overview of the significant historical events unearthed over the area:

Between 700 BC and 500 AD: the "Ketef Hinnom" caves were hewn from solid rock and used as tombs for wealthy Jerusalem families.

Between 100 BC and 100 AD: the hill of Ketef Hinnom was used as a quarry from which Herod took stone for rebuilding the Temple in the City. The tombs continued to be used as mortuaries.

Between 100 AD and 300 AD: Ketef Hinnom functioned as a cremation burial area for the 10th Roman Legion.

Between 500 AD and 600 AD: the construction and destruction of a Byzantine church.

A fortified watchtower was built on the site and used to guard the southern approach to Jerusalem. Excavations of the tower indicated that

Turkish troops had been stationed there until 1917 and an adjacent cave had been used for storing arms and ammunition.

Immediately to the east of the large entrance gate leading up from the main road to the Church and Guesthouse lie the remains of a previously unknown large Byzantine church. There is very little evidence of the stone outer walls as it would appear that the site had been turned into a "quarry" during the Ottoman period with the cut stone being used for other purposes, including the building of the nearby watchtower. Despite that, the plan of the church has been identified and during exploration pieces of superb mosaic tile work which had decorated the floor were discovered:

'One particularly beautiful mosaic fragment depicts a partridge pecking at a bunch of grapes, surrounded by vine tendrils and vine leaves. The hindquarters of a ram can also be glimpsed. Also of special interest were dozens of marble stone tiles in different colours cut in various shapes and sizes: rectangles, triangles, circles, squares, floral designs and even tooth shapes. These pieces once formed part of luxurious decorated floors adorned with inlaid designs, a flooring technique called opus sectile. Coloured glass tesserae, many of which were gilt, represented the remains of vibrant mosaics that had once decorated the walls of the church. And below the church's narthex the plastered walls of three graves were painted with depictions of metal crosses inlaid with coloured, semiprecious stones.' [15]

Gabriel Barkay has identified the church as "The Church of St George Outside the Walls" maintaining that this is the church mentioned in literary accounts of the Persian invasion of Christian Jerusalem in 614 AD, where Christian Clergy were massacred and the church destroyed. Prior to this it was one of a number of churches situated along the pilgrim road between Jerusalem and Bethlehem.

The network of burial caves, immediately to the east and below the level of the Memorial front courtyard, provided a mass of artefacts dating from 700 BC. Although they had been desecrated and looted in ancient times the caves revealed many items which had been overlooked by the raiders. However one burial chamber within one of the caves had remained unopened with its contents untouched. With over one-thousand artefacts belonging to at least ninety-five individuals the find was described as an archaeologist's dream. It proved to be a veritable treasure trove of jewellery, the largest collection ever found in Jerusalem, and included more than one-hundred silver and gold objects of very fine quality and artistry.

The stars of the find, however, were two tiny amulets. When found they were rolled up like small scrolls with a hole down the middle through which a necklace could be threaded. Both were of very thin almost pure silver and after specialised treatment they were each rolled out to expose lines of writing. One measured 97mm x 27mm, the other was smaller. The writing was minute, measuring between 1.7mm to 5mm and lightly scratched onto the silver. Using fibre-optic and other modern technology the texts were eventually revealed and translated.

The larger amulet contained traces of the first two blessings of the tripartite priestly blessing from the Book of Numbers (Ch. 6 vv 24 to 26):
'The Lord bless you and keep you.
The Lord make His face to shine
upon you and be gracious unto you.'

The smaller amulet had the trace of the third blessing:
'The Lord lift up his countenance
upon you, and give you peace.'

In addition, the large amulet contained a variation of the verse in Deuteronomy (Ch. 7 v 9):
'Know, therefore, that only the Lord your God is God, the steadfast God who keeps his covenant faithfully to the thousandth generation of those who love Him and keep His commandments.'

With a series of further tests using latest technology it has been asserted that the silver amulets date back to the late 700 BC, to the time of the Prophet Jeremiah. The earliest Biblical texts among the Dead Sea Scrolls date to about 250 BC. That means that the Ketef Hinnom texts are older than the next oldest Biblical texts by nearly four-hundred years and are the oldest composition of words recognisable as Biblical verses in existence.

—— APPENDIX THREE ——
Memorial Construction Costs

THE FOLLOWING is an extract from the Final Account drawn up by the Clerk of Works, Captain Pearcey, and agreed by Messrs De Farro and the various Sub-Contractors.

GENERAL WORKS

No	Description	1930 Amount £PA	2014 mount £Stg
1	Excavation	330.00	18,270.00
2	Filling	98.00	5,426.00
3	Water Proofing	643.00	35,599.00
4	Mass concrete	1,875.00	103,808.00
5	Reinforced concrete	2,479.00	137,248.00
6	Masonry	7,160.00	396,408.00
7	Brickwork	522.00	28,900.00
8	Plastering	1,183.00	65,946.00
9	Metal Work	1,105.00	61,178.00
10	Electrical Installation	624.00	34,547.00
11	Drainage and Water Supply	538.00	29,786.00
12	Tiling and Skirting	696.00	38,534.00
13	Terrazo and Cement Floors	390.00	21,592.00
14	Marble Work	146.00	8,083.00
15	Artificial Stone	298.00	16,499.00
16	Glazing	118.00	6,533.00
17	Painting and Decorating	239.00	13,232.00
18	Church Fittings	103.00	5,702.00
19	Miscellaneous	76.00	4,207.00
20	Stone balast	295.00	16,332.00
		18,918.00	1,047,830.00

SUB-CONTRACTORS

No	Description			1930 Amount £PA	2014 mount £Stg
21	Central Heating	945.00	52,319.00		
22	Joiner & Carpenter	721.00	39,918.00		
23	Roller Shutters	68.00	3,767.00		
24	Ceramic Tiles	165.00	9,135.00		
25	Sanitary Fittings	140.00	7,715.00		
26	Windows & Ironmongery	206.00	11,405.00		
27	Iron Lectern	18.00	997.00		
28	Sky Light	13.00	720.00	2,276.00	125,976.00
	Construction Costs			21,194.00	1,173,806.00
	ARCHITECT'S FEES			2,235.00	123,740.00

CLERK OF WORKS' FEE	987.00	54,645.00
PURCHASE OF LAND & ASSOCIATED COSTS	3,851.00	213,208.00
	28,267.00	1,565,399.00

To arrive at the total cost of the Memorial buildings should be added, for example, the cost of all the hard and soft furniture for the Hospice or the chairs for the Church manufactured by the "CMJ Industrial Workshop". In addition the costs do not include any management or sundry expenditure incurred by the Committees in Edinburgh or Jerusalem.

It would be fanciful to imagine that the Memorial could be built today on its current site or anywhere else in Israel or Palestine for £1.56m. This calculation simply compares the value of currency in 1930 against its value today taking inflationary factors into account and ignores market forces.

—— APPENDIX FOUR ——

Style and Sustainable Design Overview

Building Design Style and Details Generally – Chen Barnett

Chen Barnett, born in Israel, is a graduate of the Camera Obscura Art School in Tel Aviv and has a B.A., magna cum laude, in the History of Art from the Hebrew University, Jerusalem. As part of her advanced studies in the department she researched 19th century Anglican churches in Jerusalem and has continued to investigate other churches in Israel. Chen selected to focus on St Andrew's Church for her Master Degree in Historical Geography at the Hebrew University, and also sometimes guides at St. Andrew's as part of the Jerusalem "Open House" project. Chen is married and a mother of 4.

As a result of her research into St Andrew's Church Chen has provided a report of which the following is an extract. The fully annotated and illustrated report will be posted on the St Andrew's Church Blog.

Overall Style

Unlike the Ottoman regime which not only encouraged modernisation in Palestine and its surroundings and had no problem ruining property despite its historic value, the British Mandate came with a completely different set of values. This attitude was due mainly to Ronald Storrs, the Governor of Jerusalem. Storrs managed to bridge the gap between the British imperial colonial intentions and his unique love of the Holy city which enabled him to keep that which existed and in renewing what was necessary to look authentic. Nothing revolutionary would be acceptable. He felt it was his job to preserve the Holy City as a precious gift and was responsible for maintaining and preserving its historic and aesthetic values. Storr's vision, together with the people he brought to work with him, held a combination of romantic fascination with the traditional lifestyle of the local population and the beauty of the local scenery, even if leaving it all "natural" or "traditional" was at a cost to the local inhabitants who wanted to move ahead and develop comfortable modern living.

Jerusalem of the 19th century was full of "recycled" styles brought over from foreign countries. The different states trying to gain power in the Holy Land not only built in their local style from home, but in revived historical styles, which were very fashionable in the 19th century, for example, Augusta Victoria built by the Germans in mediaeval Romanesque, the Russian Compound in Jerusalem looking like a little Moscow, and St George's Cathedral, built by the British missionaries in a Gothic revival style looking like a small college in Oxford or Cambridge.

For Storrs and the Pro-Jerusalem Society the fascination of Jerusalem was that for them it seemed as if it had not changed for centuries, the land of the Bible. They wanted to believe that this is what Palestine looked like in the days of Christ and they were prepared to invest much effort in keeping it "authentic" and preserve its "beautiful treasures". During this period British architects in the Colonies developed a new approach to architecture referred to as "Regional Colonialism", integrating local elements of building into the foreign style brought from abroad. This style is evident in the British Government buildings in New Delhi and the colonies in Africa. In Palestine this style is noticeable in two iconic British Mandate period buildings, Government House and the Rockefeller Museum, both designed by Austen St. Barbe Harrison

Dr Ron Fuchs is a senior lecturer in art history at Haifa University and has written extensively on colonial architecture in Palestine. For him the Church of Scotland's Memorial buildings create an impressive structure with the Apse "growing" out of the natural rock with the rigid geometric elements of the buildings contrasting vividly with the natural shapes of the hilly landscape – more apparent when originally built than today when the buildings are enclosed by trees and later developments. Reminders of the local arched shapes are evident in the large windows, the opening below the stairway to the Church and on the Terrace of the Hospice. More "local reminders" are the half dome of the Apse and the full dome above the Church crossing.

Internal Space

In his detailed letter of 1928 to the architect, Ninian Hill is concerned to provide Holliday with the sources of his inspiration as to how the buildings should look when completed. Hill favours the "early Christian and Byzantine" style and mentions elements from churches in

Rome as examples. He is not inspired by "Norman" or "Gothic" styles both common in Scotland and England.

A major source of inspiration for Hill was the Roman Catholic Westminster Cathedral. Opened in 1903 it was built in a unique Neo-Byzantine style – impressive externally and very authentic to the style internally. He notes the Apse in Santa Sabina in Rome, in addition to Westminster Cathedral, being covered with vertical marble white slabs with delicate dark veins and, in the Cathedral, green marble with white veins. According to his correspondence, Hill intended to cover the walls of the Apse with textured marble similar to Santa Sabina but with white marble with green or "reddish" veins from Aberdeen.

Westminster Cathedral has horizontal rows of decorative marble separating the Apse from the internal face of the semi-dome. In both Westminster Cathedral and Santa Sabina the Apse is covered with coloured mosaic scenes or decoration, with hints of gold, as in traditional Byzantine art. The decorative marble and the mosaic to the Apse were elements which Hill wished included in the design of the interior of the church, all in one colour, gold. The cost of undertaking this work proved to be beyond the resources of the Committee. The stone wall to the Apse was later covered with a golden silk velour drape personally funded by Hill.

Hill's plans for the Transept of the Church, including the number and measurements of the steps leading to the Communion Table were very precise and modelled on the design at Westminster Cathedral. Simplicity and symmetry were the objectives in Hill's design.

Windows

With the passage of time it was thought that the unique coloured windows to the Church were made in the workshops set up by Storrs and Ashbee, among them the glass workshops in Hebron. In this current research documents were found, letters and quotations, proving correspondence between Ninian Hill and Dr. Douglas Strachan and his brother, Alexander, two Scottish brothers who were leading figures in the art of stained glass at that time. The Strachan Brothers had designed the stained glass windows in many Scottish Churches, and most important, a large set of windows in the Scottish National War Memorial in Edinburgh Castle initially built to commemorate the deaths of Scots of the World War 1. There is also a letter from Holliday to Hill from 1929 requesting the windows to be designed by those who designed the windows of the National Memorial. Of the brothers Douglas was more well known but according to the documents it is clear that Alexander was also involved in the design and planning as well as the business side:

Letter dated the 17th July, 1929, to Ninian Hill from Douglas Strachan, Lasswade, Midlothian:

'Dear Mr Ninian Hill,

'I shall be very pleased to see you here any time and to advise you to the best of my ability regarding the treatment of the windows in the Chapel in Jerusalem.

'I was greatly impressed by some of the stained glass I saw in the mosques in Cairo (I don't recollect seeing any in Jerusalem). I don't mean the rather footling "Cairo glass" (domestic work) that one sees in the museums and elsewhere in this country: but really <u>monumental</u> stained glass of the first ranks: yet evolves on almost purely geometric patterns. Something of <u>that type</u> would seem to be the right treatment for your Windows but you would have to see to it that the colour arrangement and quality are good – else having practically nothing but colour to give it meaning, the effect might be awful.

Yours sincerely, Douglas Strachan.

Letter dated the 25th July, 1929, to Ninian Hill from Alexander Strachan:

'Dear Sir

'My brother, Douglas Strachan, called yesterday evening with the architectural drawings of the Scottish Churches' Memorial in Jerusalem and explained to me the type of glass he had suggested might be used for the windows at the St Andrew's Church.

'I am working on the colour schemes meantime but before preparing the estimates I should be glad if you could call and see the different qualities and textures of glasses, which might be used.

Yours faithfully, Alexander Strachan.'

Letter of the 30th July, 1929, to Ninian Hill from Alexander Strachan:

'Dear Mr Hill,

'I have much pleasure in sending you herewith my colour scheme suggestions, for glasswork in cement, for the West Window and North and South transept Windows, and my design for the eight Clerestory lights above the Church.

'As you will noticed I have prepared three different arrangements for the transept Windows for your selection,-viz; there's A, B and C, and if desired two of these designs may be used, i.e.' one window to design A or B and the other to designs C. My price to any of these designs will be the same – £45 Stg. for each transept window. The glass to be chiefly in Norman Slabs, with a little Antique glass used as a foil to give a change of texture.

'The West window (Design D) also in Norman Slabs and Antiques will be £18 Stg.

'My price for making eight clerestory lights in leaded glass to design E or F will be £50 Stg, the glass to be Norman Slabs, Antiques and 5" and 6" Roundels.

'It might, I think, be advisable to use extra wide leads for the Clerestory Windows to be more in keeping with the cement astragals of the other windows and I suggest that 3/8" should be used for the roundels and ½" width for lead elsewhere.

'A summary of the above is:

'2 Transept Windows at £45 each	£90
'1 West Window	£18
'8 Clerestory Windows in leaded glass	£50
	Total £158

'The above prices are FOB Edinburgh and include for packing and supply of cases or boxes, which are not returnable.

'According to my calculations the measurements of the Windows are:

'2 Transept Windows each 14 feet high by 8 feet wide.

'West Window 8 feet in diameter

'8 Clerestory Windows each 4'2" by 2 feet

'During our conversation this afternoon you mentioned that the architect could supply me with a full-sized drawing of these Windows, and also a section of the cement astragals showing the depth of checks.

'I have endeavoured to keep my prices as low as possible and trust that you may find them acceptable, as I am keenly interested in the whole scheme, and should like very much to be associated with it.

Yours faithfully, Alexander Strachan.

Letter of the 1st August, 1929, to Ninian Hill from Douglas Strachan:

'Dear Mr Hill

'It was a pleasure to be able to assist you in any way with the glazing of the Church at Jerusalem: and I am glad that you are satisfied with the results as shown in my brother's colour drawing. He brought it out to show me before sending it to you and save for one or two slight alterations which I suggested; it seemed to me that it ought to produce an interesting effect in glass.

'You can rely on it producing a still finer effect when seen in position: and my brother has an excellent "glass sense" – by which I mean a kind of instinctive sense in the grouping of the glass tones and textures that go to produce a jewel like quality – as compared with the flat tinted effect that results when the sense is absent.

Yours sincerely, Douglas Strachan.

It must be mentioned though, that despite all this correspondence no actual plans or drawings have been discovered. Apart from the correspondence there is no definitive proof that the work designed and quoted for was carried out and that these are Strachan windows. However there is no evidence to suggest that they are not the work of the Strachan Brothers.

There are two arch shaped windows on each side of the nave, and one perfectly round window high up on the West wall of the Church. All have stone latticework in geometric shapes - squares, circles, and elements dividing the squares such as rhombuses or internal stone cross and X shaped lattice lines. Most of the colouring is shades of blue, with the odd single red or green square shining like a ruby or an emerald. The glass softens the internal light giving it a diffused atmosphere as in the historic medieval use of stained glass in Cathedrals. Douglas described his brother as having "a kind of instinctive sense in the grouping of the glass tones and textures that go to produce a jewel like quality ". One nave window has a definite shape of a cross made of white roundels fitting into the design. The other one more of a free form, and the round rear window has a short-armed cross in it, perhaps representing the Greek Orthodox cross. The white roundels, appearing scattered in the large windows, are set into order in the set of 8 Clerestory Lights. In softer light one can see they have green centres and blue background outside the white circles.

Many models can be accounted for being the inspiration for either Hill instructing or the Strachan brothers bringing their own thoughts to the process. One potential source could be "Église Notre-Dame du Raincy", built in 1922-1923 in the outskirts Paris. Designed by another set of brothers, the French architects Auguste and Gustave Perret, it is an excellent example of an attempt at "pouring" Christian spirituality into modern architecture - not just modern design and forms but also using contemporary techniques and materials. There was excitement in the challenge of building the clean-lines of a modern church from reinforced concrete, a post industrial revolutionary material which was also cheaper than masonry. The stained glass windows for the church, a unique pioneering use of simple geometrical forms in the traditional Christian related art of stained glass, were built by Marguerite Huré. As an artist working alongside others, including the Perret brothers, she set out to find modernist and contemporary ways of portraying the Christian faith in the design of new churches. This model of "Notre-Dame du Raincy" as a modern form of church building began to be copied in a few places, and one can clearly see the resemblance in the windows of St. Andrew's Church.

Armenian Ceramic Tiles

David O'Hannessian, the Armenian ceramic artist arrived in Palestine as a refugee from Haleb, Syria, after escaping from Turkey during the First World War. He was introduced to Governor Storrs of Jerusalem by his friend Sir Mark Sykes, who had hired O'Hannessian in 1912 to build a "Turkish Room" in his country house "Sledmere House" in Yorkshire. Sykes was a great traveller and inspired by the orient. Storrs and Ashby (his civic adviser) welcomed O'Hannessian in Palestine and integrated him in the "Arts and Crafts" style workshops run by the Pro-Jerusalem Society, specialising in local traditional arts. O'Hannessian was involved in building an entire "Armenian Pottery" workshop, where he and his team made many painted tiles and artefacts and even new tiles for the Dome of the Rock which required renewing.

In her M.A. thesis on David O'Hannessian, the founder of the Armenian Ceramic style in Jerusalem, Dr. Nirit Shalev-Khalifa, an art historian and researcher of visual culture in the Holy Land in the 20th century, notes that he was usually given the "traditional" elements to integrate into the structures designed by the local British architects, including Clifford Holliday. These elements would include the

Mechrab, prayer niche; Sebil, a local form of public drinking fountain and the Matstaba, low benches on the sides of an entrance to a building.

Clifford Holliday knew David O'Hannessian well through their common connection with Ronald Storrs and employed his skills particularly within the Hospice. The first piece of art one encounters on entering the Hospice are the two low benches, perhaps Mastabas, and above each is a niche, perhaps a Mechrab.

According to Shalev-Khalifa the low front part of the benches are boxed inside a thick floral framework with elements taken from the decorated tiles in the Rustem Pasha mosque in Istanbul, being one of the key monuments demonstrating the important Isnik pottery style at its best. Within the frame are three medallions with foliage elements creating a cross, while long serrated "saz" leaves and flowers float around them as if in a light wind, a design taken from benches in Topkapi Palace. The work is all in blue and green shades over a white background. The niche above is completely plain turquoise-blue, surrounded by an arch containing a border with a repetitive design of red, green and blue flowers, surrounding another repetitive design of flowers and squares of four small leaves flowing towards each other, also taken from a panel design in Rustem Pasha.

In the side entrance of the guesthouse and below the stairs leading to the Church there is an archway in which the entire inner wall is covered with turquoise-blue tiles. In the wall are three small vertical niches and one horizontal one in different heights, all with stylised pointed top edges. The inner wall is framed by a border of arabesque pattern. According to Shalev-Khalifa this entire work is inspired by the green covered tiles in the Sultan's tomb in Bursa, Turkey.

At the side of the veranda of the Hospice is another distinctive work. A fountain the lower part of which is a Sebil and the upper shaped in the form of a niche, containing yet another internal niche with tiles shaped as corbels, Mukarnas in Islamic architecture. The rest of the niche is decorated with a repetitive pattern of small lotus flowers bordered by two tulips and two other flowers. This design is identical, according to Shalev-Khalifa, to decoration on the main columns in the Rustem Pasha Mosque.

Shalev-Khalifa considers that with O'Hannessian's use of so many elements from Rustem Pasha it was an important source of inspiration for shapes, decoration and design which he then went on to incorporate in his creation of a new "local" style, firstly in the Dome of the Rock and later in all of his other works.

Bio-Climatic and Sustainable Design – Gil Peled

Gil Peled is an architect and founder of Eco-Challenges Sustainable Design and Consultancy. Born in Jerusalem and raised in Bonn and Vienna. Completed his architecture studies with distinction at the Robert Gordon University in Aberdeen specializing in sustainable and affordable housing. (MSc.) Experienced architect, urban planner and sustainability coordinator. Designed sustainable buildings and environments at micro and macro levels. Pioneered the first green retrofit of an existing building in the Holy Land. Has been involved in several public campaigns and initiatives for community gardens urban nature and architectural heritage. Presented his work internationally. Is currently researching World Heritage Sites.

The following are key extracts from an extensive report produced by architect Gil Peled in researching Clifford Holliday's application of contemporary bio-climatic and sustainable design in the buildings constructed in 1930. The full report will be published separately and a reference will be listed in the St Andrew's Church Blog.

Introduction:

The design of St. Andrew's Scots Memorial Church and Hospice includes both western and eastern architectural features. It is a fine example of the "fusion architecture" developed by British architects during the Mandate period in Palestine which they incorporated in their public buildings in Jerusalem, i.e., the Government House, the Rockefeller Museum, the City Hall, the Central Post Office and the YMCA, innovative technologies with local traditions. Of particular interest is how Holliday related to the local climatic and environmental conditions of the site.

Site Selection and Orientation:

In bioclimatic design, orientation of buildings aims to minimize penetration of solar heat in the summer while maximizing it in the winter and making best use of prevailing winds for ventilation. The Church is orientated on a SW-NE axis with its apse, similar to synagogues, facing the Temple Mount. The hospice is at a right angle to the Church and with a NW-SE axis with views to the Old City walls. Holliday was probably familiar with the merits of the eastern orientation of the building and its openings. These can be found in the nearby, previously built, Mishkanot Sha'ananim compound. The north easterly orientation of the Hospice enables warming up of night chilled spaces by the early morning sun, and its stepped elevation shelters it against the westerly sun and protects from the prevailing winds. In comparison the western elevation has less surface area and has been, to some extent, protected from the south west by the hill, the planted trees and the adjacent ex-Consulate building. Holliday succeeded in overlapping the spiritual and climatic orientations with the functional layout.

Layout:

The layout consists of three distinct elements: the Church, the Hospice and the Bell Tower. The Church and the Hospice are connected via a stairwell under the Bell Tower. Church and Hospice are grouped into an L shaped floor plan, creating a semi enclosed terrace-courtyard and a support structure for the Church. The main functions of the Hospice, i.e., central lounge, library and dining room, as well as most guest rooms, face Mt Zion and the Old City. Most spaces are accessed through the double height entrance hall, which, with the staircase, forms both the circulation and orientation hub of the Hospice as well as an essential component of its passive ventilation. The arrangement of functions creates a clear hierarchy of spaces, the public, the semi public and the private, typical of local Islamic architecture and culture. The emphasized Hospice entrance and entrance hall is one example, as well as the option to enter the building also through the front terrace.

Thermal comfort:

The building's envelope consists of its walls, floors and roofs. Together they form its thermal mass in which solar heat is stored during the day and radiated during the night. A building with thick masonry walls will have a high thermal mass that evens out the rate at which the walls and spaces heat up or cool down, thus eliminating the extreme fluctuations of outdoor temperatures and creating thermal comfort for its occupants indoors. In bioclimatic design, the aim is to balance between increasing the thermal mass storage capacity and heat resistance, while reducing heat losses through surface areas of walls and roofs exposed to the elements. Holliday seems to have achieved this balance with the solar heat stored mainly in the Church's south eastern and the Hospice's south western masonry walls. Over-heating in these walls is evened out due to their deviation from a southern orientation; they are cooled by morning eastern and afternoon western air flows and are partially shaded during the day. Interestingly, the walls of the Church and Hospice vary in width, from 30 to 40 cm around the Hospice and 50 up to 90 cm around the Church, the reason seems to be both structural and thermal. The roof areas are also a significant surface for absorbing and releasing heat, their shape and thermal resistance must be optimized to avoid the heating up of the spaces underneath them. Holliday adopted the local tradition of shaded terraces on the roofs which enables cooling the spaces underneath, and adding extra recreation spaces.

Holliday also incorporated a dome and vaults in the Church design. These increased the height of the space they cover and the release of warm air through the roof far above the heads of the visitors. The whitewashed domed roof acts as a reflective surface and due to its volume is always partially shaded from the sun. Any heat absorbed on its sunny side is released on its shaded side. Skilled use of materials and colours in the building's envelope can reduce heat gains and glare. Holliday created, on the front elevations of the Church and Hospice, self shading walls which reduce the glare from the reflective stone surface and provided for planting trees and vegetation around the area.

Ventilation, cooling and heating:

Holiday addressed the need for natural ventilation and lighting through placing shafts in the thick stone walls, up to 90 cm in width, in the ceiling and with openings in the apse and the large dome. The Church was designed with clever, yet discreet ventilation. It included passive sub floor ventilation and cooling (a system also used in traditional country houses in Britain) with air discharge through a double membrane dome. The Church was intended to be ventilated using the stack effect, and cooled through under-floor air ducts along its two long walls, bringing into the church fresh and cooled air from outside through iron grills in the floor. The air inlets are still visible from the outside under the apse, built above ground over the sloped terrain. The air was chilled while passing under the stone floor and along the foundation walls of the Church. The rising warm air in the Church sanctuary is discharged through the cupola opening in the inner membrane of the dome and out through windows on the outer dome membrane. This sub-floor system may have also been intended for heating; pipes in the ducts are visible, perhaps intended for pre-heating the air in winter. This ventilation system is significant considering that the Church windows cannot be opened and are solely for bringing in filtered light. It may have had some drawbacks, or was forgotten over time. The ducts have since been covered with carpets, perhaps to minimize outside noise and dust. Permanent radiators have been installed along the walls and movable electric fans are placed along them during the summer. This ventilation system could be reinstated and upgraded with new devices. For centuries, in this climatic region, domes were used in residential, public and religious buildings for ventilating and cooling spaces underneath them, yet constructing a dome over a new church was quite unusual. It has become a distinct architectural feature of the church and has proven to be effective for passive cooling.

In the Hospice cross ventilation on the ground and upper floors is created by placing NE and SW windows opposite each other, with direct lines of air passages. The public areas on the ground floor have high ceilings and at least two openings each, i.e. windows and openings above the doors. For example, the lounge room is shaded and cooled by the north east facing arcaded terrace, (now glazed in) and can be cross-ventilated through openings over the doors. A common practice in this region was to create, at ground level, air flow between front and back courtyards through the lounge space. Here the back courtyard is larger than the front terrace, air heats up quicker in the back yard and rises up, drawing in cool air from the terrace through the lounge, thus creating a steady cool breeze. For this to occur, the SW facing back door of the lounge, or window above it, needs to be opened.

The lounge was heated by an open fireplace with a closed chimney penetrating through the second and third floors, providing radiant heat to a cluster of rooms. An additional fireplace was used for heating the dining room and the rooms above it, both are no longer in use. All floors are ventilated through the entrance hall and stairwell. Over the entrance hall there is an octagonal opening penetrating through to the second and third floors with a fenestrated lantern window on the roof, which also lights up the entrance space with plenty of natural day light. It is possible that the lantern window could have been opened for natural ventilation, now it is sealed. Most Hospice rooms have, in addition to their main window, "Taka" windows. These are small openings at the upper part of a wall, usually above a main window. The "Taka" allows for light and air to enter while the main window is shut or screened against the heat. These small openings increase the speed of air movement and cross-ventilation, especially effective for night ventilation and cooling down of the spaces heated during the day. There are two kinds of "Taka" in the Hospice, the smaller ones are for ventilation and the larger ones also for light. In the original plans all wet rooms were directly ventilated to the outside. Since then, the renovated rooms have en suite facilities and some have individual air conditioning units. The lounge, library, kitchen, dining room and reception office now also have air condition units, however not all units are always required. Wind catchers or towers, "Malqaf", were also used for cooling buildings especially in hot and arid climates. Some brought in air from one direction and others from varying wind directions. Hot air could rise and be funnelled out, or cool air brought in. It is not clear whether Holliday intended the Bell Tower to double up as a wind catcher, however from the 1928 blueprints we learn that there was a possibility of continuous air flow upwards through the stair well and out of the Bell Tower's grilled openings. In any case this has been partially blocked with a guest room.

Reference to additional aspects appear in the full report.

Conclusions:

This study has revealed the various bioclimatic and sustainable features Holliday incorporated in the design of the Church and Hospice. Most of the identified features originate from local traditional buildings in this region and a few originate from western knowhow. Holliday succeeded in integrating traditional techniques with contemporary requirements. The outcome is impressive and durable. It is an example of best practice for architects designing today in this region. In a 1911 address to the Royal Institute of British Architects on indigenous building techniques, Ernest Richmond, then director of public buildings in Egypt, and from 1927-1937 Director of Antiquities of the Government of Palestine, said, 'If local methods do not provide all that is needed in an age of change and activity, they are at any rate adapted to the physical conditions of the country and an architect will lose nothing by studying them respectfully'. Now, just over a century from then, we can appreciate architect Clifford Holliday's masterful study of indigenous building techniques and their implementation in the design of the Memorial buildings. Holliday's skill and these techniques enhance the spiritual experience of those who visit it and dwell within its walls. His design is a legacy from the past to the future, perhaps in keeping with Psalm 48 vv 12 to13 which is also the motto of the Pro-Jerusalem Society, "People of God, walk about Zion and go round about the towers thereof, mark well her buildings, set up her houses that ye may tell them that come after."

—— APPENDIX FIVE ——

Special Committee on Church Property

REPORT TO THE GENERAL ASSEMBLY
OF THE
SPECIAL COMMITTEE ON
CHURCH PROPERTY IN PALESTINE
MAY 1949

The Committee has to report that, following on the verbal report to the last General Assembly, representations were made to the Colonial Office, the Foreign Office, the British Consul General at Haifa, the Jewish Agency and the Arab League concerning the Church of Scotland properties in Palestine. Full details were given of these properties, and their values, and the various parties to whom representation was made were asked to do all in their power to protect Church of Scotland property. Favourable replies were received.

Properties about which representations were made are as follows:

Jaffa

(a) Tabeetha School and the Memorial House – Property owned by the Jewish Mission Committee.

(b) Abarbanel Street Mission – Property on lease to the Jewish Mission Committee.

(c) German Church – Property handed over to the care of the Rev. A. Scott Morrison in 1939 and used for Church of Scotland Services – Property registered with the Custodian of Enemy Property.

Tiberias

(a) Church, Manse and Halls – Property owned by the Jewish Mission Committee.

(b) Hospital Properties and Residences – Property owned by the Jewish Mission Committee.

Safad

(a) Church and Mission House (now destroyed) – Property owned by the Jewish Mission Committee.

(b) Ford House – Property owned by the Jewish Mission Committee

Haifa

German Church, Manse and Compound – Property handed over to the Rev. J. Patterson in 1939, and used for Church of Scotland Services – Property registered with the Custodian of Enemy Property

Jerusalem

(a) St Andrew's Church and Hospice – Property owned by the Committee on the Scots Memorial, Jerusalem (St Andrew's Church and Hospice).

(b) Manse – Leased from the Greek Patriarchate

All these properties are in areas now administered by the Israeli Government.

Events Since The Last General Assembly

After the departure from Palestine of the British Administration in May 1948 information was received that the Tabeetha School, Jaffa, and the Church and Hospital Buildings at Tiberias were under the Red Cross flag, the Jaffa property being used for refugees and the Church in Hospital Buildings at Tiberias for hospital purposes. The Church and Mission Building at Safad was destroyed in the fighting which took place there, and no official information was obtainable concerning the other Safat property belonging to the Church (Ford House) which was leased to the Government of Palestine as auxiliary hospital premises. The St Andrew's Church and Hospice, Jerusalem, remained in Church possession throughout the past year. The Abarbanel Street property at Jaffa was bombed and, after evacuation by the Church of Scotland personnel, occupied by refugees. The German Churches at Haifa and Jaffa were used throughout the year for Church of Scotland services.

In December 1948 information was received that the Lutheran World Federation was making general representations concerning German property rights in Palestine to the Secretary General of the United Nations. These included the future ownership and use of the German Churches in Haifa and Jaffa.

The Church Commission on International Affairs (formed by the World Council of Churches and the International Missionary Council) also submitted a Memorandum on Church properties in Palestine to the United Nations, and was informed that approach should also be made to the Government of Israel. It is not known what, if any, action the United Nations is likely to take in response to these approaches.

In the meantime the Committee is taking advantage of the contact which has been established between the Jewish Mission Committee and the Israeli representatives in London. In February 1949 the Jewish Mission Committee of the General Assembly was in communication with the Israeli representatives in London regarding the possibility of a return to work in Palestine and received permission to send representatives to Palestine to negotiate concerning the resumption of work. The Rev. A. Scott Morrison was sent out at the end of February under the auspices of the Jewish Mission Committee and the Scots Memorial, Jerusalem Committee, and kindly agreed to investigate the possession of all Church properties in Palestine and to report.

Report On Position Of Properties At 17th May 1949

Mr. A. Scott Morrison has reported that the Tabeetha School property at Jaffa has been returned to the Church of Scotland and that the way is open for resumed work. The Abarbanel Street property is at present occupied by refugees. The Israeli authorities are ready to return the Church and Hospital properties at Tiberias, but they have required the return of Dr. H.W. Torrance to complete the negotiations. Dr Torrance returned to Palestine in 1st May and his report is awaited. At Safad, the Church and Mission House has been destroyed and the Ford House is in the hands of the Jewish authorities and some Jewish immigrants are quartered their meantime. The Scottish Church and Hospice and Manse at Jerusalem are all substantially sound although considerable damage has been sustained. In regard to the German Lutheran Church properties at Haifa and Jaffa, negotiations are being continued.

There seems, therefore, every prospect that all properties actually belonging to the Church of Scotland will be returned before the autumn.

The Committee desires to place on record its great indebtedness to Mr. A. Scott Morrison for the valuable services rendered to the Church in this matter and for his detailed report. The Committee desires also to acknowledge the helpful co-operation of the Israeli authorities and, in particular, the Israeli Ministry of Religions.

J. Frederick Strachan, Convener.

R. Clephane Macanna, Hon. Secretary

—— APPENDIX SIX ——

President Carter's Visit to St Andrew's Church

ON THE 12th March, 1979, the Jerusalem Post reported on President Carter's attendance at worship in St Andrew's Church the previous day:

'St Andrew's Church Filled as Carters Attend Service

'When Jimmy Carter went to church yesterday the service began with a hymn set to a traditional Jewish melody and ended with a benediction in Hebrew.

'All 150 places were filled for the service at St Andrew's Church of Scotland, situated on a hilltop overlooking Mount Zion. Long before the 10a.m. service began, a crowd of would-be worshippers gathered at a gate leading to the church where regular congregants of St Andrew's, and the guest Baptist congregation, were being admitted. (Carter is a Baptist.)

'Not all the Baptists were able to enter, however. A St Andrew's official said 14 Baptists arrived at 8a.m., before security had been imposed. With only 25 seats allocated to the Baptists, this left little room for others from the visiting congregation.

'Most of the worshippers, including families with small children, were in the pews by 9.30. The church bell began ringing at 9.45. President and Mrs Carter and their party entered the building shortly after 10. The President smiled, nodding briefly to those on either side of the centre aisle, as he took his place in the pew reserved near the front.

'The service began with a hymn, "The God of Abraham Praise," set to the Ashkenazic melody for the anthem "Yigdal Elohim Hai" (Praise the Living God)," a poetic rendition of Maimonides' 13 principles of faith.

'At the request of the Presidential party, the Rev. Tom Houston of St Andrew's conducted a normal service, only briefly welcoming the President, and continuing to make the usual announcements about such functions as Ladies' Guild meetings. But he did pray that Carter's visit might prove successful.

'Bible readings included Psalm 2, from the Old Testament, and Luke 22 vv 24 to 40, from the New Testament. The worshippers also sang the versified version of Psalm 122, including the words: "Jerusalem, within thy gates, our feet shall standing be; pray that Jerusalem may have peace and felicity."

'In his sermon, Dr. Robert Lindsay of the Baptist Congregation pointed out that, in Christian thought, Jerusalem is often visualised in spiritual terms. But, he stressed, the prayer for the peace of Jerusalem was for the physical city, with its 360,000 inhabitants.

'"Mr Carter would have been more successful in his mission," Lindsay said, "if we had been more faithful in our prayers." At the opening of his sermon, Lindsay welcomed the "expanded congregation," and jested that perhaps the U.S. president could come every week to boost church attendance.

'Another hymn, "The Service of the Kingdom," gave yet another possible allusion to the Carter mission. "Help me the slow of heart to move by some clear winning word of love," read one line.

'The service ended with a benediction in Hebrew by Dr. Lindsay. The Baptist minister recited the threefold priestly blessing without English translation.

'After the service the congregation remained standing while the Carters left. The Carters paused briefly in the courtyard to pose for photographers against the background of the walls of the Old City. Within minutes the Carter motorcade sped on its way.

'St Andrew's Church was opened on November 30, 1930. The foundation stone, obtained from King Solomon's quarries, was laid three years previously by General Allenby. The Church was built to commemorate Scottish soldiers killed in Palestine during World War I.

'Security reasons prevented Carter from attending services at the Baptist congregation on Rehov Narkiss in central Jerusalem.'

—— APPENDIX SEVEN ——
Regimental Memorial Plaques

THE FOLLOWING Memorial Plaques are placed around the Church building on the floor of the Sanctuary or on the walls. The "Hamilton/Stirling" Memorial is situated on the wall of the vestibule of the Church.

1914-1918
TO THE GLORY OF GOD
AND IN PROUD
AND AFFECTIONATE MEMORY
OF THE OFFICERS
NON-COMMISIONED OFFICERS
AND MEN OF THE
52ND LOWLAND DIVISION
WHO GAVE THEIR LIVES
IN THE GREAT WAR

IN MEMORY
OF THE
SEAFORTH HIGHLANDERS
WHO FELL IN BATTLE
WHILE SERVING WITH THE
FIRST BATTALION
IN PALESTINE AD1918
+S SIEMH SUAIN NA SONN+

THIS STONE IS PLACED HERE
BY THE FIRST BATTALION
+JERUSALEM + AD1934+

IN MEMORY OF
THE BLACK WATCH
ROYAL HIGHLANDERS
WHO FELL IN BATTLE
IN PALESTINE, 1917-1918
AND NOW REST IN PEACE

THIS STONE WAS INSCRIBED BY THEIR
COMRADES IN THE 1ST AND 2ND BATTALIONS
SIR ARTHUR WAUCHOPE, GENERAL, AD1937

IN COMMEMORATION OF
THE OFFICERS WARRANT OFFICERS AND SOLDIERS OF
THE ARGYLL AND SUTHERLAND HIGHLANDERS
—— (PRINCESS LOUISE'S)
WHO SERVED AND DIED IN PALESTINE

1916-1918	1939-1945	1945-1948
NE OBLIVISCARIS		SANS PEUR

TO THE GLORY OF GOD
AND
THE UNDYING MEMORY OF THE OFFICERS AND MEN
OF
THE LONDON SCOTTISH REGIMENT
WHO LAID DOWN THEIR LIVES
IN THE PALESTINE CAMPAIGN

JERUSALEM

GAZA		JERICHO
EL MUNTAR		JORDAN
NEBI SAMWIL		TEL AVIV
1917		1918

PALESTINE

TO THE GLORY OF GOD
AND IN MEMORY OF
THE MEMBERS OF THE ARMED FORCES
AND OF
THE PALESTINE POLICE FORCE
WHO WORSHIPPED HERE
AND GAVE THEIR LIVES
IN THE SECOND WORLD WAR
AND DURING THE BRITISH MANDATE
1920-1948

GREATER LOVE HATH NO MAN THAN THIS
THAT A MAN LAY DOWN HIS LIFE FOR HIS FRIENDS

SACRED TO THE MEMORY OF
ALISTAIR MUNGO
CAPTAIN, THE BLACK WATCH
CAPTAIN, THE BLACK WATCH M.C.
WHO FELL IN THE DEFENCE OF CRETE
WHO DIED ON DECEMBER 14TH 1941
ON MAY 28TH , 1941
OF WOUNDS RECEIVED AT TOBRUK
AGED 27AGED 26
ONLY SON OF BRIG. GEN. J G H HAMILTON ONLY
SURVIVING SON OF COL. SIR GEORGE STIRLING
OF SKENE
OF GLORAT

THEY WORSHIPPED TOGETHER IN THIS CHURCH
NOVEMBER 1937 – JUNE 1940
AND THEIR COMRADES IN THE BLACK WATCH WHO
SERVED WITH THEM IN JERUSALEM
AND GAVE THEIR LIVES IN THE GREAT WAR
1939-1945

"ALL THE TRUMPETS SOUNDED ON THE OTHER SIDE"

─── APPENDIX EIGHT ───

Ministers of St Andrew's Church, Jerusalem

THE FOLLOWING is a list of Ministers appointed to St Andrew's Church, Jerusalem, from 1930 to 2014. It has been prepared based on available records and is acknowledged as not being definitive. Subsequent information which may come to hand updating the list, for example with the names of Locum Ministers, will be posted on the St Andrew's Church Blog. When on the list the Rev. Herbert Minard of the Y.M.C.A. appears these are periods when he was requested by the Committee in Edinburgh to assist with the arrangements for Sunday worship and pastoral care of the Congregation during prolonged vacancies.

Ninian Hill	1930-1931
Ninian B. Wright	1931
William Ewing	1931-1932
Ninian Hill	1932-1933
David L. Cattanach	1933-1934
William Ross	1934-1936
R. S. Calderwood	1936-1937
W. Neil Sutherland	1937-1938
J. F. Alexander	1938-1939
Norman Maclean	1939-1940
Duncan S. MacGillivray	1940-1945
Roderick Murchison	1945-1946
W. Clark Kerr	1946-1948
Herbert Minard (Y.M.C.A.)	1948-1949
A. Scott Morrison	1949-1953
Herbert Minard (Y.M.C.A.)	1953-1954
J. Nelson Hall	1954-1955
William Gardiner Scott	1955-1960
John Gray	1960
R. M. Brown	1960-1961
T. Gibson	1961-1963
Herbert Minard (Y.M.C.A.)	1963-1964

William MacIntyre	1964-1965
William Gardiner Scott	1966-1975
Tom C. Houston	1975-1979
Robert Craig	1980-1985
John Miller Scott	1985-1988
Colin Morton	1988-1997
Iain F. Paton	1997-1998
Maxwell D. Craig	1999-2000
Clarence W. Musgrave	2000-2006
Jane Barron	2006-2008
George Shand	2011-2014
Paraic Reamonn	2014-

---- · APPENDIX NINE ----

Gifts and Miscellany

1. Memorial To Robert The Bruce

> **IN REMEMBRANCE OF**
> **THE PIOUS WISH OF**
> **KING ROBERT BRUCE**
> **THAT HIS HEART SHOULD**
> **BE BURIED IN**
> **JERUSALEM**
> **1329+7TH JUNE+1929**
>
> **IN CELEBRATION OF THE SIXTH CENTENARY OF HIS DEATH**
> **GIVEN BY CITIZENS OF DUNFERMLINE AND MELROSE**

The Scotsman of the 21st March, 1932, reports:

'"In remembrance of the pious wish of King Robert the Bruce that his heart should be buried in Jerusalem." These are the words engraved upon the bronze tablet which is to be placed in the Church of St Andrew, Jerusalem, and which was yesterday at the forenoon service in St Cuthbert's Church, Edinburgh, unveiled by the Earl of Elgin, head of the family of Bruce, and handed over for conveyance to the Holy City. Thus, 600 years after, has been fulfilled in some measure the task which Robert the Bruce, on his deathbed, laid upon his trusted lieutenant, Sir James Douglas, that he should convey his heart to Jerusalem, since he himself had been unable to undertake a crusade. Sir James, history tells us, while undertaking the pilgrimage, fell in Spain in battle with the Saracens.'

Prior to the unveiling of the tablet a sermon was preached by Dr. Norman Maclean following which, 'The Earl of Elgin said that in the inspiring address of Dr. Maclean they had listened to the story of King Robert the Bruce and the times of 600 years ago when Scotland became and was made a united nation. There still remained at the end of a life spent for his country that undying wish to do something for that greater cause, the cause of the Lord in the Holy Land. And so on his deathbed he gave to the trusted knight, Sir James Douglas, the duty of taking his heart to that place where he wished to be. The tablet which he was to unveil had been subscribed by the citizens of Dunfermline and Melrose and the family or house of Bruce. It sought to fulfil the unfinished mission of Sir James Douglas.

'What was the value to us of history and tradition? Surely the value of thinking back to these troublous times was that we might try to inspire in our country in the heart of every individual that same spirit of courage, determination, and hope. Those were the days of chivalry. Was there no need today of that same sort of chivalry to meet our difficulties? He thought that if they could inspire that same spirit of devotion to the great urge to do something for our Lord and Master and for our neighbour, they would be able to surmount the difficulties in the same way as they were surmounted 600 years ago.

'He had brought with him that day the sword of King Robert. The sword was the emblem of attack but in the Christian armour it was designated the Sword of the Spirit – the Word of God. In fulfilling this old-time undertaking, let them dedicate themselves that day to that same service. That day was the first of a week of special effort which would be made, he hoped, by every Scotsman to do all he or she could for the benefit of our native land. Let them take with them that same spirit of enterprise, devotion, and courage, and they would overcome as they did in the past. It was his privilege to unveil the tablet, and asked Dr MacLean to accept it and forward it through his committee in charge of St Andrew's Memorial Church in Jerusalem, there to be placed in the place prepared for it.'

2. St Bride's Bell

Manufactured by Messrs Taylor & Co, Loughborough, the Church bell was a gift from Isobel Hutchison and the text on the small plaque next to the bell rope in the vestibule of the Church reads "To the Glory of God and in Memory of Thomas Walter Hutchison of Carlowrie, Kirk Liston, Captain, 1st 10th Battalion The Royal Scots (T) who gave his life in the Great War 22nd November, 1915. This bell is given by his sister Isobel. 'The Spirit and the Bride say come'"

3. Prayer Desk And Chair

Within the records of the Memorial Committee Dr. Norman MacLean notes that 'on the 10th March (1940), a Prayer-desk and Chair were dedicated in St Andrew's Church, Jerusalem, as a memorial of the late Dr. (Alexander) Barclay, Minister of Dalserf. A beautiful product of the best craftsmanship, the chair bearing in relief a carved Columban coracle, these complete the lovely chancel which is floored chiefly with Iona marble. The Prayer-desk is the gift of friends in the Congregation of Dalserf, who chose this romantic way of commemorating their Minister in that city where the springs of his life had lain.'

4. Wrought Iron Gates At Entrance To The Church In Stairwell From Lounge

In a Memorandum dated October 1940 Ninian Hill provides the background to the set of gates following receipt of a letter from Miss Annie Menzies:

'The Rev. A. MacKenzie, Minister of St John the Baptist Church, Ayr, saw the gates in an art decorator's showrooms in Ayr and, being interested in the Jerusalem Memorial Church, he thought they would look well in some part of it: so he mentioned the matter to the two Misses Menzies who enquired as to the cost. Miss Louisa Menzies wished to have the pleasure of presenting the gates so Miss Annie gave way. The gates were offered to the Committee, accepted and sent to Jerusalem. A year or two later the donor died, and her sister provided for a small bronze plaque recording the gift which was placed near the gates in the Church. Miss Annie Menzies also gave £10 for a chair to bear the name of "Ayr, St John the Baptist" in memory of her sister.

'As far as Miss Menzies could learn the gates were the work of a celebrated iron artist in Milan and were made for a ducal palace there. The family fell on evil times and the gates were sold. A Colonel Bennet of Ayr then bought them for his own place but found they were too light in structure for his purpose, so he tried to sell them and then Miss Menzies bought them.'

Wrought iron gates

5. Sanctuary Chairs

The following is the list of names of Congregations, Regiments and various groups each of which donated £10 to have their name inscribed on a bronze plaque and fixed to the back of a Sanctuary chair. The list is set out in alphabetical order:

Abbotshall; Aberdeen; Aberdeen:Gilcomston St Colm's; Airdrie:Flowerhill; Alloa; Almondbank; Alness; Alvie; Angus:Inverarity; Annan; Arbirlot; Argyll and Sutherland Highlanders; Auchterarder; Auckland (NZ); Avoch; Ayr:St John the Baptist.

Blackbraes; Blairgowrie; Blantyre (Nyasaland); Boddam; Bridge of Allan; Broughton; Buckie.

Cairo; Callander; Cambusnethan; Camelon; Canonbie; Carstairs; Cathcart; Cavers; Coatbridge; Coats; Connel Ferry; Craigrownie; Crieff; Cromarty; Culcairn; Cumbrae; Cunninghame House; Curry.

Darnaway; Dingwall; Dornoch Cathedral; Drumoak; Dundee:St Mary; Dunkeld:Eastferry; Dunning.

Elie; Errol.

Fern; Fetteresso; Forres; Forteviot; Forth Valley

Gartsherrie; George Street Club (Edinburgh); Grange; Grantown on Spey; Greenock; Greenock:St Mark.

Haddington; Hamilton Old; Hawick; Hillhead; Huntly.

Inverallan; Inverary; Invergowrie; Isle of Skye.

Johnstone

Kabete; Kalimpong; Kells; Kilmodan; Kilwinning:Canongate; Kingussie; Kinkel; Kinnaird; Kinross; Kippen, Kirkliston; Kirkmichael; Kirkoswald;

Laggan (Badenoch); Langholm; Lawrencekirk; Lauriston; Liff; Lilliesleaf; Linlithgow; Linton (Teviotdale); Lister House; Liverpool; London:Crown Court.

Maxwelltown; Mazoe-Lomagundi (S Rhodesia); Methlick; Moffat; Monklands; Monkton; Montrose; Monzievaird; Motherwell:Dalziel; Murrayfield.

Nairobi; Newbattle; Newhills; New Monklands; North Berwick;

Oban; Old Kilpatrick.

Paisley Abbey; Paisley:St George's East; Penicuick; Pitlochry; Polmont.

Rattray; Renwick Glasgow; Roslin; Rothesay; Rothiemay; Royal Air Force.

St Andrews; St Andrew's Drumsheugh (Edinburgh); St Colm (Edinburgh); St Cuthbert (Edinburgh); St John (Glasgow); St Madoes; St Mathew (Edinburgh); St Mungo (Glasgow); Salisbury (S Rhodesia); Scoonie; Skirling; Sleat; Souden Kirk; South Morningside (Edinburgh); Southend; Sothwick (Stewartry); Stepps; Stirling; Stornoway; Strath; Strathallan; Strathearn.

Tarbert (Loch Fyne); The Cameronians-Scottish Rifles; Troquair; Tullamore.

Urray and Kilchrist.

Victorian Scots.

Waverley (NSWales); Wellington (Glasgow); West Kilbride; Whittinghame.

6. *Various Gifts*

a) Gift from the "Tyneside Scottish Brigade" to fund the large coloured window on north wall of the nave of the Church.

b) £500 [£27,500] Gift from "The Girls' Association" to fund the large coloured window in the south wall of the nave of the Church, the organ, Iona marble for the floor in the Chancel and the font.

c) £20 from Mrs Scott, Kippen, towards the cost of the cast iron lectern in memory of her husband, Judge J.H. Scott. The lectern was designed by the architect, Clifford Holliday.

d) Bronze Alms Dish from Mrs McClymont in memory of her husband, the Very Rev. Dr. McClymont, C.B.E.

e) Anonymous gift of funds towards the cost of the Communion Table.

f) Gift of silver head to the Beadle's baton from Dorothea Sloan in memory of Agnes Mary Richardson Harper

g) Gift of solid silver Communion vessels, cup, paten and flagon, from Ninian Hill and taken to Palestine and used for the first time in the Church of the Redeemer on the occasion of The Church of Scotland's first worship service in Jerusalem on the 18th March, 1923.

—— REFERENCES ——

[1] "The Long, Long Trail" by Chris Baker and Milverton Associates Ltd. (www.1914-1918.net)

[2] "The Deliverance of Palestine" published in Edinburgh, 1927, by the Committee for the Scottish Churches' Memorial.

[3] "The Significance of Our Victory in Palestine" published in Edinburgh, 1927, by the Committee for the Scottish Churches' Memorial.

[4] "Records of Scotts Engineering Co., Ltd., Greenock." in the University of Glasgow Archives Hub.

[5] "The Last of the Windjammers" by Basil Lubbock, published in 1927 by Brown, Son and Ferguson, Ltd., Glasgow.

[6] "The Story of the Old West Kirk of Greenock 1591-1898" by Ninian Hill, published in 1898 by James McKelvie & Sons, Greenock.

[7] "Poland and the Polish Question. Impressions and Afterthoughts" by Ninian Hill, published in 1915 by George Allen and Unwin, London.

[8] "The Story of the Scottish Church from the Earliest Times" by Ninian Hill, published in 1919 by James MacLehose & Sons, Glasgow.

[9] Pro-Jerusalem Society Report 1918-1920

[10] "Letters from Jerusalem During the Palestine Mandate" by Eunice Holliday, edited by John Holliday and published in 1997 by Radcliffe Press, London

[11] "In The Steps Of The Master" by H.V. Morton, published in 1934 by Rich & Cowan Ltd., London.

[12] "Mission Work Under Difficulties In The Holy Land", an article by Andrew Scott Morrison published in 1948 by World Dominion Press, London, in their Occasional Papers Series (No.4).

[13] "Experiment In Anarchy" by R.M. Graves, published in 1949 by Victor Gollancz, London

[14] "Shards" by Tanya Gardiner Scott, from "Children of Israel, Children of Palestine – Our Own True Story", edited by Laurel Holliday and published in 1998 by Pocket Books, New York.

[15] "The Riches of Ketef Hinnom" by Gabriel Barkay, from the "Biblical Archaeological Review, 200th Edition", 2009.

9 781784 561116

An environmentally friendly book printed and bound in England by www.printondemand-worldwide.com

PEFC Certified

This product is
from sustainably
managed forests
and controlled
sources

www.pefc.org

PEFC/16-33-415

This book is made of chain-of-custody materials; FSC materials for the cover and PEFC materials for the text pages.

Reprint of # - C0 - 234/156/21 - PB - Lamination Gloss - Printed on 15-Dec-17 07:26